AMERICAN
MUSICAL INSTRUMENTS

in The Metropolitan Museum of Art

AMERICAN MUSICAL INSTRUMENTS

in The Metropolitan Museum of Art

LAURENCE LIBIN

THE METROPOLITAN MUSEUM OF ART
NEW YORK
W. W. NORTON & COMPANY
NEW YORK   LONDON

This publication is made possible through the generous support of Mr. and Mrs. Gordon P. Getty.

Published by The Metropolitan Museum of Art, New York, and W.W. Norton & Company, Inc., New York. Published simultaneously in Canada by Penguin Books Canada Ltd, 2801 John Street, Markham, Canada L3R 1B4.

The Metropolitan Museum of Art

Bradford D. Kelleher, Publisher
John P. O'Neill, Editor in Chief
Barbara Burn, Project Supervisor
Dinah Stevenson, Editor

Library of Congress Cataloging in Publication Data

Libin, Laurence.
American musical instruments in The
Metropolitan Museum of Art.

Bibliography: p. 213
includes index.
1. Musical instruments—United
States. I. Metropolitan
Museum of Art (New York, N. Y.) II. Title.
ML476.L5 1985   781.91'0973   85-4817

ISBN 0-87099-379-8   (MMA)

ISBN 0-393-02277-3   (W.W. Norton)

The photographs for this volume were taken by the Photograph Studio of The Metropolitan Museum of Art and by Stewart Pollens of the Museum's Department of Musical Instruments, unless otherwise credited.

Composition by David E. Seham Associates, Inc.
Colorplates printed by Colorcraft Lithographers, Inc.
Black-and-white pages printed by Rae Publishing Company
Printed in the United States of America
1 2 3 4 5 6 7 8 9 0

Contents

Foreword

Although small in comparison to other departments within the Metropolitan Museum, the Department of Musical Instruments exerts an influence that transcends size and place. Recordings, broadcasts, and concerts presented on many of the Museum's instruments in recent years have earned widespread recognition for advancing the cause of historically authentic performance. Except for these instruments, no objects in the Museum's collections currently serve the practical purposes for which they were designed. Hence, our instruments constitute a unique "living" repository whose effects reach beyond the Museum's walls. Such activity has been made possible by the Department's concern with scientific conservation and restoration, the result of daily collaboration between the Department's curator, Laurence Libin, master restorer Stewart Pollens, and a highly skilled staff.

As it has been for nearly a century, the musical instruments collection remains a place of pilgrimage for instrument makers, musicologists, and performers seeking information and inspiration. The beautifully installed André Mertens Galleries for Musical Instruments also offer a rare visual refreshment for casual visitors. Those who follow Curator Libin's entertaining and instructive audio guide cannot remain unmoved by the aural effect of the eight hundred instruments on display. These include such treasures as the oldest extant piano, invented by Bartolomeo Cristofori at the Medici court in Florence, and a Stradivari violin of 1693, the only "Strad" thus far to have been restored to its original Baroque condition. It is a revelation to hear early music played on the instruments for which it was intended; the effect is akin to cleaning away layers of discolored varnish to reveal a painting's vivid, true colors.

No less attractive to the eye than to the ear, the Museum's many European instruments dating from the Middle Ages through the nineteenth century enrich our understanding of decorative arts and the vital place of music on all levels of Western society. Further, non-Western instruments, constituting nearly two-thirds of the entire collection, represent an astonishing wealth of unfamiliar forms, materials, significant ornaments, and acoustical principles that testify to mankind's inventiveness and aesthetic impulse. Covering six continents and more than four thousand years, this assemblage runs a gamut unsurpassed at any other museum.

It may seem strange that only a relatively small part of this comprehensive collection is devoted to instruments of our own country. Partly this reflects some reluctance to acquire commonplace material; indeed, acquisitions today must be limited to a few outstanding products of exemplary quality, lest scarce storage space be overwhelmed by readily available commercial items better preserved at a museum of American history than of fine art. There will be time enough in the future to single out those American instruments of recent manufacture that best express our musical aspirations; right now our priorities favor preserving rarer artifacts of a vanishing past. But there is always room for new creations that meet the criterion of outstanding quality.

Another reason American instruments have been underrepresented, not only in this museum but in others as well, has been the unfortunate bias of previous generations, who, having been reared in a European tradition, tended to assume the superiority of foreign-made instruments. As the present book shows, such prejudice is unjustified, and Laurence Libin through his musical and scholarly acumen has made a vigorous effort to redress the imbalance. The scores of American instruments he has acquired for the Museum demonstrate a commitment to excellence and curatorial fairness that Mrs. John Crosby Brown, the founder of the collection, would have applauded.

It is a pleasure to thank those who have supported the publication of this book, notably Gordon and Ann Getty, whose generous gift has been responsible for its expeditious appearance. Other contributors are gratefully acknowledged in the author's introduction. There remains only to express my personal delight that an often overlooked aspect of the Metropolitan Museum's holdings, and of American culture, is now being brought before the public. I hope this book will stimulate further interest and research, and thus fulfill the Museum's fundamental goals.

Philippe de Montebello
Director

Preface

This book, which documents only a small part of one of the world's great musical collections, gives for the first time a comprehensive overview of America's instrumental heritage. From toy kazoos and minstrel "bones" up to the most sophisticated keyboard and orchestral instruments, the distinguished author describes the form and construction of each example, discusses musical and social functions, and relates important biographical facts about makers, some of whom were virtually unknown before Laurence Libin's extensive researches. Mr. Libin has not let sound scholarship overwhelm us with details, however, but has provided a highly readable story, using the remarkable objects in his care as the focal point for a wider discussion of America's accomplishments in instrument manufacture from colonial times to the present.

Until now, little of a general nature has been published on this interesting aspect of American material culture, made up as it is of strands from many different nations, social classes, and levels of technology. We should be proud of this diversity and grateful that it is represented so well in the following words and illustrations. When my German ancestors started making pianos in New York in the middle of the last century, they soon found that simply making a superior instrument was not enough; they had also to convince influential musicians and the public that any such product made in America could really be as good as what came from European factories. The idea that anything musically good has to come from Europe unfortunately lingers even to our day,

but this book and the objects it describes will help overcome that old prejudice. For a long time American pianos have been regarded as a world standard. Here, other sorts of instruments of equal significance receive the attention they deserve. In the Metropolitan Museum they are displayed side by side with foreign counterparts and do not suffer by comparison. When played in the Museum's musical programs and recordings, their tonal virtues too become apparent.

In going further, American craftsmen have fostered the development of instruments such as the Appalachian dulcimer, banjo, electric guitar, and certain types of rotary-valved brasses and reed organs, thus giving the world something musically unique and enriching. Ensembles such as the post–Civil War brass band or the jazz and "jug" bands of earlier in this century would have been unthinkable without America's contributions, discussed here with respect and affection. Also considered are some curious patented novelties of little enduring usefulness but showing much Yankee ingenuity, as well as sound-producing implements such as sleigh bells that are not essentially musical but deserve a place in this catalogue owing to their aural purpose.

Truly, in this rich collection everyone will find something surprising, something familiar but seen in a new light, something revealing of over two centuries of musical endeavor. I hope that other readers will take as much pleasure and pride as I do in learning more about the fascinating tools of America's musicians.

Henry Steinway

1. *Anders Zorn*. Mrs. John Crosby Brown *(Mary Elizabeth Brown, 1842–1918), c. 1900 (60.85)*

Introduction

Musical instruments serve a great many functions. Musicians, of course, regard them as refined, sensitive tools. For the musicologist they embody tangible evidence of how music sounded before the advent of recording. Making and selling instruments provides a livelihood for craftsmen, the best of whom express aesthetic aims through their products. Transcending craft, rare masterpieces such as Stradivari's violins combine the visual and tactile appeal of sculpture with the added dimension of aural beauty. But to some purchasers an instrument represents only a silent mark of status. The mere presence of a handsome grand piano in a parlor makes a statement about the household's values and wealth, even if the piano is seldom played. Such conspicuous instruments figure prominently as furniture, challenging designers of the stature of Duncan Phyfe to cloak their unwieldy innards in fashionable cases. Smaller instruments, richly ornamented or elegantly shaped, may be collected for investment or displayed as objets d'art.

Often made for casual private use rather than for sale, folk instruments offer personal amusement and give scope for creativity outside daily labor. A cherished heirloom such as a homemade banjo can instill a sense of family pride; played in a domestic jam session, it reinforces camaraderie even as it shows off an individual's prowess. But among austere fundamentalist sects instruments may represent sinful pastimes. Associations with lascivious dancing and empty virtuosity have given fiddles, for example, a bad name; hence expressions such as "fiddlesticks" for nonsense and "fiddling away" for wasting precious time.

In more worldly societies many instruments echo serious purposes. Trumpets and kettledrums still call to mind the pompous processions of royalty. Bugles, fifes, and snare drums summon the image of battle. Horn passages in classical music may recall the hunt and other virile outdoor pursuits. Plucked and bowed strings evoke the seductive aura of Orpheus's fabled lyre. Organs resound with ecclesiastic overtones, while harps convey an impression of heaven.

The same instrument can connote different things depending on time and place. For example, though for most of us a harp conjures up a vision of angelic grace, it can also suggest more down-to-earth concerns. To an Irishman the harp has patriotic meaning; it is his national instrument. Thus it often appears in advertisements for Irish products or tourism. As an emblem of the successful joining of the American colonies into a federation of thirteen United States, a thirteen-string harp appears on a Federal-era banknote together with the motto *Majora minoribus consonant* ("Greater and lesser harmonize"). Similar emblematic uses of instruments, political, spiritual, or mundane, are evident throughout the visual arts, where pictorial devices such as the trumpet of Fame convey symbolic messages.

In life, as in art, the use and repertoire of certain instruments reinforce social stereotypes. Raucous bagpipes and awkward hurdy-gurdies were long associated with Europe's peasantry, while expensive keyboard instruments such as the virginal (a small harpsichord) were, as the name suggests, proper for well-bred young women to play. Surprisingly, until well into the nineteenth century flute playing was chiefly a masculine prerogative, a sporting amateur accomplishment with which to beguile the ladies.

As Mozart well knew, skill on the right instrument allows one to climb in society; this purpose prompts many music lessons today. More important, instruments serve the goals of formal education by teaching dexterity and discipline while acquainting pupils with concepts of mathematical scale and proportion. Toy instruments introduce children to a magical realm of tone, opening their ears to music's power to rouse and soothe. Instrumental music's kinesthetic potential, recognized in prebiblical times, has been exploited in all cultures. Playing an instrument can be invaluable for physical rehabilitation and emotional therapy. Often, professional instrumentalists continue to perform for many years after normal retirement age; theirs is a healthful occupation.

Nearly everywhere, certain instruments have been endowed with supernatural virtues to avert evil and attract good luck and longevity. Apotropaic bells and jingles, rattles, and so on date back to prehistory. Many efficacious noisemakers have doubled as signal instruments, a function partly usurped today by automatic electrical devices. Traditional instruments have also been replaced in many circumstances by radios, phonographs, and tape recorders, which have made music more widely accessible than ever before. But because playing, say, the piano or violin, unlike producing sounds automatically, rewards effort and concentration and allows self-expression, such instruments endure as a source of pleasure for us all.

In America musical instruments partake of all these attributes. To view them merely as playthings is to miss the greater part of their significance. The study of American instruments involves investigating many aspects of American life: immigration and acculturation, nationalism and warfare, handicraft and industry, entertainment and worship, tradition and innovation. By revealing universal human aspirations and accomplishments, musical instruments illuminate our broad heritage. They reflect moral and aesthetic values and express an unflagging cultural vitality. For these reasons many museums count instruments among their treasures, to be preserved, displayed, interpreted, and appreciated.

The Metropolitan Museum of Art was one of the first major repositories of historic instruments in the United States. In 1889 a notable assemblage entered this Museum through the generosity of two foresighted private collectors, Joseph W. Drexel and Mrs. John Crosby Brown (Fig. 1). Drexel's gift of forty-four European and American instruments was chiefly of decorative merit; Mrs. Brown's more diversified 276 items were the nucleus of The Crosby Brown Collection of Musical Instruments of All Nations, which had an educational aim. Imbued with Darwinian confidence in human progress and a passionate love of music, Mrs. Brown charted the history of instruments in one of the world's most comprehensive holdings, numbering over three thousand examples by the time she died in 1918. Here Mrs. Brown accumulated an extensive variety of American instruments to illustrate the developing musical landscape of her country. Her goal complemented the Museum's chartered obligation to promote American arts and manufactures. These objectives have been maintained ever since.

American exemplars (not counting aboriginal ones, which form a culturally separate, much larger group) comprise fewer than 5 percent of the Museum's present four thousand or so instruments. This proportion reflects the collection's enormous scope, rather than any negative judgment. In contrast to the attitude of those Victorian snobs who considered the United States to be a musical backwater, Mrs. Brown insightfully celebrated the achievement of American builders whose innovations in areas as diverse as pianos and banjos had a real effect on musical style and were enthusiastically welcomed by progressive performers. The novel pianos of Chickering & Sons, for example, earned accolades abroad at a time when, paradoxically, American-trained pianists had difficulty making headway even at home.

Naturally Mrs. Brown concentrated on collecting instruments of her own day. In the later nineteenth century, although American concert artists were still struggling for recognition, domestic instrument makers were flourishing. Their technological advances, for example in the construction of inexpensive, durable keyboard instruments, did not necessarily reflect purely musical demands but arose largely from new tools and industrial processes, improvements effected for the sake of economy and efficiency. Mechanized production, standardization, and use of modern materials kept costs and prices down, in good times enabling nearly everyone to purchase instruments of reasonable quality. It is in economical manufacture and mass marketing that American ingenuity excelled. Tonal design was often only a minor consideration. Tone quality, after all, is a highly subjective matter that allows wide latitude of choice, but mechanisms can be tested quite objectively. Still, structural developments often lead to new tonal and virtuosic possibilities, for which in the last 150 years or so the United States has become a testing ground.

Early in the nation's history instruments were much used to accompany dancing and singing. Probably many players made their own simple instruments or used ones brought from abroad. Military "bands of musicke" (distinct from fife and drum corps) that entertained at official and social functions provided a pool of trained musicians, who continued as performers, teachers, and purchasers of instruments after the Revolutionary period. By the nineteenth century, as amateur music making increased, employers often hired workers on the strength of musical ability, as contemporary want ads attest (Fig. 2); an employee who also played the clarinet could have been a real business asset.

In the colonies commercial instrument making was generally a sideline for carpenters, turners, mechanics, and smiths such as Paul Revere, whose bells "rang in" the Federal era. Only a few builders were specialists, and these—represented in the Museum's collection by Johannes Clemm and John Harris—usually had learned their trade abroad. As public concerts became an established feature of community life, demand for professionally made instruments grew. In the South concentrated wealth supported the importation of high-quality instruments, but in the less affluent North local production had the advantage over more expensive foreign manufactures. To supply the music-loving populace (despite some religious opposition), some Yankee craftsmen began to devote themselves more and more to instrument making, a respectable occupation that as a rule required no tedious formal apprenticeship. While workmanship might perhaps have suffered from lack of expert supervision, democratization paid dividends in fostering private initiative.

Free of Old World guild regulations, protected after 1790 by patents and sometimes by favorable tariffs, American instrument manufacture prospered, with a distribution network extending by rail and (after 1896) by rural free delivery to a swelling population. Many American makers were foreign-born and trained in German or British factory methods; they applied modern technology to operations previously performed by hand, using machines such as the circular saw, introduced to the States perhaps in 1814, to compensate for a chronic shortage of skilled labor. Trade fairs and grand expositions, like the one at New York's Crystal Palace in 1853, showcased their instruments before the public. Influential juries, for example at Philadelphia's Franklin Institute, conferred prestigious awards upon deserving makers. Newly organized manufacturers' associations dealt with labor problems and methods of maximizing profit; raising industry standards and ethics was a secondary concern. Musical instruments had become important "positional goods" for an aspiring, increasingly affluent society.

Boastful advertising and aggressive marketing spurred sales. Aaron Montgomery Ward's innovative mail-order price list (1872), directed to the rural Grangers (the cooperative National Grange of the Patrons of Animal Husbandry), introduced a flood of wholesale postal catalogues of useful goods, including instruments. In 1905, when in-

2. *"Musicians and Situations Wanted," from* Trumpet Notes XV/4 *(April, 1888). Published by the band-instrument manufacturer C. G. Conn, Elkhart, Ind.*

WANTED—A Bb or Eb cornet player who is ether a painter, jeweler, or barber. Good location for either. Address O. F. Hurlon, Horton, Kansas.

WANTED—At once, clarinet player who is a wagon painter by trade. Steady employment for right man. Address O. A. Peterson, Carthage, Mo.

WANTED—Situation by a good Eb cornet player and band director. Can furnish good reference as to ability, character, etc. Address Geo. P. Bradford, Claremont, Surry Co., Va.

WANTED—To correspond with harness maker who plays leading band instrument. Address, stating trade and instrument. Chas. S. Dole, Danville, Vt.

WANTED—A situation in live town as solo cornet player. Am a jeweler by trade and desire a situation where there is steady employment. Address F. D. Wermuth, New Metamoras, O.

WANTED—A good clarinet player who is a machinist or painter. The same can hear of a good situation by applying to undersigned. Must be sober and reliable. Address Mechanics' Band, Marion, Ohio.

WANTED—A situation to lead some enterprising band by a good cornet player of fifteen years' experience, am willing to do any kind of ordinary work. Address J. F. Chesdic, box 787, Kankakee, Ill.

WANTED—A good flute player who is a first-class shoemaker by trade. Must be sober and reliable. Good situation for suitable person. Address Walter A. Mestrezat, Morgantown, W. Va.

WANTED—An engagement at some summer resort for the ensuing season to furnish band and orchestra or as solo cornet. Address, Musician, Lock box 52, Frankfort, Kan.

WANTED—Violoncello player, first class cigar maker by trade. Good situation in orchestra and factory for the right man. Address Walter A. Mestrezat, Morgantown, W. Va.

WANTED—Clarinet players, who are carpenters or brick and stone masons, to communicate with the undersigned. Big boom, plenty of work, will secure employment for first class musicians only. Address E. M. McCune, Dixon, Ill.

WANTED—To start a barber shop in a small town of from five hundred to three thousand inhabitants. I play solo baritone in band and clarinet in orchestra. Sober and reliable. Geo. Schoefel, Millersville, Sandusky Co., Ohio.

WANTED—A good druggist, blacksmith and barber, to play Eb or Bb cornet, baritone and tuba. Must be good musicians. Places vacant are in K. of P. Band. Address Jeff. Smith, Ashland, Mass.

WANTED—At once, band men, Eb cornet and Eb bass players preferred. A good opening for harness maker's shop, or jewelry store. No opposition. Address E. L. Miller, Hammond, St. Croix Co. Wis.

WANTED—To correspond with a competent E or Bb cornet player who is a moulder and foundryman by trade. None but sober and industrious men need apply. Address Brand & Smith Waitesburg, Wash. Ter.

WANTED—To correspond with a competent E, or Bb cornet player, who is a moulder and foundryman by trade. None but sober and

struments peaked at 6.09 percent of the annual value of new domestic consumer-durable goods (up from 3.71 percent in 1862 and 5.89 percent in 1892, the highest percentage before the panic of 1893 and subsequent depression), the massive "wish book" of Richard W. Sears and Alvah C. Roebuck included sixty full pages of ads for instruments, clear evidence of their sales appeal. Distributors such as Chicago's Sears, Roebuck & Co. and specialized musical outlets such as C. Bruno & Son in New York apparently monopolized the entire output of some instrument manufactories. They were also major wholesale customers of larger manufacturers such as Lyon & Healy in Chicago and the Boston Musical Instrument Company, both of which were also successful wholesalers in their own right.

Mass production and impersonal merchandising did not always imply low quality and did indeed create significant economies of scale. But alongside the large commercial operations there was always a body of independent craftsmen who worked on commission, making truly distinctive instruments in labor-efficient small shops. These often old-fashioned individuals did not necessarily enjoy higher income or better working conditions than factory laborers, and the depressions of 1893 and 1929, coupled with increasing competition from nonmusical entertainment, bankrupted many. Some shifted to military production during World War II and never went back to making instruments. But the social and economic climate of the 1960s fostered a crafts movement even more pervasive than the Arts and Crafts trend early in the century; this leisure-related movement brought renewed interest in custom-made instruments—folk as well as classical types—and today, despite an unsettled economy, many instrument workshops again thrive around the country.

Interestingly, no large-scale manufacturer anywhere has excelled at producing bowed stringed instruments. Selecting, cutting, assembling, and finishing costly violin woods involve constant judgments over each piece of material; these critical operations, to which power tools are ill adapted, have not been successfully automated for high-quality mass production. Until about a hundred years ago American purchasers of fine violins shopped mainly on the Continent or in London. Most production in the United States was done on a part-time or amateur basis, and middle-class buyers often made do with medium-quality imports sold by dealers such as the Gemünder family in New York. Like many other dealers the Gemünders made some instruments themselves in this country but also put their label on violins made abroad. This Museum's quartet of Gemünder instruments bear New York labels but were almost certainly made in Germany. Because fine European violins as well as lesser ones were readily available through dealers, no great need was felt for domestic violin production until the mid–twentieth century, when demand outstripped supply and prices rose alarmingly. Now several schools in the United States train violin makers.

Manufacturing standards for popular plucked instruments such as mandolins and guitars vary widely, and construction has been easier to automate. By the late nineteenth century plucked instruments made in America dominated the market almost to the exclusion of imports. Demand for these instruments seemed insatiable, and one type after another made the transition from ethnic specialty to commercial property. The banjo, for example, once disparaged because of its racial associations, eventually became the vogue among all classes, leading to modifications of design and construction that took it beyond the realm of rural tradition. New varieties of zithers, among them the Appalachian dulcimer, arose to fill the need for even cheaper instruments capable of chording simple accompaniments. Relatively easy to learn to play, plucked fretted instruments of all sorts provided entertainment for innumerable amateurs until around World War II, when the public's interest swung toward nonparticipatory amusements. The increasing popularity of radios and phonographs in particular hurt the sale of instruments, but in the second third of this century electronics opened a new frontier, notably for the guitar industry, as rock and country-and-western styles came to the fore. Following in the footsteps of the inventor and sometime musician Benjamin Franklin, Les Paul and other electronics wizards set the pace for innovation in musical electronics, now a fertile field for tonal experiment.

Wind instrument construction, which can be mechanized to a substantial degree, has been affected by still other considerations. Whereas native forests and imported hardwoods were already providing materials for ordinary wooden instruments in the eighteenth century, American mines, as yet undeveloped, were not yielding the ores needed for brass winds and pewter organ pipes. Lead, tin, and zinc were not produced in adequate quantity in the United States until well into the nineteenth century. Before about 1825 nearly all brass, for example, came from England and was subject to wartime embargoes; hence American trumpet and horn manufacture got off to a slow start. Foreign pewter, in great demand for household utensils, was constantly being recycled, and little was available for nonessential products such as organ pipes. In any case, before the last century few metal-pipe makers were active in America. Likewise, tools for rolling and cutting sheet metal were scarce. But by the second quarter of the nineteenth century the American sheet-metal industry was getting on its feet, and a period of heavy demand for brass winds and large pipe organs was beginning. Churches sprang up in the wake of westward expansion, opening opportunities for organ builders, who now easily undersold foreign competitors. Cheap brass reeds made possible the ubiquitous melodeon or "American organ" that never went out of tune.

The brass band movement of the 1840s prospered with the times, and the Civil War created a previously unparalleled demand for band instruments of all kinds. Veterans of that war included many trained bandsmen who kept on playing and teaching. The flamboyant John Philip Sousa, son of a Marine bandsman and leader of the U.S. Marine Band from 1880 to 1892, attracted a huge following; his own band was world famous by 1910. At the same time, conductors such as Leopold Damrosch and Theodore Thomas cultivated orchestral music that involved instruments and skills foreign to the band idiom. As adults flocked to band and orchestral performances, children were learning the rudiments of music in public school programs initiated by Lowell Mason. Private conservatories joined in inculcating musical performance, taking over where religious "singing schools" left off. During the later nineteenth century music was fostered institutionally on every level of society but the most disenfranchised, which nevertheless had a vigorous musical life of its own, perhaps less instrumental than vocal. In the present century, thanks to the easy availability of sheet music, reasonably priced instruments, and liberal education, popular American music making shows no sign of slowing down.

This brief introduction touches on musical, technological, and social matters that are discussed more fully hereafter in relation to particular instruments in the Museum's collection. This account is in no way complete, just as the collection is not complete; completeness is not possible, for the pursuit of objects, as of knowledge, is an endless task, infinitely exciting. If this book encourages these ends, an important function of the text will be fulfilled.

As no comprehensive study of American musical instruments has yet been written, much preliminary work was needed for this book: identifying makers, tracking down patents, culling contemporary descriptions and advertisements, selecting illustrations that give the flavor of the times. Most of this work I undertook during twenty weeks' travel supported by the National Museum Act through the Smithsonian Institution and by a grant from the Catherine Lorillard Wolfe Art Club administered by the Metropolitan Museum. I ordered my material during a further period of leave granted through the Theodore Rousseau Memorial Fund of the Metropolitan Museum.

Since I could not possibly approach the whole range of instruments with equal familiarity, I sought help from specialists too numerous to thank individually. Among those who contributed most to my education, I am particularly grateful to my research assistants Deborah Autorino and Anna Miller, whose tenures in the Department of Musical Instruments were provided by the Museum's graduate assistantship program. During two years as an Andrew W. Mellon Fellow in this department Nancy Groce compiled invaluable data on New York City instrument makers for her Ph.D. dissertation, on which I relied most appreciatively.

Colleagues at other museums were generous with facts and advice. Curator Cynthia Hoover and the staff of the Division of Musical Instruments at the National Museum of American History (Smithsonian Institution), and Robert Eliason, curator of musical instruments at the Henry Ford Museum in Dearborn, Michigan, were especially kind in sharing the fruits of their pioneering research. Among private collectors Frederick R. Selch offered notable encouragement by underwriting preparation of a checklist of this department's American holdings, which include items not discussed here.

Craftsmen or their descendants and other informants whom I interviewed gave much precious information that has not previously been published. I am grateful to them and also to the helpful professionals at several dozen historical societies, libraries, universities, patent repositories, and museums in the United States and in London, where I searched for the backgrounds of certain artisans. The officers and members of the American Musical Instrument Society helped locate sources and inspired me by their enthusiasm.

The donors of instruments and purchase funds credited herein allowed me to expand considerably the scope of the American collection, building on the nucleus provided by Mrs. John Crosby Brown. Notable acquisitions in the Department of American Sculpture and Decorative Arts have added strength to the Museum's representation of fine makers and have greatly enriched the content of this publication, in which many objects are described for the first time.

The fundamental task of cataloguing the American instruments was supported in its initial stages by the National Endowment for the Arts and the National Endowment for the Humanities, whose grants permitted expert consultants to inspect the collection systematically. Of my own staff, master restorer Stewart Pollens examined many of the instruments and provided measurements and materials identifications. His analytic skills have added immeasurably to the accuracy of the text, though I take full responsibility for the inevitable errors and hope readers will point them out. My senior administrative assistant, the late and sorely missed Mary McClane, read several versions of the text and made many improvements; her successor, Susan Snyder, helped similarly, while departmental secretary Anne McIlvaine retyped innumerable drafts. Assistant curator J. Kenneth Moore and principal technician Helmut Hauser assisted greatly in handling objects and photo orders. During my research absences and fitful bouts of writing my staff shouldered many additional responsibilities; I am deeply appreciative of their support and forbearance. The editorial finesse of Dinah Stevenson finally brought my manuscript into focus; to her belongs the credit for clarifying my often convoluted thoughts and prose.

Note: Throughout this book, pitch and range are indicated according to the following system:

BB C—B   c—b   c¹—b¹ c²—b² c³—b³ etc.
CC

Where no specific octave is implied, capital letters alone are used; it will be clear from the context whether or not these refer to octave placement.

1. *Grand Harmonicon, style of Francis Hopkinson Smith. Baltimore, Md., c. 1830. W. 45½ in. Several glasses are missing (1980.504)*

3. *Clarinet in E-flat of ivory, silver, and rosewood by Theodore Berteling or successors. New York, N.Y., 1880–90. L. 18¹⁹/₃₂ in. (1982.18)*

2. *Snare drum. Late 18th century? Diam. 16⅞ in. (58.82)*

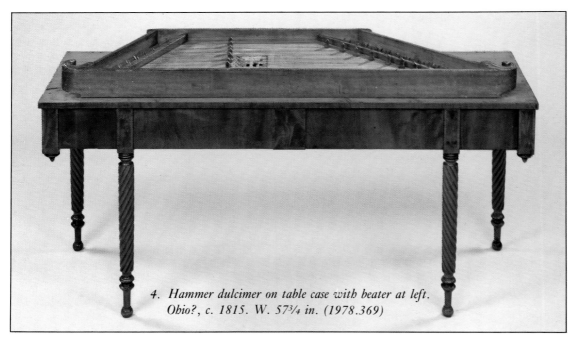

4. *Hammer dulcimer on table case with beater at left. Ohio?, c. 1815. W. 57¾ in. (1978.369)*

5. *Lyre-mandolin or Mandolira by Nicòla Turturro. New York, N. Y., c. 1904. L. 25½ in. (1975.357.1)*

6. *Mandolin by Angelo Mannello. New York, N. Y., c. 1900. L. 24⁹⁄₁₆ in. (1972.111.1)*

7. *Yankee bass viol or "church bass" by William Darracott, Jr., or George L. Darracott. Milford, N. H., 1861. L. 52¹⁄₁₆ in. (1979.204)*

8. *Cornet with maker's mark of J. W. Pepper on bell, c. 1900. L. (without tuning shank and mouthpiece) 12¹³⁄₃₂ in. (1977.246.1)*

9. *Electric guitar by Bruce BecVar (two views). Cotati, Calif., 1973–74. L. 39¹⁄₈ in. (1980.544)*

10. *Bentside spinet by John Harris. Boston, Mass., 1769. W. 79½ in. (1976.229)*

11.   Piano by Firth, Hall & Pond. New York, N.Y., c. 1835. H. 84⅞ in. (44.57)

12.   Piano by Nunns & Clark. New York, N.Y., 1853. W. 87¹⁵/₁₆ in. (06.1312)

13.   Parlor grand piano by Steinway & Sons. New York, N. Y., 1872. L. 86 in. (N. A. 11.1983)

14. *Cylinder piano by George Hicks. Brooklyn, N. Y., c. 1860.*
H. 36½ in. A panel enclosing the strings has been removed.
(89.4.2048)

15. *Virginal by Chickering & Sons under the direction of Arnold Dolmetsch. Boston, Mass., 1906. W. 68 in. (60.51)*

16. *Barrel organ by brothers named Beach. East Hamilton, N. Y., c. 1800. W. 34⅝₁₆ in. (1972.166)*

17.   Chamber organ by William Crowell. Mont Vernon, N. H., 1852. H. 81½ in. (1974.193)

18. Church organ by Thomas Appleton. Boston, Mass.,
1830. H. 16 ft. 1 in. (1982.59)

NOISEMAKERS, TOYS, PERCUSSION, AND MISCELLANEA

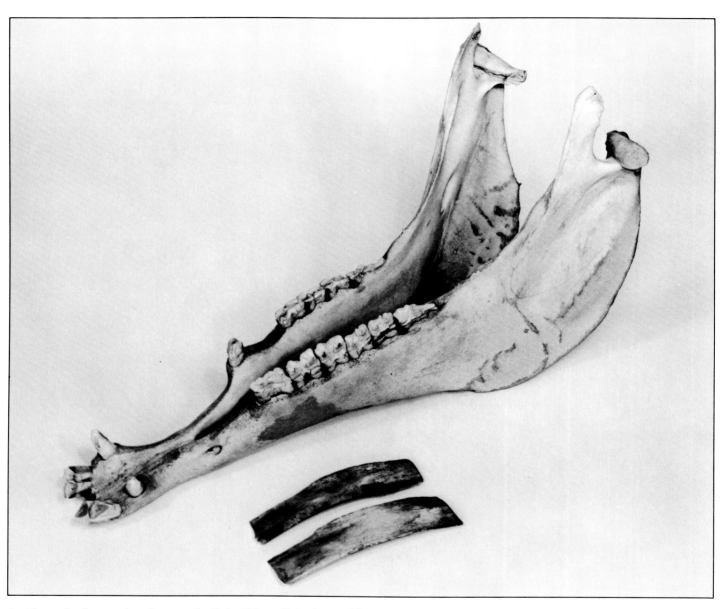

3. Above: *Jawbone rattle and scraper. L. 18 in.* Below: *Pair of natural bone clappers. L. 5 in. Late 19th century (89.4.1351, 89.4.1348 a,b)*

Noisemakers, Toys, Percussion, and Miscellanea

Today's Americans share with people of all lands and every age the knowledge that practically anything solid can be turned to the purpose of producing sound. Incidental noises from primitive tools enticed cave dwellers to explore the mysterious sonic potential of stones, bones, hollow logs, and the like. Soon the unaided sounds of human bodies—voices, whistles, clapping hands, stamping feet—were intentionally being extended by sonorous natural objects. As creative hands refined multipurpose implements to elicit pleasing sounds more effectively, prehistoric technology produced the first specialized musical instruments.

Nature's uncrafted prototypes remain to be discovered anew by each generation. Especially in nonurban cultures and among children, tonal exploitation of found objects supports the concept of a universal human musical impulse. Throughout America's history, on every social level, crude or unsophisticated instruments have been wielded to produce delightful sounds.

Jawbone percussion was introduced to this hemisphere by African slaves and is still heard in Latin America. A large jawbone (Fig. 3), often the whole mandible of a horse or donkey, weathers outdoors until its teeth loosen. The dried-up jawbone can then be played as it was by E. P. Christy's famous minstrel troupe, organized in 1842 in Buffalo, New York: "The Christy minstrels held the instrument at the point of the jaw by the left hand; the stick or beater was held in the right hand between the cheek bones, striking one cheek bone for a single beat and both for a double beat. There was also a varying pitch of the sound

according to the point struck, the sharper sounds if struck near the teeth and . . . lower . . . if struck near the joint over which the jaw was hinged. Occasionally the beater was rubbed across the teeth like a notched stick rattle."[1]

To vibrate the loose teeth, a player hit the jaw as he would a tambourine, with the heel of one hand. Rasping the teeth with a stick (also suggested in a grotesque illustration in the Book of Hours of Jean d'Evreux, from about 1325) has a counterpart in scraping a corrugated washboard with a thimble, as was done in rustic jug bands early in this century. While the tone quality of all such casual rhythmic contrivances is haphazard, sheer dexterity made a spectacle of their use. No doubt a virtuosic display enlivened the Christy Minstrels' Broadway renditions of Stephen Foster's sentimental song "Angelina Baker" (1850):

> Angelina Baker! Angelina Baker's gone,
> She left me here to weep a tear
> And beat on de old jaw bone.

Nineteenth-century minstrels—white performers in blackface makeup who mimicked southern black dialect and manners—also mastered the bewildering art of playing paired bone clappers, long known simply as bones (Fig. 3). Found even in ancient Egypt, these clappers were mentioned in Shakespeare's *A Midsummer Night's Dream* in connection with "rurall musicke" and were described in 1636 by the French scholar Marin Mersenne, who told of bones held between the fingers and "handled so dextrously and quickly and with such regulated cadence that it is impossible to explain them." Introduced from Europe,

4. *William Sidney Mount. The Bone Player, 1856. Courtesy Museum of Fine Arts, Boston, Mass. M. and M. Karolik Collection*

bones were already familiar in the United States in 1843, the debut year of Daniel Decatur Emmett's famed Virginia Minstrels. At their first performance in New York, Emmett's "Ethiopian Band" featured Frank Brower playing bones alongside banjo, fiddle, and tambourine. "Mr. Bones," as Brower's stereotyped character came to be called, sat opposite "Mr. Tambo" and imitated horses' hooves, snare drums, gunfire, and other riveting effects by clashing castanetwise two pairs of short rib bones or shinbones from cattle. William Sidney Mount's painting *The Bone Player* (Fig. 4) evokes the snappy gesture and rhythmic ecstasy implied in another of Foster's

"plantation melodies," "Ring de Banjo" (1851):

> De time is nebber dreary if de darkey nebber groans;
> De ladies nebber weary wid de rattle ob de bones.

Like old-time players of barroom spoons, the ambidextrous maestro of the bones might be part acrobat. An eyewitness to one performance recalled, in barely repressed amazement, "He stands upon his chair in his excitement frantically rattling the bones, he dances to the tune, he throws open the lapel of his coat, and in a spasm of final delight, as the last stroke is given to the sleigh bell by the others, he stands upon his head on the chair seat, and for a thrilling moment and evanescent instant extends his nether extremities in the air."[2]

Brittle, crisp-sounding cattle bones of uniform heft and shape were not always available to urban minstrels, who therefore bought factory-made artificial bones cut from dense hardwoods. In 1896, when "Old Dan" Emmett finally retired, Sears advertised five kinds of wooden bones (Fig. 5). Five and one-half to seven inches long, these were sold by mail in sets of four priced by size and material. Ebony, the most expensive, cost thirty-five cents for a seven-inch, seven-ounce set; rosewood bones retailed for twenty cents, while the Museum's set of stained oak (Fig. 6) would have cost about a dime at the turn of the century. More expensive these days but still being made—notably by the Dexter, Michigan, farmer Raymond Schairer—neatly finished hardwood bones can be heard today in the capable hands of such folk musicians as Percy Danforth.

Pickup bands even now occasionally include household articles that can be played with little or no modification: spoon clappers, washboard scrapers, jug tubas, musical saws, and so on. In the past poverty and frontier isolation fostered do-it-yourself instrumentation in which cast-off utensils found new life. Since no two homespun instruments sound exactly alike, every rustic jug band has a unique sound. Instead of blending like a string quartet, each band's instruments contrast sharply in tone, giving clarity to the already normally thin texture of much Anglo-American folk music. Distinctive sonorities complement the musicians' idiosyncratic styles, sustaining interest through repeated performances of familiar tunes.

Like bone, cane and cornstalks offer rural youth an inexhaustible free resource for fashioning instruments. Cane, which is hollow, is well suited to making whistles. A slight bevel cut at one rim gives a sharp blowing edge that produces a clear tone. An internal node blocking the tube defines the cane's sounding length and pitch. A cane without finger holes can with luck be overblown to sound one or two shrill harmonics, but for melodic playing pierced finger holes or a pennywhistle-type plunger are needed.

Canes of different lengths can also be tied together raft-style to make a panpipe, an ancient, widely dispersed instrument cultivated today especially in South America. Writing of plantation workers in central Georgia in 1883, Joel Chandler Harris (author of the "Uncle Remus" tales) reported, "I have heard them make sweet music with . . . Pan's pipes." The Museum's examples (Figs. 7, 8), from the southern United States, have five and seven canes respectively, sounding approximately the notes g^1, c^2, c-sharp^2, e-flat^2, f^2; and g^1, a^1, b^1, c-sharp^2, e-flat^2, f^2, g^2. Such pentatonic (five-note) and whole-tone scales are

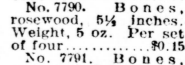

Bones and Clappers.

No. 7789. Bones, hardwood, 5½ inches. Weight, 5 oz. Per set of four.............$0.12

No. 7790. Bones, rosewood, 5½ inches. Weight, 5 oz. Per set of four.............$0.15

No. 7791. Bones, rosewood, 7 inches, large. Weight, 6 oz.

No. 7789. Per set of four...$0.20

No. 7792. Bones, solid ebony, 5½ inches. Weight, 6 oz. Per set of four......................$0.25

No. 7793. Bones, solid ebony, 7 inches large. Weight, 7 oz. Per set of four..................$0.35

5. Sears, Roebuck & Co. mail-order catalogue advertisement for wooden bones. Chicago, Ill., 1896

6. Two pairs of commercial oak bones. Late 19th century. L. 6 in. (89.4.522.1–4)

common in folk music. Tuning often seems random; in the United States, where the panpipe usually plays alone, the pipes are tuned in whatever manner pleases their makers.

Many Americans reared in corn country remember cornstalk fiddles. These desiccated, fragile toys do not last long but can be replaced on the spur of the moment. With a pocketknife, the maker cuts two shallow parallel lines lengthwise between two nodes, defining a narrow strip of fibrous surface. This strip, separated beneath but left attached at both ends, is raised by short sticks that free it to vibrate. More "strings" can be loosened in this manner, to be plucked gently by the finger or scraped with a rolled corn leaf. In the Museum's example (Fig. 9) an uncut internode section serves as a handle. Stalk fiddles, like panpipes, are found in many parts of the world; in North America they were childhood artifacts. A generation ago youngsters in rural Pennsylvania used them at harvest time to ac-

company barnyard plays. Interestingly, a similar but larger fiddle was made of agave stalk by nineteenth-century Apache Indians; its origin is uncertain, but may be owed to contact with white settlers.

Novelty instruments amuse children with their intriguing shapes and sounds, and bring good profits to dime stores. Musical toys have even been incorporated in orchestral scores by such composers as Leopold Mozart and Darius Milhaud. The noted pedagogue Carl Orff employed specially designed juvenile instruments in his system of teaching music. Today's musical juvenilia have thus moved from the realm of folk craft into commerce and schooling. But their ancient archetypes possessed even more formidable social significance. Many noisemakers now considered children's property—whistles, jingles, rattles, and the like—formerly had important roles in adult ceremonies, courtship, hunting and food gathering, and communication. Though today's

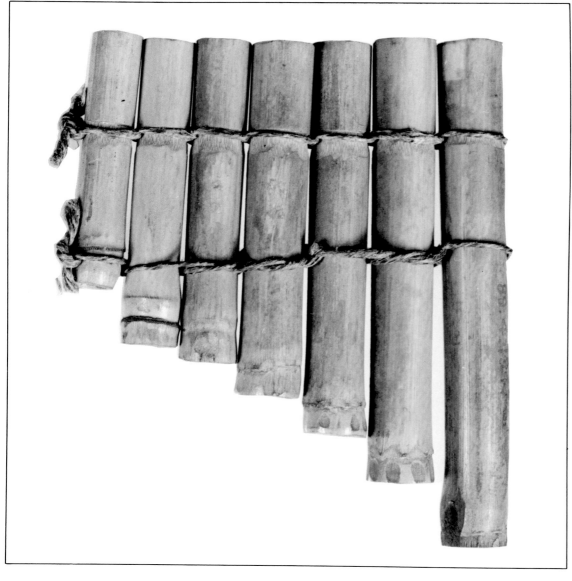

7. Seven-note cane panpipes. Georgia, before 1900. L. 4¼ in. (89.4.3295)

noisy toy might merely indicate a child's where-abouts to a busy parent at the other end of the house, its precursor may have been a charm against evil.

The whistling rattle, an amusing bauble for infants, was a traditional gift at eighteenth-century christenings. These treasured keepsakes, first advertised in the American colonies by the Charleston goldsmith John Pennefather in the *South-Carolina Gazette* for November 16, 1738 ("a child's whistle and chains"), came to the colonies with early settlers. Before the Revolution American newspapers carried many ads for infants' "whistles-and-bells" imported from England. In 1791, after federal tariffs cut imports of luxury goods, Martha Washington commissioned the Philadelphia silversmith Joseph Anthony to make one such rattle for twenty-five dollars, a substantial price.

Some pre-Revolution New York artisans made these highly prized items of gold. The Museum's

9. Cornstalk fiddle with two "strings." Late 19th century. L. 11¹³/₁₆ in. (89.4.2495)

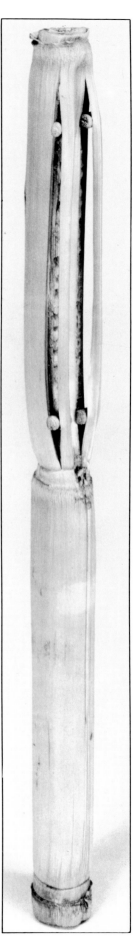

8. Five-note cane panpipes. Georgia, before 1900. L. 4⅜ in. (89.4.1347)

40

whistling rattle by Nicholas Roosevelt (1715–69) is one of only three gold examples known today (Fig. 11). Its unusually ornate chinoiserie and rocaille engraving and repoussé work would not have impressed a toddler, but reflected his elders' refined taste. A whistle with shield-shaped mouth caps the central baluster, on which eight pear-shaped jingles hang from loops in two rows. At the opposite end a smooth orange coral finger served as a cool pacifier and teether and as a good luck charm; coral amulets are still worn by the superstitious to ward off the evil eye and promote health. This whistling rattle was worn suspended from a ring held by a tiny screw behind the whistle.

Around 1750 a second Dutch-surnamed New Yorker, Richard van Dyck (1717–70) of Hanover Square, made a silver whistling rattle (Fig. 12) that bears in addition to his hallmark the scratched initials *IS*, perhaps those of the child for whom it was destined. The octagonal stem, embellished with leaf appliqués, holds eight round jingles, an orange coral at one end, and a whistle with traditional heart-shaped mouth at the other. A suspension ring is fastened at the back of the whistle. This opulent noisemaker and its gold counterpart exemplify the lavish gifts bestowed upon such privileged tots as the little girl in William Johnston's portrait of Mrs. Jacob Hurd and daughter (Fig. 10). Wielded like royal scepters in tiny fists, these aristocratic playthings inspired these lines from Longfellow's "To a Child":

With what a look of proud command
Thou shakest in thy tiny hand
The coral rattle with its silver bells
Making a merry tune!

10. *William Johnston. Mrs. Jacob Hurd and Daughter, c. 1765 (64.114.2)*

11. *Whistling rattle by Nicholas Roosevelt. L. 6⅛ in. (47.70)*

12. *Whistling rattle by Richard van Dyck. L. 6⅛ in. (33.120.361)*

41

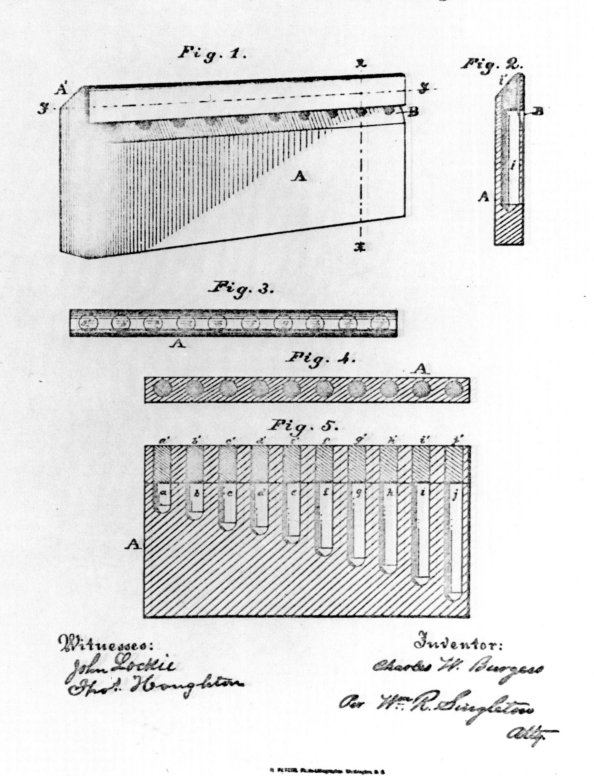

C. W. BURGESS.
MUSICAL INSTRUMENT.

No. 409,315.   Patented Aug. 20, 1889.

Fig. 1.

Fig. 2.

Fig. 3.

Fig. 4.

Fig. 5.

Witnesses:
John Lockie
Thos. Houghton

Inventor:
Charles W. Burgess

Per Wm. R. Singleton
Atty.

Nineteenth-century technology brought commercial mass production of musical juvenilia. The Bostwick & Burgess Manufacturing Company of Norwalk, Ohio, a general woodworking concern specializing in Victoria Venetian Blinds, struck a bonanza in the late 1880s when Charles W. Burgess created the Calliope, a ten-note diatonic panpipe (Figs. 13, 14). Its economical design involves ten holes of graduated depth drilled into a rectangular hardwood block. A V-shaped channel runs across the lightly varnished block near the drilled end, intersecting the holes to form sharp-edged mouths, below which the shorter tube segments are partly plugged to make whistle-type windways. The block's lower edge is chamfered to provide a comfortable surface for the player's lips.

Interestingly, a Japanese panpipe of nearly identical design exists in the Pitt Rivers Museum, Oxford, England; apparently contemporary with the Metropolitan Museum's Calliope, it may indicate a cross-cultural influence. Some Calliopes in other American museums bear labels lithographed by the Laning Printing Company, picturing Uncle Sam handing out these panpipes by the crateful at a midwinter fair. The label on our example, which bears the wording *patent applied for*, shows that Calliopes were in production before Burgess's patent was granted on August 20, 1889 (patent number 409,315). These little toys retailed throughout the East and upper Midwest at up to twenty-five cents each ($1.70 per dozen, wholesale, in 1898). Isaac W. Bostwick earlier gave up his marble works (listed in *Bailey's Northern Ohio Gazetteer and Directory* of 1871–72) to become president of the woodworking firm. Perhaps he supplied the capital, and vice-president Burgess the ideas and skills. Burgess was not listed in local directories before 1900; by that time, presumably, he had gained some wealth. The small company exists today only in the memory of some older Norwalk residents.

In Buffalo, New York, the toy panpipe assumed its most ephemeral form. The Victory Siren (Figs. 15, 16) produced by Glenn Confections was an edible, or at least chewable, eight-note panpipe molded of a 1¼-ounce trapezoidal slab of artificially colored and flavored wax. The name Victory Siren was applied to this confection during World War II, when a former curator of prints presented one to the collection as a lighthearted gift. Accessioned in a rare moment of frivolity, it was consigned to storage wrapped in a rubber band that eventually squeezed its sides out of shape. The transient orange coloring has faded almost completely. Happily, these panpipes are still being made and sold, mainly around Halloween. The ingredients have changed somewhat, and the current product called the Wowie Whistle weighs only half as much as its forty-five-year-old ancestor. Certainly no musical virtue explains the longevity of this novelty, but its ability to

13. *Patent drawing of Calliope invented by Charles W. Burgess*

14. *Calliope (panpipe) by Bostwick and Burgess. Norwalk, Ohio, late 19th century. W. 6⁷/₃₂ in. (1977.246.2)*

15. *Victory Siren (chewing-gum panpipe) by Glenn Confections. Buffalo, N. Y., 1944. W. 3½ in. (44.119)*

16. *Label for Victory Siren in Fig. 15*

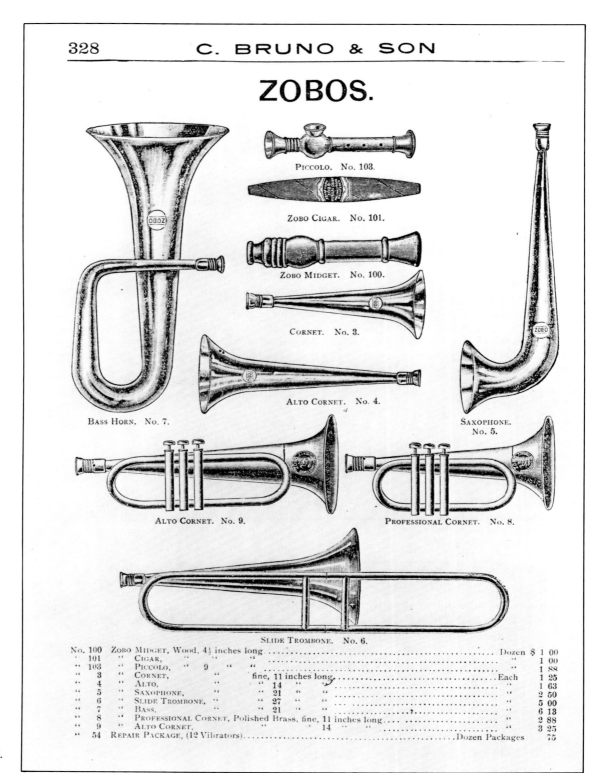

C. BRUNO & SON

ZOBOS.

PICCOLO. No. 103.

ZOBO CIGAR. No. 101.

ZOBO MIDGET. No. 100.

CORNET. No. 3.

ALTO CORNET. No. 4.

BASS HORN. No. 7.

SAXOPHONE. No. 5.

ALTO CORNET. No. 9.

PROFESSIONAL CORNET. No. 8.

SLIDE TROMBONE. No. 6.

No. 100	Zobo Midget, Wood, 4½ inches long				Dozen $ 1 00
" 101	" Cigar, " " "				1 00
" 103	" Piccolo, " 9 "				1 88
" 3	" Cornet, " fine, 11 inches long			Each	1 25
" 4	" Alto, " " 14 " "			"	1 63
" 5	" Saxophone, " " 21 " "			"	2 50
" 6	" Slide Trombone, " " 27 " "			"	5 00
" 7	" Bass, " " 21 " "			"	6 13
" 8	" Professional Cornet, Polished Brass, fine, 11 inches long			"	2 88
" 9	" Alto Cornet, " " 14 " "			"	3 25
" 54	Repair Package, (12 Vibrators)			Dozen Packages	75

17. *Wooden Zobo of Warren H. Frost's design for Bruno & Son Zobo Midget model number 100. L. 4²¹/₃₂ in. (89.4.2586)*

18. *C. Bruno & Son wholesale catalogue advertisement for Zobos. New York, N. Y., 1903–4*

sound while being consumed must be its major attraction, akin to the satisfying pop of bubble gum.

Zobo was a turn-of-the-century brand name for a toy later called the Sonophone and today generally known onomatopoeically as the kazoo. A kazoo is a voice modifier that consists of a flexible, inelastic membrane, like waxed paper, attached to a tube. Vocalizing into the tube excites the membrane to buzz loudly, disguising and intensifying the voiced tone. The use of such a membrane modifies the tone of instruments as varied as Chinese flutes and African xylophones. In a simple form it exists as the comb-and-tissue mirliton concocted by generations of schoolchildren.

Kazoos have occasionally been included in modern scores such as Leonard Bernstein's *Mass*

ZOBOS.

(NEW MINIATURE STYLES.)

Cornetto No. 102.

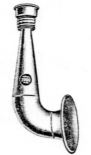

Saxonette No. 105.

Altonette No. 104.

Trombonette No. 106.

Bassonette No. 107.

Prof. Cornetto No. 108.

No. 102	Zobo Cornetto,	Polished Brass,	5	inches long		Dozen	$ 5 25
" 104	"	Altonette,	"	6½	"	"	10 00
" 105	"	Saxonette,	"	7¾	"	"	10 63
" 106	"	Trombonette,	"	9¼	"	"	20 00
" 107	"	Bassonette.	"	6	"	"	20 00
" 108	"	Prof. Cornetto,	"	6½	"	3 Pistons	"	20 00

━ KAZOO. ━

(THE 1903 MODEL TRUMPET.)

NEW MODEL TRUMPET **KAZOO** (FULL SIZE.)

AN ENTIRELY NEW INSTRUMENT. All metal, nickeled. Do not confuse this with the old style Kazoo or any other instrument of a like nature. It is easier to play, far more musical and powerful and will last longer than any instrument of its kind ever introduced. Plays any tune. Any one can play it without instruction. Imitates any bird or animal, bagpipes, snare drum and Punch and Judy. Bands using it as mouth-piece on brass or tin horns produce excellent music without fingering keys. Used with astonishing results at society meetings, home, club or church entertainments, dances, serenades, picnics, outings, excursions; by campaign, bicycle and marching clubs, quartettes, choruses and shows.

No. 75 Nickel Plated..Dozen $ 1 85

19. C. Bruno & Son wholesale catalogue advertisement for Zobos. New York, N. Y., 1903–4

20. Plated brass Zobo of Warren H. Frost's design for Bruno & Son Zobo Cornetto model number 102. L. 4²⁹/₃₂ in. (89.4.2585)

(1971) and Maurice Wright's *Like an Autumn Sky* (1980). Less formally, the University of Chicago recently fielded a kazoo marching band. Earlier in this century, kazoos imitated cornets and trumpets in jug bands. Otto Langey's Zobo tutor, advertised in the 1902 Sears catalogue, contained scales and exercises to make good the "wish book's" glowing encomium:

Anybody can play, anybody can buy; brilliant martial and orchestral music at small cost; best and cheapest sacred music. The Zobo Musical Instruments are the latest addition to the Zobo [line], and are rapidly becoming the most popular amusement in the novelty and musical way, as the tone is produced by singing into them. Anyone can play them without difficulty, and produce good music or many imitations if so desired; with Zobo Brass Band Instruments a brass band can be organized with men or boys who have

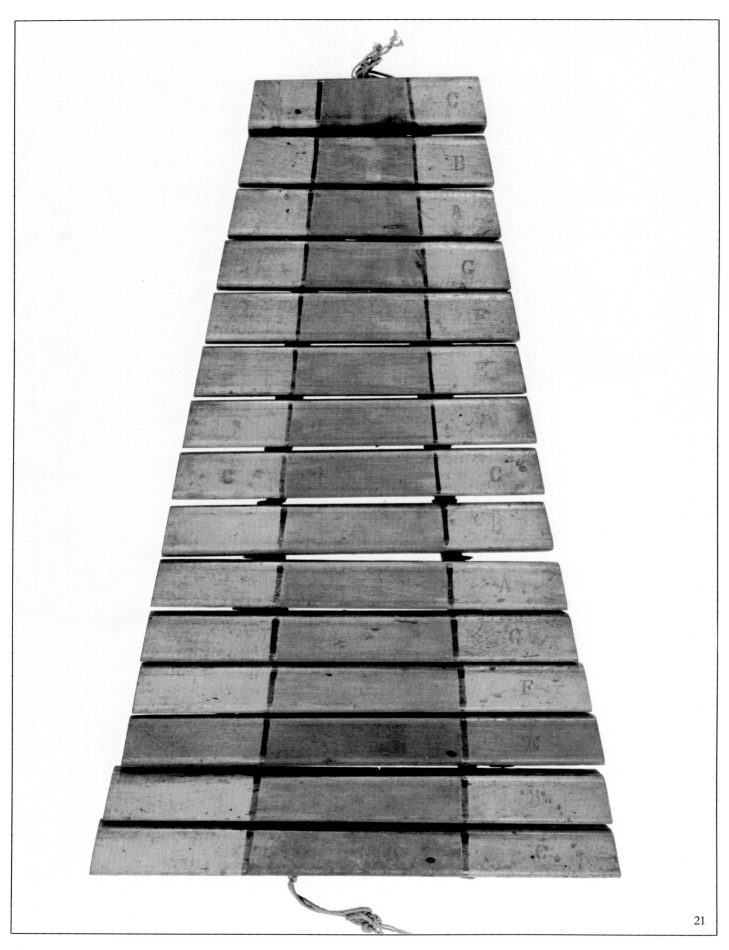

no knowledge of musical instruments whatever, but with a few rehearsals are capable of rendering brilliant music, and producing instrumental effects possible hitherto to none but the best brass band and orchestra.

All the various Zobos—C. Bruno & Son's 1903–4 wholesale catalogue (Figs. 18, 19) illustrated sixteen forms—were related to Chicagoan Warren H. Frost's patent of January 7, 1896 (552,612). Two examples in the collection represent the types shown in Frost's patent: one of varnished wood (Fig. 17), the other of plated brass (Fig. 20). The former has a side aperture that lets the sound out, while a tiny vent hole near the mouthpiece allows breath to escape without distending the membrane and thereby preventing its vibration. Blowing hard will rupture the thin diaphragm, so the more expensive metal Zobos were often stamped *Do not blow but sing or speak* or *Don't blow simply* hum *into the mouthpiece.* Most models had threaded wooden mouthpieces in which the membrane could be secured more or less tightly; Frost maintained that a female voice required a tighter diaphragm than a male voice. Spares could be purchased in anticipation of a blowout.

More durable and more strictly "instrumental," xylophones have been played in Europe at least since the Middle Ages. One called a "straw fiddle" is pictured among other rustic instruments in the *Theatrum Instrumentorum* (1620) of Michael Praetorius. (The slang name "fiddle" is applied to all sorts of implements, not just stringed instruments.) Xylophones were widespread in Africa much earlier. Transported slaves were making them in the West Indies by the mid-seventeenth century and in Virginia by 1775.

Because they are almost unbreakable, are not too loud, and visually suggest the "size" ratios of scale pitches, xylophones are much used in teaching elementary school music. In 1898 C. Bruno & Son sold eight varieties of two-octave xylophones having fifteen diatonic bars or twenty-five chromatics (Fig. 23). The bars were made of ash, walnut, maple, or rosewood in order of increasing cost, from $1.05 to $25 per set. These retail prices were subject to a standard trade discount, usually 60 percent, plus another 5 or 6 percent off for cash payment. Sears' price for a fifteen-bar xylophone like the Museum's example remained stable at ninety-five cents from 1896 to 1902 (Fig. 22).

This typical maple set (Fig. 21) has bars strung on cord and separated by felt washers. Two felt strips stapled along the bottoms of the bars provide acoustic insulation. Each bar is stamped with its pitch; curiously, this set sounds a half step above nominal pitch (the lowest note, marked C, plays c-sharp[2]). The tops of the bars are varnished on either side of a dark striking surface marked off by black lines. Each bar has a shallow saw kerf

across its underside to render it more flexible. The beaters are missing.

In essence a mechanized xylophone, the conventional toy piano is a good example of a musical plaything that emulates a serious adult instrument. Toy pianos were preceded in the Baroque era by diminutive spinets with narrow keys suiting a child's handspan. These expensive siblings of the fashionable harpsichord needed frequent tuning and regulation and belonged mainly to children of wealthy families. The piano's rise to popularity shortly before 1800 coincided with the stirrings of an economically advantaged bourgeoisie whose offspring, too, wanted miniature instruments. As the sentimental cult of childhood mushroomed in the Victorian era, toy pianos became common articles of middle-class commerce, and ways to reduce their cost were

21. *Fifteen-bar maple xylophone similar to C. Bruno & Son model number 0 and Sears model number 7787. L. 17¾ in. (89.4.3393)*

22. *Sears, Roebuck & Co. mail-order catalogue advertisement for xylophones. Chicago, Ill., 1896*

23. *C. Bruno & Son wholesale catalogue advertisement for xylophones. New York, N.Y., 1898*

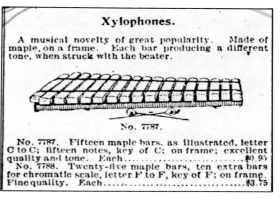

Xylophones.

A musical novelty of great popularity. Made of maple, on a frame. Each bar producing a different tone, when struck with the beater.

No. 7787.

No. 7787. Fifteen maple bars, as illustrated, letter C to C; fifteen notes, key of C; on frame; excellent quality and tone. Each................$0.95
No. 7788. Twenty-five maple bars, ten extra bars for chromatic scale, letter F to F, key of F; on frame. Fine quality. Each................$3.75

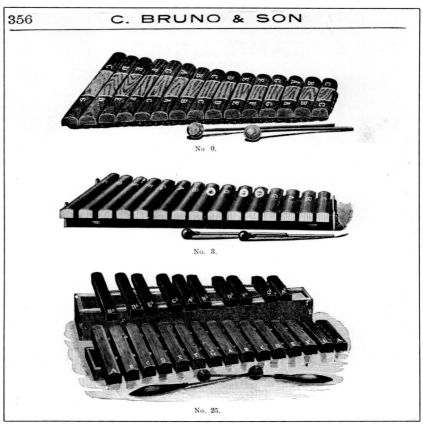

356   C. BRUNO & SON

No 0.

No. 3.

No. 25.

sought. To save tuning and simplify manufacture, the piano's strings were dispensed with. Instead, sound came from struck metal bars. The hammer mechanism was reduced to two moving parts per key, and the soundboard was omitted. The remaining works were enclosed in piano-shaped cases: grands, uprights, and squares. Though usually no more than two or three octaves in range, such toy pianos proved useful in fostering basic music appreciation, as reflected by Schroeder's devoted practicing in Charles Schultz's comic strip "Peanuts."

Albert Schoenhut (d. 1912), America's leading manufacturer of toy pianos around 1900, began making toys and dolls in Philadelphia in 1872 when that city vied with New York as the coun-

try's toy-producing capital. Schoenhut's catalogues show many styles of toy pianos as well as other novelties employing struck metal bars. His products, small and light enough for cheap posting, were widely sold by mail.

A Schoenhut upright piano (Fig. 24) made shortly after the turn of the century incorporates the specially treated wrought iron bars he patented on October 28, 1873 (144,148) and a mechanism of which the patent (September 18, 1900; 726,905) covers improvements in keyboard construction and hammer design (Fig. 25). This mechanism was assembled with a minimum of separate parts and operations. Instead of having a separate pivot pin through each key, Schoenhut's keyboard balances on a single long fulcrum that runs through

24. *Toy piano and stool by Albert Schoenhut. Philadelphia, Pa., c. 1900. Piano: W. 20¹⁵/₁₆ in.; stool: H. 9 in. (1977.266.1, 2)*

25. *Patent drawing of toy piano mechanism invented by Albert Schoenhut*

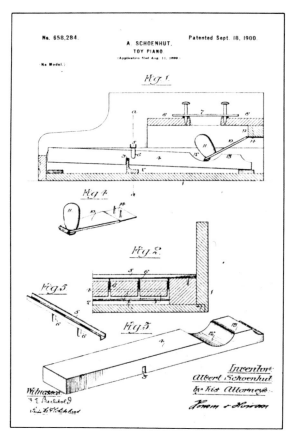

a notch across the keys' lower surfaces. Prongs descending from a stamped metal rail hold the keys apart. Oval wooden hammers are glued to flexible pasteboard strips covered with a piece of muslin that forms a hinge stapled to a rail over the keys. A vertical stick on the back of each key thrusts the hammer upward to strike the bottom of its iron bar. There is no damper. In principle the mechanism resembles the "single action" of eighteenth-century English pianos.

This toy piano's twenty bars, resting on yarn pads and held loosely in place by nails, are tuned diatonically half a step above normal pitch, like the bars of the xylophone previously discussed. The 2½-octave keyboard has false black accidentals painted on the white natural keys. Con-structed without time-consuming screwed and glued joints, the piano's frame was notched and nailed. The vertical front panel is covered with embossed simulated-wood-grain paper on which Apollo and his nine Muses dance between flute-playing cherubs. Below this the name *Schoenhut* in Gothic-style letters is flanked by gold medal-lions stating *Trade mark established* and *National Export Exposition*. The donor of this toy received it from her older sister around 1902 along with a larger-scale piano stool of comparable workman-ship. By her own account, for a five-year-old black child growing up in Orange, Virginia, this beloved instrument opened the door to a lifetime of musical enjoyment.

The harsh ratchet sounded by children at cer-

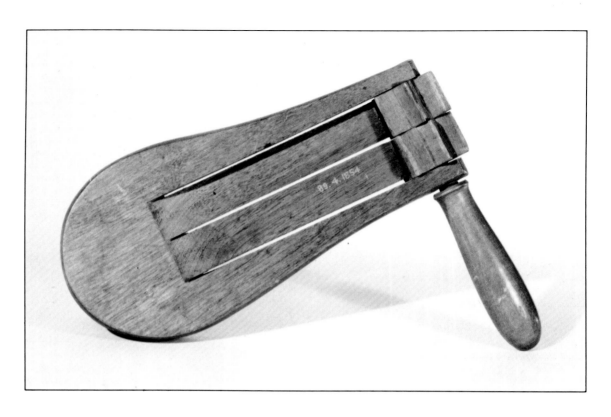

26. *Two-tongue ratchet. Late 19th century. L. of frame 8⁹/₁₆ in. (89.4.1854)*

tain holidays and celebrations represents a much older noisemaker that once announced the approach of lepers and watchmen. It found a place in the orchestra as well, notably in Beethoven's *Wellington's Victory*, Strauss's *Till Eulenspiegel*, and William Walton's *Façade* (1923). Little-changed since the Middle Ages, a ratchet consists of a frame holding a stiff tongue that scrapes over a stationary gear when the frame is swung by a handle extending from the gear's axis. Paired tongues or paired gears with dissimilar teeth give a ratchet tonal individuality, allowing it to be identified at a distance by its particular timbre. The Museum's nineteenth-century example (Fig. 26) has two six-toothed gears of beech and two tongues fixed in a horseshoe-shaped walnut frame. Because the teeth are isosceles, the ratchet can swing in either direction. Easily whittled at home, wooden ratchets such as this never became important articles of commerce.

More tedious to make, metal megaphones and coach horns used for signaling were a specialty of Pennsylvania tinsmiths. Tinned, rustproof sheet iron, available in America after about 1830, was bent around mandrels and soldered to produce long conical tubes. Short flared bells, shallow mouthpieces, and arched handles were soldered on to complete these undecorated, cumbersome horns. Lacking melodic potential, they conveyed their signals as rhythmic blasts. The Museum's black japanned horn (Fig. 28) was sounded on the coach running between Lancaster and Philadelphia around the middle of the nineteenth century. Many similar ones can be found in Pennsylvania museums.

Firemen's "trumpets," actually wide-throated megaphones, amplified shouted orders. Their ample mouthpieces surrounded the shouter's lips and reached to the cheeks. No less than helmet, bucket, and hose, a megaphone was an indispensable part of the Victorian fire brigade's paraphernalia. During parades its upturned bell was filled with flowers, but it could also serve as a drinking horn and as a formidable weapon in brawls. Some engraved silver examples commemorate heroic deeds and notable disasters. The Museum's plainer trumpet of sheet brass has incised foliate and symbolic designs (Fig. 27). According to the 1874 catalogue of the New York dealer Moses Slater, a seventeen-inch "service trumpet" like this would have cost six dollars.

Like megaphones, bells had a vital role in communication a century ago. The American bell-casting industry formerly centered in the Connecticut River valley around East Hampton, the "Bell Town of America." In the spring of 1808 William Barton erected next to his house, on the hill that now bears his name, a small manufactory said to have been the first in the country exclusively devoted to bell making.

The ingenious William Barton (b. Wintonbury, later Bloomfield, Conn., November 26, 1762; d. East Hampton, July 15, 1849) learned gunmaking from his father, who served at the Springfield arsenal during the Revolution. Barton moved to New York City in 1790 and there made and sold brass goods until he bought his East Hampton house in 1807. Eighteen years later, having trained his sons and other young men in his craft, he moved to Cairo, New York, to establish another bell factory. Late in life he returned to East Hampton, where his former apprentices were

27. *Fireman's trumpet or megaphone. Mid-19th century. L. 16¾ in. (89.4.1813)*

28. *Japanned iron coach horn or megaphone. Philadelphia, Pa., mid-19th century. L. 58 in. (89.4.3321)*

27

28

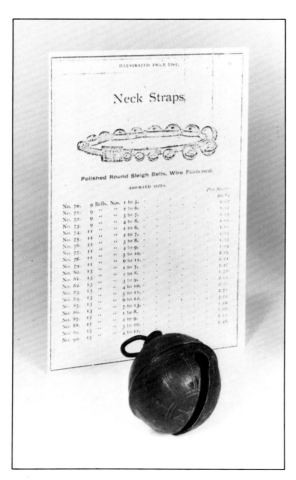

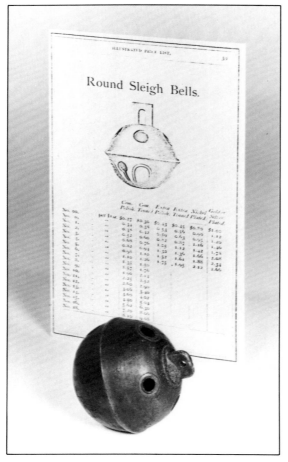

29, 30. *Bronze pellet bells (jingle bells). Connecticut River Valley, 19th century. Diam. (above) 2⁹/₁₆ in., (below) 2¹⁵/₁₆ in. (89.4.1418, 89.4.1419)*

actively expanding their trade. Between 1854 and 1873 fifty bell-related patents originated there from over thirty closely related individuals and firms.

Barton's specialties were hand and sleigh bells, the latter really globular jingles, each enclosing a loose pellet. Jingle bells (Figs. 29, 30) were cast in sizes ranging from one to four inches in diameter; the smallest were sold by the pound or dozen. Hung singly on livestock or in rows on horse trappings, they could identify unseen animals and carriages by means of their different pitches. Customarily, if a wagon suffered an accident, its bells were given to people who stopped to help; thus, to arrive "with bells on" meant a safe, unhampered journey.

Normally of plain bronze, these hardware items could be had in various finishes at extra cost: brightly tinned or polished, or plated with nickel, silver, or gold. Otherwise their appearance was quite uniform. The globe was made of two hemispheres joined at a circumferential ridge, the lower half opened in a straight or crossed slit terminated by circular enlargements and surrounded by radiating "petals" outlined by double grooves. Sometimes the maker's initials were cast in. The upper dome had a protruding eyelet or stem for attachment, two or four sound holes below, and a numerical size designation. Originally the hemispheres were cast separately and joined after the iron pellet was inserted. Barton reportedly invented a process in which the pellet was embedded in a sand core, the globe was cast in one piece around this core, and the sand was then shaken out to free the pellet.

It is hard to overestimate East Hampton's impact on America's ears. Perhaps 90 percent of all bells manufactured in the United States and Canada before 1900 came from the area. Abundant power and cheap transport contributed to the community's success. Waterways and roads carried the heavy goods to market before a railroad, begun in 1867, created a local boom. Bell makers then diversified their wares, stamping lightweight toys from sheet brass or steel and casting finer bronze hardware from melted scrap that included old bells. Smelting was done in charcoal furnaces that yielded alloys of exceptional quality; indeed, the town's foundries fostered improvements in smelting that were adopted throughout American industry. In 1940 the five surviving firms produced well over 52 million bells and jingles of various types.

Around 1900 large stationary sirens were supplanting bells as navigation aids. By 1910 North American coastal shipping was protected by forty-nine powerful sirens audible for miles offshore. (Ironically, the name *siren*, applied to these devices by Charles Gagniard de la Tour around 1819, derives from the half-female monsters of Greek mythology whose beguiling song lured sailors to shipwreck.) Aware of the siren's economic and acoustic importance, the organizer of the Museum's collection, Mrs. John Crosby Brown, sought one for display. Obtaining a marine siren with an amplifying horn twenty feet long that terminated six feet in diameter was out of the question, so she settled for a mouth-blown, pocket-size exemplar (Fig. 31). Made of brass, it has an elliptic mouthpiece and a five-bladed disk inside. Spinning behind a perforated partition, the disk interrupts the wind stream to give an infinitely variable pitch that rises or falls as the disk's rotation speeds or slows.

De la Tour's siren was a scientific instrument used to measure the frequency of musical tones. The Museum's, marked *Mossberg Wrench Co. Attleboro, Mass. U.S.A.* and *'The Develine' patent pending*, is simply a noisemaker. When blown gently, it sounds a spooky, wavering wail. Others like it were attached to cardboard cones decorated with Halloween symbols, indicative of their holiday function. An undated (1920s) catalogue of the Rudolph Wurlitzer Company illustrates just such a siren among drummers' traps (Fig. 32); priced at ten cents, it was called a Cyclone Whistle—"Rendering a perfect imitation of a heavy windstorm." Used for sound effects in vaudeville and silent films, versatile sirens ultimately assumed a truly musical role in Edgard Varèse's avant-garde composition *Ionisation* (1931).

Musical glasses, an occasional feature of vaudeville acts early in this century, enjoyed a great vogue in the Romantic era, although they were blamed for causing fits in sensitive females whose fingertips were irritated by rubbing the glasses' rims. The eerie, ethereal tones of rubbed goblets have fascinated people at least since the seventeenth century, when they were mentioned in Galileo's *Discorsi e dimostrazioni*, written in 1634. Thanks to the Irish virtuoso Richard Puckeridge, musical glasses became the rage in eighteenth-century England. The composer Christoph Willibald Gluck played a concerto in London on April 26, 1746, "upon Twenty-six Drinking Glasses, tuned with Spring Water, accompanied with the whole band, being a new instrument of his own Invention; upon which he performs whatever may be done on a Violin or Harpsichord."[3]

Inevitably this fad was imitated by Americans, notably Benjamin Franklin. While living in London, Franklin invented an improved Glass Armonica with nested, treadle-rotated bowls. This may have been the type of musical glasses unveiled at a concert by Stephen Forrage announced in the *Pennsylvania Gazette* of December 27, 1764. The statesman Francis Hopkinson (1731–91), a signer of the Declaration of Independence, accomplished harpsichordist, composer, and inventor, corresponded with Thomas Jefferson on the subject of adding a keyboard to Franklin's armonica. Hopkinson had a variety of musical interests: He developed a new method of quilling harpsichords, dedicated songs to "His Excellency"

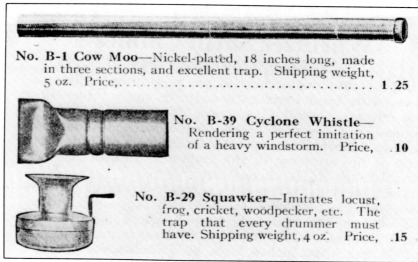

No. **B-1 Cow Moo**—Nickel-plated, 18 inches long, made in three sections, and excellent trap. Shipping weight, 5 oz. Price, ... 1.25

No. **B-39 Cyclone Whistle**—Rendering a perfect imitation of a heavy windstorm. Price, .10

No. **B-29 Squawker**—Imitates locust, frog, cricket, woodpecker, etc. The trap that every drummer must have. Shipping weight, 4 oz. Price, .15

31. *Siren or Cyclone Whistle. Distributed by the Mossberg Wrench Co., Attleboro, Mass., c. 1905. L. 2⁷/₃₂ in. (89.4.2723)*

32. *Wurlitzer wholesale catalogue advertisement for drummers' traps, including Cyclone Whistles. New York, N.Y., c. 1920*

George Washington in 1788, and invented a Bell Armonica and "a contrivance for the perfect measurement of time." His musical bent was inherited by his son Joseph, who wrote the text "Hail Columbia" to the tune "The President's March," and by his grandson Francis Hopkinson Smith, Sr. (b. Baltimore, Md., March 14, 1797; d. Eastville, Va., February 14, 1872), who became the nation's foremost maker of musical glasses.

Smith's Grand Harmonicon, patented on April 7, 1825, had been played by its inventor during the previous December at concerts in the House of Delegates and elsewhere in Richmond, Virginia, where these instruments were sold through William Henry Fitzwhylsonn, later mayor of Richmond. Smith's *Preceptor for the Grand Harmonicon, or Musical Glasses* contains instructions for playing the glasses, a selection of sacred and secular tunes, and an advertisement for instruments with sixteen or twenty-five glasses, sold with or without a mahogany case. The case could be placed on a table, or equipped with four turned legs or a pillar base on claw feet, or mounted like a pier table on two columns and a carved lyre. Prices in 1831 ranged from eighteen to twenty-five dollars, with extra glasses two dollars each.

Judges William Norris, Jr., Abraham Ritter, and J. C. B. Standbridge reported favorably on Smith's entries in the catalogue of the seventh exhibition of Philadelphia's Franklin Institute (1832):

> No. 198. The metrotone invented by Mr. Francis H. Smith, is an instrument of ingenious contrivance, capable of describing to a well cultivated ear, *seventy-two distinct sounds in one whole tone.* We consider this invention a useful one, as it will enable Mr. Smith to present to the public his grand harmonica in perfect tune.
> No. 197. The grand harmonicon, or musical glasses, patented by Mr. Francis H. Smith, is a pleasing instrument, differing essentially from, and superior to, the musical glasses heretofore brought before the public. The quality of tone is rich, and with its sweetness combines great power. This instrument, we are of opinion, *deserves a medal.*

Smith described his harmonicon similarly in his *Preceptor,* adding, "So soft are its tones, that some have called it '*the Æolian Harp harmonized,*' while others on hearing its rich and powerful tones have been deceived by supposing it a well toned organ. Though capable of executing the most rapid passages, it is to soft and plaintive music that it is best adapted; affording a rich treat to the lovers of Scotch and Irish melody." Smith further claimed that two or three weeks' study were sufficient to learn the instrument.

Despite their fragility, over twenty sets of musical glasses attributed to Smith survive today. Two of the Museum's three unsigned sets represent styles offered by Smith: one on a pedestal with four shaggy paw feet (Fig. 33) and one on a handsome lyre-and-column base (Fig. 34, Colorplate 1). No doubt the mahogany bases and cases

33. *Grand Harmonicon, style of Francis Hopkinson Smith. Baltimore, Md., c. 1830. W. 35⅝ in. (89.4.1820)*

34. *Grand Harmonicon, style of Francis Hopkinson Smith. Baltimore, Md., c. 1830. W. 45½ in. Several glasses are missing. (1980.504). See also Colorplate 1*

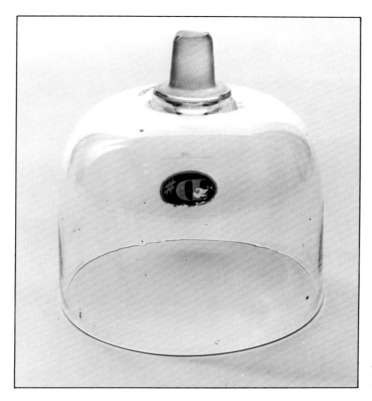

35. *Musical glass from Grand Harmonicon, Fig. 33, with decal and water-level line; pitch letter scratched on bottom of bowl next to stem, opposite accession number. Shown resting on rim. Diam. 5 in.*

were supplied by independent cabinetmakers; the lyre-and-column stand resembles a Boston style, while the pedestal has parallels in New York furniture. Many of Smith's cases are crossbanded and have glass knobs in front. Inside, the soundboard, perhaps of Spanish cedar, often gives a spicy fragrance that fades moments after the case is opened. The blown flint glasses have thin, graduated bowls three to five inches in diameter attached to blunt stems that fit holes in the soundboard (Fig. 35). Commonly in Smith's instruments a pitch letter appears in gold in a black, gold-ringed oval on each bowl, matching a letter engraved on the stem where it joins the bowl. Some bowls have a horizontal scratch indicating the proper level for water used in tuning. Empty, the bowls ring about a half step below modern pitch. An occasional glass displays decoration ". . . richly cut for an additional charge of $10 [per set]," or is more deeply ground near the base, showing that the pitch was adjusted during manufacture.

Smith's sets of twenty-five glasses arranged five-by-five are presumed to date from 1828 or earlier. Later sets held twenty-four glasses six-by-four; the extra note (an alternate high B-flat) was stored separately. Smith remarks that only sixteen glasses at a time were played. The others were alternate notes, used to change the key from the normal E major to keys with fewer sharps. Rarely, a set of twenty-eight glasses was manufactured.

Listed in Baltimore directories of 1824 and 1827 as a dry goods merchant (perhaps in partnership with John D. Toy, publisher of the *Preceptor*), Smith was called a "professor of music" in 1829, when he maintained a manufactory and warehouse on South Frederick Street. By 1833 he was a teller for the Bank of Maryland, and between 1835 and 1853 he was an agent for the Franklin Fire Insurance Company. By 1854 he had become merely a brickmaker and salesman, and his son F. H. Smith, Jr., faced with the family's financial hardship, gave up college to work as a clerk. The son nevertheless later distinguished himself as an artist, writer, and engineer of the Statue of Liberty's foundation.

The Museum's third set of musical glasses (Fig. 36), numbering twenty-five in a plain stained poplar case without base, is markedly dissimilar to the other two and may have been made by a lesser-known man such as Alexander Coger, listed in New York directories as a "harmonica glass" maker only in 1821. Though unsuited by their nature to the modulatory, chromatic music of the late Romantic era, musical glasses remained in popular use into the early twentieth century, when in Chicago, for instance, costumed Bavarian family ensembles played them in vaudeville shows.

Sounding not unlike musical glasses when struck softly, but intended chiefly for outdoor playing, West Indian piano pans developed relatively recently from African and, ultimately, Indonesian prototypes made of various materials. Piano pans, often miscalled "steel drums" although they lack the membrane that defines a true drum, are novel in that they incorporate on a single gonglike surface many distinct areas, each of which emits a different pitch when struck. This economical design originated with black musicians in Trinidad and Tobago, where before World War II single-note gongs were made from empty paint cans and other metal containers. Large oil drums discarded by military installations provided the islanders' raw material for recycling as piano pans.

The Trinidadian Ellie Mannette, now a New York resident, is credited with having originated the new instrument around 1946. Mannette sawed the end off a fifty-five-gallon drum, hammered the head concave to increase its surface area, then raised segments with a hammer and center punch while heating the metal to improve its ductility. One head thus treated can comprise several large,

deep-toned portions or twenty or more small, high-pitched areas. The depth of the rim's edge varies with the pitch of the pan. Today the government of Trinidad and Tobago is said to subsidize the manufacture of high-quality steel drums just for making these pans.

Colorful pan ensembles ranging from bass to soprano enliven festivals wherever West Indians have settled. The growing popularity of such bands in the United States is owed largely to virtuoso performers such as Vincent Taylor (b. Success Village, Laventille, Trinidad, 1944), who started making pans at the age of sixteen. After three years' apprenticeship with master Bertie Marshall, Taylor spent another few years perfecting his skill before coming to New York in 1967. One of only three or four expert pan makers

36. *Musical glasses, table model with lid removed. Mid-19th century. W. 29¹/₁₆ in. (89.4.2885)*

in New York, he took nine weeks to fabricate the pair of tenor pans (Fig. 37) he presented to the Museum in 1974. Taylor outlines his procedures thus: He bought two chemical drums in New Jersey (chemical drums are made of better steel than oil drums, according to Taylor) and cut off the unpierced heads with a power saw, keeping a rim of consistent depth. After heating the heads and beating them concave, he raised the individual segments and fine-tuned them by hammering until their pitch matched a tuning fork. Finally he scoured and polished the pans and waxed them to prevent rust. He made rubber-tipped beaters and ordered the protective cloth covers and the pipe frame from which the pans hang side by side on strings.

These pans, with sixteen and seventeen notes respectively, have a combined chromatic range c-e^3. On them Taylor has played classical arrangements, calypso and show tunes, and original compositions. Self-taught and unable to read notes, he learns and plays by ear, from memory. Practicing four hours daily, Taylor has acquired an astonishing technique that draws crowds at

37. Piano pans (double tenor pair) and beaters by Vincent Taylor. New York, N. Y., 1974. Diam. 22⅞ in. (1974.114)

street performances. Although at first he depended on street performance and taxi driving for income, today he appears in clubs, on college campuses, and on television programs, including one produced by the Museum that also features Mannette and his "discoverer," Pete Seeger. Taylor makes pans only for his own use, not for sale; to do otherwise, he feels, would steal time from musical responsibilities. Although now a professional, he has the reliance on aural transmission of repertoire and on instruments made by himself that generally characterizes folk musicians.

Conventional drums with one or two skin heads are represented in the American collection only by the cylindrical types most commonly seen in bands. All of the Museum's examples—snare, tenor, and bass drums—have two heads, unlike Afro-Cuban conga drums, which have only one and are played by hand rather than with sticks. In contrast to orchestral drums, which are normally placed out of sight at the back of the stage, band drums are invariably positioned so as to seize the eye and therefore are often decorated.

38. Snare drum with regimental banner. Mid-19th century. Diam. 17 in. Leather "ears" on ropes partly deteriorated (89.4.2162)

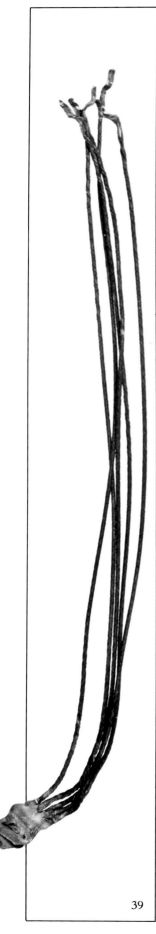

39

Their showiness is enhanced by playing techniques that involve extravagant flourishes of the beaters; any football halftime show will provide examples of these techniques, descended from the drumming style of the Turkish janissaries whose music inspired Mozart and Beethoven.

American-made drums were much in demand locally after the mid-eighteenth century. Soldiers took drumming seriously; in 1777 army drummers at Germantown, Pennsylvania, practiced as much as four hours daily. By 1783 thirty-three regiments in New England, New York, and New Jersey required 158 drummers. Traditionally paired with fifes on the march or used alone to transmit signals, military drums were more than rhythmic instruments. Prominent in battle, like flags they displayed meaningful emblems and embodied the honor of the troops. Capture of its drums left a regiment demoralized, as of course did the loss of the drummers, sometimes unarmed ten- or eleven-year-old sons of officers. Thirteen drummers were killed at the Battle of Bunker Hill alone.

In moments of civic excitement citizens formerly mustered to the unifying beat of drums. Said the painter John Trumbull (1756–1843), "the sound of a drum frequently called an involuntary tear to my eye." But the social messages drums convey, once of transcendent patriotic significance, change with the times. Today rock drummers rouse the blood with orgiastic rhythms that may shout of anger and alienation.

The Museum's oldest American drums were obviously intended for military use. A snare or "side" (slung at the player's side) drum said to date from the Revolutionary period bears on its birch shell a worn painting of an eagle with wings outstretched below an arch of clouds (Colorplate 2). With its left talon the eagle supports an escutcheon displaying thirteen red and white stripes below a faded blue field. Its right talon holds a stylized olive branch. These symbols of federal aspiration recall the Great Seal adopted by the Continental Congress on June 20, 1782, and approved in another version by the first Congress of the United States on September 15, 1789. The American eagle became a common embellishment of military drums and paraphernalia.

To the side of this naive painting is another typical drum decoration, a geometric pattern of domed brass tacks arranged around the air hole. The tacks are clinched inside to fasten the shell's overlapped ends, supplementing a row of iron nails along the outer seam. Two interior rings reinforce the cylinder at its rims. A discoloration visible inside, opposite the air hole, shows where a label had been affixed; this is the label's usual position in cylindrical drums, protected but visible through the air hole when the translucent heads are held to the light. The vellum heads with their thin wrapping hoops are missing, but the larger cord hoops of ash (the upper one colored red) remain in place, each pierced with nine holes through which the tension or bracing rope passed. Two notches at opposite sides of the bottom rim allow clearance for the missing snares, which vibrated sympathetically against the lower head to intensify the sound. These snares could have been either separate gut or rawhide strings or a single strip of skin cut into twisted strands but still attached at one end. The example of the latter type shown here (Fig. 39) was salvaged from a drum attributed to F. M. Smith of Pittsfield, Massachusetts, perhaps the same F. M. Smith who ran a bicycle shop in Pittsfield in 1901. Because wooden snare drums changed so little in structure during the eighteenth and nineteenth centuries, it is impossible in most cases to date them with certainty.

A slightly taller Civil War–era drum (Fig. 38) is similarly constructed and better preserved. A spread eagle on a blue background holds in its beak a banner reading *Reg: U.S. Infantry*. A space before the abbreviation of "Regiment" was left blank for the unit's number to be filled in. The eagle holds arrows in its left talon and an olive branch in the right; as usual it stands behind an escutcheon with thirteen red and white stripes below a blue field, and its head is surrounded by stars under an arch of clouds. The drum is intact except for its snares and their adjustable clamp, but a leather tab with five holes in which the snares were knotted is still wedged between the lower rim and cord hoop. The cords are squeezed together by leather buffs or "ears" that slide up and down to adjust the tension. The air hole, through which no label can be seen, is surrounded by a pattern of domed tacks.

Another nineteenth-century example, much shallower, has a tantalizing label within, its top and bottom lines obscured by internal rings. The unidentified seller's label reflects the frequent commercial association of instruments with umbrellas, fabrics, and dress apparel, a combination of merchandise sold simply as dry goods. The label reads: . . . *[Manuf]acturer, No. 6, Court, near Washington Street, Boston. Offers at low prices, wholesale and retail, an extensive assortment of umbrellas, silk, gingham, and oil cloth . . . . . Fashionable and desirable styles. Parasols, every variety of fashion, color and quality. Walking canes, with and without swords . . . . . mounted with gold, silver and ivory. Musical Instruments, violin, bass viol, and double bass strings, of the very best quality. Every article . . .*

This drum (Fig. 40) has a plain varnished cylinder and orange cord hoops to which a hemp rope is secured through nine holes and held Y-fashion by leather buffs. The air hole, bushed with a bone ring, is surrounded by domed tacks. A brass clamp and screw tighten five gut snares, while a braided "drag" or carrying cord is tied at the lower edge. A loop of leather by the top hoop may have held the sticks.

Typical of turn-of-the-century orchestral

40

39. *Five snares cut from a single piece of drum skin, taken from a drum by F. M. Smith. Pittsfield, Mass. Approx. vibrating L. 15 in. (Inst. 1975.22)*

40. *Snare drum, shallow model. Boston, Mass., mid-19th century. Diam. 16³/₁₆ in. (89.4.590)*

41. *Snare drum and sticks by Henry Eisele with bird's-eye maple shell, eagle, and escutcheon decal. New York, N. Y., c. 1885. Diam. 16¹/₈ in. (1981.479)*

41

drums, a good commercial one of nickel-plated brass with a soldered seam has wooden hoops with decal bands representing fancy inlay (Fig. 42). The hoops are secured with metal hooks clamped by ten key-turned bolts (drum rods) in the so-called Prussian manner that replaced less stable cords and buffs. Ten twisted gut snares are stretched or released by a thumbscrew (snare strainer); the snares would have been relaxed to make the drum sound dull and somber when appropriate, as for a funeral march. All other things being equal, a shallow drum like this has a brighter tone than a deeper drum and cuts better through the sound of a full orchestra. Al-

most too thin to hang securely by a marcher's side, this drum would very likely have been placed on a stand. In the 1903–04 C. Bruno & Son catalogue, a very similar sixteen-inch orchestral drum was advertised at fifteen dollars. In that and other contemporary catalogues rope-tensioned and Prussian drums are shown at generally equal prices, but metal shells were more expensive than wood.

John G. Pike made one of the few attributable American drums in the collection (Fig. 43). Inside its shell is Pike's printed label, listing his stock in trade: *Premium Drums. Bass Drums! for brass and martial bands—2 to 3 feet Head. SNARE DRUMS,*

the double or lined stave drums, Made of Rosewood and Birdseye Maple, also the common maple and Boy's drums, of all sizes, kept constantly on hand. Repairing Done on Short Notice. JOHN G. PIKE, Mitchell Street, Norwich, N. Y.

Pike (b. Plymouth, Chenango County, N.Y., December 23, 1815; d. Norwich, N.Y., July 1, 1884) married Sarah D. Haight of neighboring Smyrna. It was after their fifteen-year-old son's death in 1853 that the couple moved to Norwich, where they subsequently bought and sold several parcels of land. On November 4, 1854, the *Chenango Union* reported the opening in Norwich of the John A. King & Co. piano factory; Pike, a leading partner, owned the building. The factory did not prosper for long, and by 1867 Pike was pursuing the drum maker's trade. This occupation was not unrelated to another local industry, the making of cylindrical wooden cheese boxes. New York was the nation's leading cheese-producing state after 1851, when Jesse Williams established America's first cheese factory in Rome, Herkimer County, forty-seven miles north of Norwich. Upstate dairies used great quantities of drumlike cheese boxes, and it is probable that more than a few "white coopers" produced drums.

At any rate, the front room of Pike's East Main Street house was furnished as a salesroom, with

43. Bass drum by John G. Pike. Norwich, N. Y., 1870–80. Diam. 27¹/₁₆ in. (89.4.2523)

walls full of drums hung from nails. As late as 1883 the Norwich directory listed Pike as a drum maker, though failing health and poor vision had forced him to curtail manufacture some years earlier. A respected Republican and member of the Congregational church, Pike was known throughout town as an able mechanic. The Museum's Pike bass drum measures about twenty-eight inches in diameter, a standard small size convenient for parades. Its mahogany-colored hardwood shell has red hoops, and blue-shaded gold decoration instead of tacks around the air hole. Pike could have purchased ready-made the calfskin or cheaper sheepskin heads he used, as well as the standard Italian hemp cords, tinned iron hooks, and leather "ears," but the shell and hoops he surely made himself, carefully lapping the joints and reinforcing the laminated, stave-built cylinder with internal ribs at top and bottom. James Robb, drummer of Johnson's Band in Norwich, had a Pike bass drum like this one, which he claimed was the best he ever played.

Otto Bötticher. Seventh Regiment Drilling Washington Square, New York, *1851. Detail. (54.90.295)*

WINDS

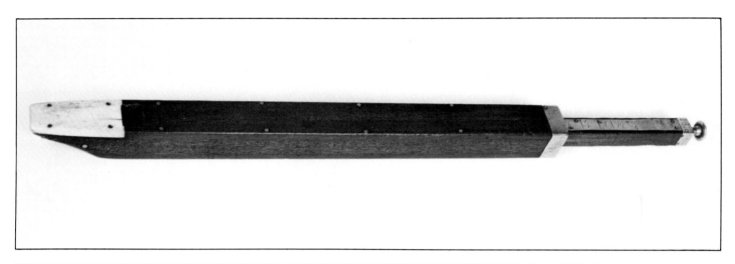

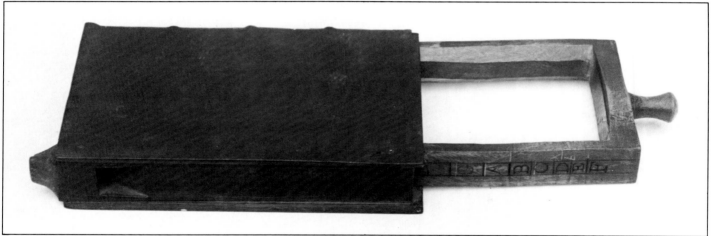

44. *Pitch pipe with metal and bone fittings, plunger inscribed with date 1816.*
New York State? L. (closed) 12⅝ in. (1980.215.1)

45. *Pitch pipe in form of a small book, with cutout plunger. Early 19th century.*
L. (closed) 6²⁵/₃₂ in. (15.132)

46. *Free-reed pitch pipe with graduated cam plunger by William Cook and D. H. Read. New York or New Jersey, after 1876. L. 2¹⁷/₃₂ in. (1981.221)*

47. *Maker's mark on pitch pipe, Fig. 46, with patent date December 26, 1876*

Traditional Anglo-American music is predominantly a vocal art. Since Pilgrim days song has eloquently conveyed our national spirit, and for our first centuries the voice was the natural model against which instrumental tone quality was measured. But vocal timbres, too, have changed over the years in response to instrumental fashions, especially in recent popular music. Instrumental accompaniment is taken for granted today, but a hundred years ago and earlier most music, from folk ballads to liturgical anthems, was sung a cappella. Some religious denominations such as Shakers and Congregationalists at times prohibited instruments altogether, deeming them worldly. Skill in instrumental performance took practice that stole time from more serious pursuits; further, any musical talent beyond the bare minimum could be a source of vanity, pride, and competition.

Among even the most orthodox communities, one exception to the instrument ban was commonly, if reluctantly, made: the pitch pipe, which required no skill to use and which could hardly play an effective tune. Wooden whistle-type pitch pipes were locally constructed in large numbers during the eighteenth and early nineteenth centuries to serve church choirs and singing schools. Their use was defended by the Boston preacher Zabdiel Adams in a 1771 sermon, *The Nature, Pleasure, and Advantages of Church-Musick*, and by America's first major composer, Boston-born William Billings (1746–1800), a tanner who was proclaimed the "father of New England music." (The frontispiece to Billings' *New-England Psalm-Singer* [1770] was engraved by the silversmith and

bell founder Paul Revere.) Introducing his *Continental Harmony* (1794), Billings warned singers that proper pitch levels were crucial to the mood of his music; if sung too high or too low, the tunes suffered a change of character. To establish correct pitch, Billings notes, "The utility of that little instrument, called a *Pitch Pipe*, is so universally known and acknowledged, that it would be needless for me to engross the reader's time in proving a thing which is already granted."[4]

For ultraconservatives, to whom even the sight of a pitch pipe was abhorrent, these essential tools were disguised as small books. At least this is how some antiquarians account for the innocuous appearance of pipes such as the Museum's flat, rectangular one of cherry (Fig. 45), with a graduated plunger that pulls out to give a range of over an octave, e¹-f². Pipes such as this had advantages over metal tuning forks: They provided many pitches rather than just one; they were easier to make, and louder.

Another example, found near Schenectady, New York, resembles a stopped organ pipe (Fig. 44). It is made of mahogany with a rubber-tipped plunger holding an engraved brass index and brass knob. The scale graduation is now incomplete, covering only six notes, d¹-b¹; the broken portion has been replaced by an unmarked copper strip. The pitch is a bit higher than today's standard. The tooth-worn mouthpiece has been repaired with bone plates. The brass index is stamped *1816*, the year in which printed songbooks began spreading into the South following publication of Ananias Davisson's *Kentucky Harmony* (Harrisonburg, Virginia) and Joseph Funk's shape-note

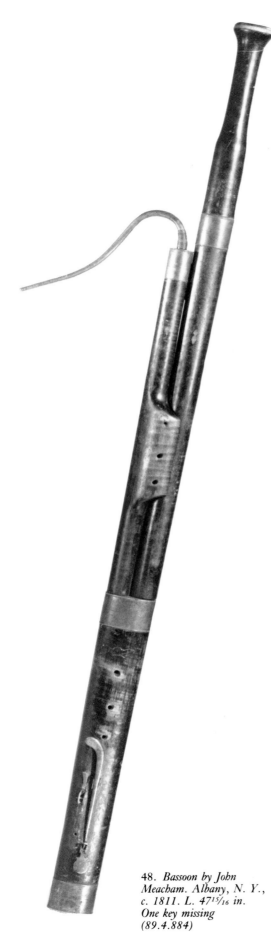

48. *Bassoon by John Meacham. Albany, N. Y., c. 1811. L. 47¹⁵/₁₆ in. One key missing (89.4.884)*

Choral-Music (printed in German at Singer's Glen, near Harrisonburg). Pitch pipes and sacred songbooks such as these went together into villages and camp meetings where religious fervor was expressed in spiritual choruses.

Few attributable woodwinds survive from before the War of 1812. Perhaps the turners and mechanics who made winds, probably as a sideline, knew most of their customers personally and so felt no need to sign their wares. In any event, many anonymous woodwinds must have been imported, and native examples so closely followed British patterns that American traits are hard to distinguish. Ivory, English boxwood, and other foreign materials were available to colonial craftsmen. Especially during the Revolutionary era substitutes such as horn, bone, and local woods were common; indistinguishable substances were also used abroad, however, so materials furnish little clue to provenance.

Warfare, hard times, and isolation brought about by embargoes led to conservatism in American instrument design during much of the first third of the nineteenth century. Many players resisted innovation, preferring their old-style, few-keyed woodwinds so long as the popular repertoire could be rendered by their familiar fingerings. Between 1816 and 1833 a 30 percent tariff on foreign woodwinds discouraged sales of the latest imports and pushed American manufacture along established paths. New machinery increased the rate of production but brought no fundamental changes in methods. After the first third of the century, though, woodwind tariffs fell to 25 percent, then briefly to 20 percent in 1842. This encouraged foreign trade, which, coupled with an influx of well-trained immigrant musicians, brought increasingly specialized American craftsmen—many of them also recent arrivals—into close touch with northern Europe's advanced designs and musical requirements. These factors challenged Americans to experiment and to patent innovations; thus distinctive styles emerged from urban manufacturing centers of the Northeast.

Due to their varied musical duties, bassoons were relatively abundant here in the early nineteenth century. The first native bassoons, copied from English models, inherited an extensive composed repertoire and an unwritten tradition of reinforcing bass lines ad lib. In organless churches—the majority—bassoons often doubled the bass singers, a responsibility shared, as in Europe, with string basses and serpents. Like bass clarinets, bassoons routinely carried the bottom part in wind ensembles. Low brasses took over in bands around 1840, but bassoons kept a secure place in theater and concert orchestras.

The Museum's old-fashioned and much-worn bassoon dating from about 1811 (Fig. 48), marked *Meacham Albany*, is one of the six earliest American examples known. Made of curly maple in four sections, it retains a soldered brass crook and three of its four brass keys, pivoted in brass saddles screwed to the tube. Brass bands reinforce edges liable to split; an eyelet on one band is for a lanyard on which the instrument could hang from the player's neck, a special convenience in parades. At the top a constriction and terminal flare suggest the contour of the otherwise conical bore. In boring the lowest (butt) section the bottom was cut through to make a U bend and then plugged by a cork sealed with wax; a protective butt plate is missing, so the cork—which had to be replaced when saturated with moisture—is now exposed.

The Meacham brothers, John Jr. (b. Enfield, Conn., May 2, 1785; d. Albany, N.Y., December 8, 1844) and Horace (b. Enfield, July 19, 1789; d. Albany? 1861), moved around 1800 to Hartford, where for several years John worked under the noted woodwind and organ maker George Catlin. Around 1810 he moved to Albany to open a business, and Horace soon joined him there. The brothers made winds for militia bands and sold other instruments and military goods as well. Surviving the panic of 1819, which shut many small factories, the Meachams diversified their trade, taking advantage of cheap transport on the Hudson River and (after 1823) the Erie Canal. In 1825 they took over a hardware store, and in 1828 they were joined in partnership by Sylvanus Billings Pond (b. Milford, Mass., April 5, 1792; d. Brooklyn, N.Y., March 12, 1871), a piano manufacturer and later a prominent music publisher and musician. Pond's activities in Albany included being foreman of Volunteer Fire Engine Company No. 1, president of the Albany Sacred Music Society, and an unsuccessful candidate for county sheriff in 1829. As part of their varied enterprise, in 1831 J. & H. Meacham & Co. restored an historic drum presented to Gen. Peter Gansevoort, a Revolutionary war hero. A couple of years later, Horace's son Roswell took over the business, and Pond moved to New York City to join the firm of Firth & Hall.

From its mark *Meacham & Co. Albany* (Fig. 51) a three-section boxwood flute in F (Fig. 50, no. 1) can be dated to around 1828–36. With its ivory rings (one missing) and ivory cap, this flute would have been called "tipped" and would have fetched a higher price than an all-wooden one. Except for the ivory mounts and turnings near the foot, the flute's slightly tapered sides are straight, its profile undistinguished in contrast to the rococo designs favored by some contemporary makers. The single key (missing) closed on a plain flat seating, a kind considered outmoded by makers of more sophisticated flutes. This high-pitched instrument most likely was meant for use in a band, not in a parlor.

John Jacob Astor (1763–1848), who first gained wealth from the fur trade, had earlier operated a music shop in New York. The sale of flutes imported from his brother George in London helped

49. *Deacon Robert Peckham*. William Cornee, *1836.*
He is holding a flute bearing the maker's mark Graves.
Courtesy The New York State Historical Association

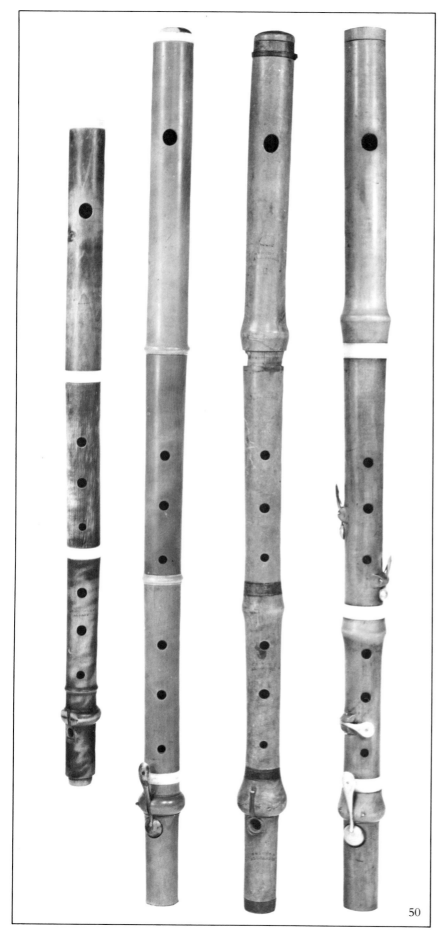

51. *Stamp of Meacham &*
Co. on flute, Fig. 50, no.1

52. *Stamp of Graves &*
Alexander on flute, Fig.
50, no. 3

53. *Stamp of William A.*
Pond & Co. on flute, Fig.
54

50. *Flutes.* Left to right: *1. Meacham & Co. Albany,*
N. Y., c. 1830. L. 18 in. Key and lowest ferrule missing
(1980.301) 2. Unknown maker. Mid-19th century. L.
24³/₃₂ in. (1975.364) 3. Graves & Alexander.
Winchester, N. H., 1830–33. L. 23³¹/₃₂ in. Key and
horn ferrule missing (1978.265.2) 4. Unknown maker.
Mid-19th century. L. 24¹³/₃₂ in. Cap replaced
(1978.552.1)

50

54. *Flute in F by William A. Pond & Co. New York,*
N. Y., mid-19th century. L. 19⁷/₈ in. (1978.136.4)

launch this enterprise in September, 1784. Flutes such as those sold by Astor were nearly indispensable in eighteenth- and nineteenth-century popular music. Made in various sizes, they conveyed cheer, patriotic defiance, or melting pathos with equal facility. One-key wooden flutes were the most plentiful of woodwinds; small, cheap, easy to play, with no reed to wear out, the flute was the gentleman's constant musical companion.

Similar in profile to the Meacham flute, but larger and pitched normally in D, an unmarked four-section boxwood flute (Fig. 50, no. 2) retains its cupped silver "salt spoon" key, which pivots in a turned ring and closes on a circular recessed seat. It has both horn and bone ferrules, indicating that some are replacements. Turned piecemeal by eye, with keys obtained from many sources, anonymous flutes such as this are not attributable on the basis of appearance. Their simple shapes hide much variety in tuning and tone, but age and wear so alter the original sound as to make attributions based on precise acoustic measurements hypothetical.

Worn to the point of being unplayable, a one-key apple or boxwood flute in D (Fig. 50, no. 3), marked *Graves & Alexander* between a Federal eagle and a lyre (Fig. 52), features the gently swelling joints seen on English instruments since the mid-eighteenth century. Its wide, flat horn ferrules, bulging key ring, and pronounced oval embouchure are stylistically unlike those of the preceding two flutes; the bore, too, is substantially narrower, likely to produce a brighter tone. A countersunk, rimmed seat suggests that the missing key was cupped rather than flat; only its brass shank remains in place. Below the domed cap an iron band clamps a crack.

This flute is among the very few products known to survive from the partnership of Samuel Graves, Jr., and Charles Alexander, joined in Winchester, New Hampshire, in 1830 and terminated in 1833. Graves (b. Andover, N. H., 1794; d. Wells River, Vt., November 18, 1878) was the son of a successful farmer and sometime state legislator whose ancestors had arrived from England before 1659. Graves started business in West Fairlee, Vermont, in 1824 and remained the company's pillar until he suffered a stroke in 1870, leaving affairs to his sons. Most Graves woodwinds were made before the mid-1840s, when brass bands began to edge out mixed ensembles. By 1851, when operations moved to Boston, the firm had begun to decline.

Samuel Graves was an able draftsman and mechanic who reportedly invented a folding bathtub, and pulled teeth as a sideline. His Winchester workshop, bought for one hundred dollars in 1830, occupied part of a four-story factory beside the Ashuelot River. His deed included rights of drawing water to run machinery. Water-powered tools helped place Graves among the most productive woodwind makers of his day; his instruments found their way far beyond the town of just over two thousand people. Unfortunately, water power was not as useful in making brass instruments as it was for woodwinds, since the manufacture of brasses relied less on rotating saws, lathes, and drills.

Deacon Robert Peckham's 1836 oil portrait *William Cornee with Flute* (Fig. 49) depicts a multiple-key, tipped boxwood flute marked *Graves* in three places. That flute closely resembles the Museum's unmarked boxwood instrument in D (Fig. 50, no. 4), with four ivory ferrules and four brass salt spoon keys, the upper three mounted in integral blocks (partial turned rings) rather than complete rings. Slightly longer and wider than the preceding Graves & Alexander flute, this one has a nearly round embouchure, perhaps altered. The flat cap is a recent replacement. This flute probably was made around 1835–40, when four-key models were becoming common here; in England their use had been established a generation earlier.

A four-section, untipped boxwood flute in F (Fig. 54) is remarkably well preserved; it has hardly been played. Its overhanging domed cap mirrors a turning at the opposite end. The brass key is mounted in an attractive ring that may reflect Renaissance Revival styles of turning. The embouchure is quite oval, and the crisp round finger holes are undercut for purposes of voicing. The flat key closes on a recessed, rimmed seat that could have been intended for a cupped key instead. The uppermost turning is flattened on the back to give the left thumb a comfortable surface. Because of its range, this small flute could substitute for a high E-flat clarinet.

The flute's mark *Wm A. Pond & Co. 547 Broadway N. York* (Fig. 53) shows that it dates from the mid-1860s to 1870s. William A. Pond (d. 1885), son of the Meachams' former partner Sylvanus Pond, became the owner of Firth, Pond & Co. when his father retired in 1850. After John Firth withdrew in 1863, William continued the business under his own name. He was a prominent music publisher—notably of Stephen Foster's songs and of Dan Emmett's immortal "Dixie" (1860)—and dealer, but the extent to which his firm actually made instruments is unknown.

His stamp appears on a flute that may have been made at "Fluteville" in the southeast corner of Litchfield, Connecticut. There in 1834 Pond's predecessors bought into the woodwind manufactory of former clockmaker Asa Hopkins, purchasing the business outright in 1845 from Hopkins's successor Jabez McCall Camp. Pond sold the subsidiary in 1867. Regardless of its origin, this elegant, pristine flute upholds a reputation for quality honored since at least 1842, when a Firth & Hall flute won a diploma at the American Institute of the City of New York.

Two technologically advanced concert flutes from New York bear the marks of increasingly

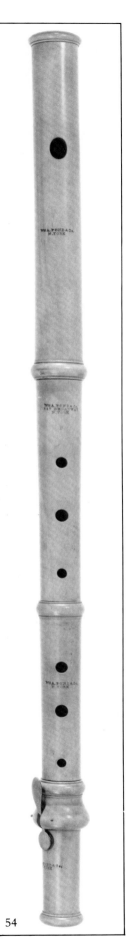

54

55. *Flute by William Rönnberg. New York, N.Y., after 1859. L. 27³⁄₃₂ in. (89.4.2173)*

56. *Flute by Alfred G. Badger with crutch on reverse side. New York, N.Y., 1866. L. 28¹⁹⁄₃₂ in. (23.153)*

57. *Stamp of William Rönnberg on flute, Fig. 55*

58. *Engraved mark of Alfred G. Badger on flute, Fig. 56*

55

56

adventurous craftsmen who, no longer content to work only in wood, accepted the challenge of metal construction. Though one- or few-key wooden flutes still served the needs of most players, such flutes were out of tune in some keys and so were unsuitable for the highly chromatic music being performed with increasing frequency by professional orchestras. As American orchestras developed, many of them staffed by European-trained musicians, serious performers and students grew numerous enough to sustain domestic production of louder, many-key metal flutes capable of sounding in tune in all keys.

William Rönnberg (b. 1803; d. ca. 1890), a German immigrant who worked in New York City after about 1834, resided in Brooklyn from 1844 to 1889, save for a period in Bloomfield, New Jersey, around 1850. He specialized in flutes but manufactured clarinets and oboes as well, while a helicon (circular bass horn) in a Swiss collection said to bear his mark suggests a broader enterprise than has yet been documented. Rönnberg received a diploma for a Boehm-system flute at the 1857 American Institute fair.

The Museum's remarkable Rönnberg flute (Fig. 55) could well have been another showpiece, though its key system is of a pre-Boehm design. Made in five boxwood sections covered with tortoiseshell, with silver-plated rings and twelve silver-plated cupped keys, the flute has a range that extends down to b, a minor third lower than usual. The three lowest keys rest open. An unusual trill key with three small cups (two of them over plugged holes) stands below the calibrated tuning barrel; this extendable section and the head section above are lined with metal tubes. The flute's sockets are likewise metal-bushed and the tenons are lapped with thread to give tight joints immune to humidity changes. The rat-tail keys pivot between pillars based on plates screwed to the tube; two plates have been removed at the back, where there was once an additional key for the left thumb. The flute's smooth, straight profile hides a conical bore that tapers markedly from tuning barrel to foot, a feature retained by German makers long after Theobald Boehm introduced the modern cylindrical bore. The mark *Rönnberg N. York* is stamped between groups of four diamonds (Fig. 57).

Rönnberg's better-known contemporary Alfred G. Badger (b. Connecticut? 1815; d. Brooklyn, N. Y., November 8, 1892) apprenticed with Ball & Douglas in Utica around 1834–37 and made flutes and clarinets in Buffalo between 1838 and 1842. Thereafter, like Rönnberg, Badger operated for a while both in New Jersey (Newark, 1844–50) and in New York City and resided in Brooklyn during his later years. He attracted a distinguished clientele, including the poet Sidney Lanier, and he was a pioneer in manufacturing and popularizing Boehm-system flutes in America. Badger made several experimental flutes of ebonite for

Charles Goodyear, and in 1859 wrote an article for *The Scientific American* concerning the merits of this synthetic material. He also wrote an *Illustrated History of the Flute* (1853 and three later editions), borrowing some information from Richard Carte's *Sketch of Successive Improvements made in the Flute . . .* (London, 1851). Badger is said to have been the first American to make a silver flute following the Boehm design brought here from England in 1845; clearly, he was an important innovator, honored for Boehm-system and ordinary eight-key flutes at five American Institute fairs between 1846 and 1856, at the Massachusetts Charitable Mechanic Association fair in 1847, and at New York's Crystal Palace in 1853. The 1855 census lists among his assets five hundred dollars' worth of tools, eight hundred dollars in silver, and two hundred dollars in woods; at that time his shop employed two men and a boy. Between 1860 and 1863, when directories show the firm as Alfred G. Badger & Co., his partner was probably Theobald F. Monzani, evidently the son of a noted London woodwind maker of the same name.

The Museum's sterling silver Boehm-system flute (Fig. 56), apparently made in 1866 and among the most advanced made in America in its day, bears the inscription *A. G. Badger & Co New-York* in a scroll engraved below the embouchure (Fig. 58). An owner's initials *J. W.* appear in a field on the engine-turned barrel, while the fitted case is embossed *W. P. Northrup* in gold. The case holds a full set of accessories: a threaded crutch that supports the slender flute on the player's left hand, a protective cover for the head tenon, a screwdriver for tightening the key axles, and a finely turned grease container. The flute's three sections are formed of soldered tubes with light, thin walls that allow no corrective undercutting of the large finger holes. Tuning is aided by joints that telescope without interrupting the bore, a problem in thick-tenoned wooden flutes. Not susceptible to humidity changes, these metal joints fit so closely that no flexible lapping is needed; grease alone assures an airtight seal.

Compared to those of older conical flutes, this one's cylindrical bore offers less resistance, greater power, more secure high notes, and more delicacy in quiet passages. Its thick lip ring gives a comfortable embouchure; this ring and the threaded cap display Badger's characteristic ornate engraving. His key mechanism incorporates a B-flat key of the type introduced by Giulio Briccialdi in 1849 and the style of G-sharp key credited to Vincent Dorus. Based on longitudinal axles introduced by Boehm in 1832, the mechanism employs both the usual leaf springs and the narrow wire ("needle") springs popularized by Auguste Buffet around 1837. The flute's range extends down to b; it may be Badger's only extant flute with five original perforated keys.

Around 1800 British amateurs had begun to

59. *Boehm-system piccolo of grenadilla with metal-lined head and barrel, nickel-silver mounts and keywork, by Theodore Berteling's successors. New York, N. Y., c. 1890. L. 11³¹/₃₂ in. (1983.267)*

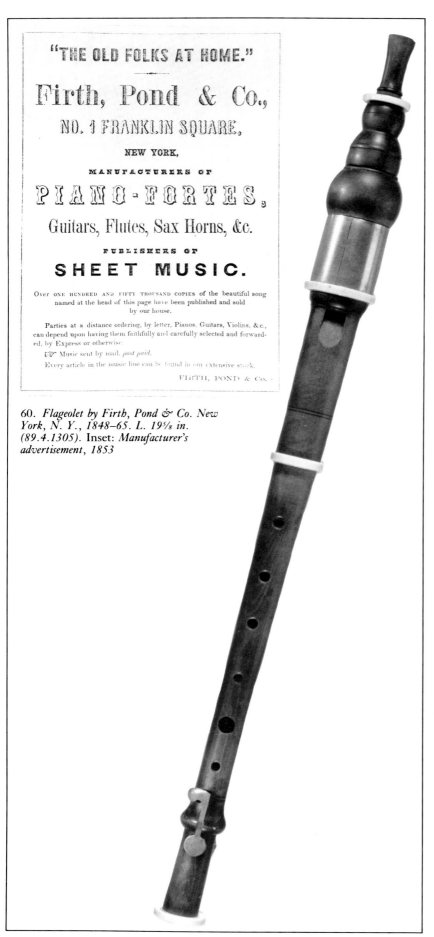

60. *Flageolet by Firth, Pond & Co. New York, N. Y., 1848–65. L. 19⅝ in. (89.4.1305).* Inset: *Manufacturer's advertisement, 1853*

replace their outmoded recorders with brighter-toned flageolets. Both types were called "English" flutes to distinguish them from transverse or "German" flutes; unlike these, the recorder and flageolet are held vertically and have whistle-type windways that need no special lip position. America lacked England's repertoire of recorder music, so improved flageolets were not made in American cities in such number and variety as in London, where multiple-key and double-tube models were common. In the States public performances such as the one in Philadelphia on November 14, 1820, in which Richard Willis played two Scottish airs on a double flageolet, were rare events.

The Museum's American flageolet of boxwood faintly marked *Firth Pond & Co. N-York* (1843–63; successors to Firth, Hall & Pond) bears decorative double score lines and squarish ivory ferrules copied from English models (Fig. 60). Normally the mouthpiece, which looks a bit like an oboe reed, would have been made of a piece of ivory or bone, removable for cleaning, but on this flageolet it is of wood and blossoms into two bulbous turnings. Inside a third, separate swelling above the windway, a small sponge was placed to absorb moisture from the breath. Below this, a nickel silver sheath clamps a crack in the tube. Ivory studs often inserted as guides between flageolet finger holes are absent from this rather plain instrument. While the brass key's offset touch is shaped much like short, angled key touches on contemporary clarinets, its raised mounting resembles those on flutes such as Graves & Alexander's. This simple flageolet may well have come from Firth, Pond & Co.'s Litchfield subsidiary.

Heinrich Christian Eisenbrandt (b. Göttingen, Germany, April 13, 1790; d. Baltimore, Md., March 9, 1860), one of America's leading nineteenth-century instrument makers, is represented in the collection by a clarinet probably fashioned before 1850. Eisenbrandt's father, Johann Benjamin (1753–1822), himself the son of a wood-turner, was an honored woodwind maker in Göttingen. The son was early introduced to flute playing and wood turning but intended to study medicine, until threatened with conscription in the war against Napoleon. Escaping to America through a series of adventures, Eisenbrandt arrived at New Castle exhausted after a voyage of ninety days. He found flute pupils in Philadelphia and married Sophie Nolte, the young daughter of family friends in Baltimore. After fighting at the battle of North Point in 1812, Heinrich settled briefly in New York around 1815; here he had some dealings with John Jacob Astor, but finding the city uncomfortable he returned to Germany after the Napoleonic War. Through his father's influence he reputedly became a court instrument maker in Hanover, a situation he had to leave because of his political outspokenness.

The couple returned to Baltimore in August, 1819, and Heinrich went into business as an instrument importer and maker specializing in woodwinds. His enterprise flourished, continuing under his son Henry William Raphael (d. 1886) and closing only in 1929's crash. Heinrich secured two patents relating to brasses (July 4, 1854, and January 26, 1858), and invented several other devices of nonmusical interest, including a coffin openable from within (an idea of 1825, when he was declared dead from yellow fever but miraculously revived after a forty-eight hour coma); a machine for raised printing for the blind; a rail car coupler; and a type of white glazed brick. An accomplished flautist, he appeared as soloist at Baltimore's Liederkranz (music club) concert in Washington Hall on March 28, 1836, and probably played in a local orchestra directed by Johann Metz, formerly first violinist under Ludwig Spohr in Germany.

Guided by his musical ability, unusual even among instrument makers, Eisenbrandt created woodwinds of exceptional merit. He exhibited them at fairs in New York (American Institute, 1837; Crystal Palace, 1853), Washington (Metropolitan Mechanics' Institute, 1853, 1855, 1857), and elsewhere. At the fourth exhibition of the Maryland Institute for Promoting the Mechanic Arts (Baltimore, 1851), he won a silver medal for a case of ornate clarinets and flutes. In 1837 he had already shown an eighteen-key clarinet. Some later models of ebony and rosewood had elegant silver keys.

Though old-fashioned in appearance and slightly warped, the Museum's clarinet in C (Figs. 62, 64) marked *Eisenbrandt Baltimore* compares favorably with a less refined but very well preserved example in B-flat (Figs. 61, 63) marked (below an eagle) *Graves & Co Winchester N. H.*, successors (ca. 1833–50) to Graves & Alexander, discussed above in connection with flutes. Both clarinets have five boxwood sections with six ivory ferrules and five brass keys, the lowest key standing open. The Eisenbrandt clarinet's turning is the more curvaceous and delicate. This instrument has thinner tenons, and its bore is more accurately centered. The numeral *XII* scratched on the edges of the joints is probably a batch number identifying parts of several unassembled clarinets. In contrast to the Graves clarinet's bell, which is conical within, the Eisenbrandt's bell flares internally like the parabolic bell of a brass instrument (Fig. 65). The Eisenbrandt's keys, mounted on blocks (partial turned rings) and a knob (the curved swelling at a joint), are of high-quality metal; the Graves's keys, on full rings and a knob, are less smoothly finished and have plain circular flaps, while the Eisenbrandt's old-fashioned flaps are square, notched, and beveled. The Eisenbrandt's long keys are straight, while the Graves's are kinked in the English style. Unfortunately the poor condition of both mouth-

61

62

61. *Five-key clarinet by Graves & Co. Winchester, N. H., 1849–63. L. 34¹⁵⁄₁₆ in. (89.4.899)*

62. *Five-key clarinet by Heinrich Christian Eisenbrandt. Baltimore, Md., mid-19th century. L. 20¹⁵⁄₁₆ in. (1979.443)*

63. *Stamp of Graves & Co. on clarinet, Fig. 61*

64. *Stamp of H. C. Eisenbrandt (here spelled Eisenbrant) on clarinet, Fig. 62*

pieces makes tonal comparison impossible, but the Eisenbrandt's relatively wider bore anticipates the proportions that give modern clarinets a louder, less covered tone. The Englishman William Gardiner, in his book *The Music of Nature* (London, 1832), characterized the tone of clarinets as resembling a female voice.

A B-flat clarinet (Figs. 66, 68) marked *E. Riley 29 Chatham St. N-York* (ca. 1830), in fine condition except for a slight warp, tends (like the Graves) toward the English style but is more rectilinear than Graves's model. The outsides of its three body sections are quite straight and parallel rather than flaring toward the joints. The lower part of the knob forms an abrupt right angle, echoed by the plain square flaps of the five brass keys. Four of these pass through blocks instead of the heavy rings used by Graves. The flare of the bell continues well up the narrow bore of the lowest body section. The finger holes are small and hardly worn by use. An especially richly grained piece of boxwood was turned for the bell; Riley's stamp appears on the prettiest side. Edward Riley, Sr., was a successful music publisher as well as an instrument seller and maker. He arrived in New York from England around 1806 and died probably in 1831; his sons continued in the trade and two daughters married the instrument makers John Firth and William Hall (Figs. 67, 69).

Theodore Berteling (b. Prussia, 1821; d. New York, N.Y., September 4, 1889), another of New York's major woodwind makers, left his homeland possibly in anticipation of the revolution that overwhelmed Germany in 1848. Establishing himself in Boston in that year, he worked successively for E. G. Wright (1850), Graves & Co. (1851–53), and J. Lathrop Allen (1854), all of whom were at that time primarily brass manufacturers. Berteling, however, won a silver medal for clarinets at the 1850 Boston Mechanics' Fair and another at the eighth Massachusetts Charitable Mechanic Association fair in 1856. Around 1857 he moved to New York and opened a shop at 219 Centre Street. Later he moved to the Bowery, where the business continued after his death until 1912. Berteling, a member of New York's Aschenbroedal Verein and Liederkranz orchestra, intended his instruments mainly for professional-caliber clients; his ad in the *American Music Directory* (1885) boasted that "in New York & Brooklyn alone there have been seventy (70) sets of our clarionets in use in the hands of musicians."

The Museum's lavish, perhaps unique Berteling ivory clarinet in E-flat (Colorplate 3) sustains its maker's good reputation. Turned in four sections (the silver-faced wooden mouthpiece with screw ligature may have been added later), the clarinet has a complex system of eighteen silver keys, including four with rollers and four delicate ring keys. The ferrules and oval name plaque stamped *Berteling New-York* are also of silver. Cupped pillar-mounted keys, cork-lapped tenons,

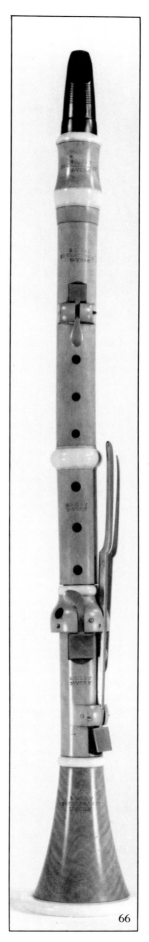

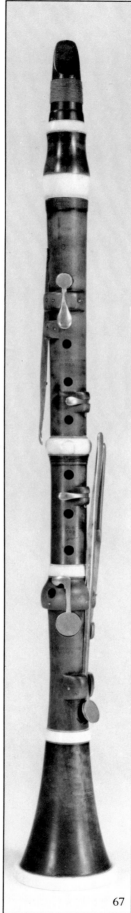

65. *X-ray views of bell and lowest body sections of clarinets by Graves & Co.* (left) *and Eisenbrandt* (right), *showing differences in bore design*

66. *Five-key clarinet by Edward Riley. New York, N. Y., c. 1830. L. 22²⁷⁄₃₂ in. (1982.42)*

67. *Eight-key clarinet by Firth, Hall & Pond. New York, N. Y., 1833–45. L. 23¹⁵⁄₃₂ in. (1983.58)*

68. *Stamp of Edward Riley on clarinet, Fig. 66*

69. *Stamp of Firth, Hall & Pond on clarinet, Fig. 67*

66

67

70. *Stamp of Theodore Berteling on plaque affixed to oboe, Fig. 71*

71. *Oboe by Theodore Berteling or successors. New York, N. Y. 1860–90. L. 22 in. (1976.7.10)*

thumb rest, wide bore, and simple profile mark this as the most modern American clarinet in the Museum collection, one that contrasts strikingly with the "classical" five-key boxwood examples. The latter remained in occasional use, however, through the end of the century.

Oboes, which had an astringent timbre that appealed to eighteenth-century sensibilities, lost ground in the Romantic era to mellower, easier-to-play flutes and clarinets. As the popularity of oboes among amateurs declined, especially after the advent of all-brass bands, American craftsmen made relatively few. Even after 1900 dealers still imported most of their stock, chiefly from France. In 1898 C. Bruno & Son advertised fifteen models of clarinets but only one standard fifteen-key oboe, still called *hautbois* in their catalogue. Nevertheless, Theodore Berteling produced some elegant oboes for discriminating musicians. The Museum's example (Figs. 70, 71), made of cocus or grenadilla (dense woods commonly used after about 1850) in three sections, has a separately turned vaselike baluster at the top, recalling Baroque designs. The bell looks like a clarinet's but has the oboe's typical inner rim. Thirteen nickel silver keys (incorporating a *brille* or pair of ring keys resembling eyeglasses, perforated half-hole plate for high C-sharp, and modern needle springs) are mounted on pillars screwed directly into the wood, just as in the Berteling clarinet. A thumb rest is similarly screwed into the back, and in front is Berteling's usual name plaque. The original leather-covered case is lined with blue plush.

Berteling was one of the first to make Boehm-system woodwinds in the United States. For mechanical improvements in these he obtained patents in 1868 (79,389) and 1882 (264,611). His ingenuity is further demonstrated by another of his rare oboes, in the Henry Ford Museum, Dearborn, Michigan, which has a key mechanism that differs substantially from that of the Metropolitan's example. Aside from innovation, personal attention and product loyalty characterized Berteling's enterprise. His widow and successor, Sophia (d. 1904), wrote to Mr. E. L. Henry of Ellenville, New York, on June 14, 1892 (letter in the New York State Museum archives, Albany):

Dear Sir!

Send herewith Your flute, it is a fine beautiful instrument, which will give good satisfaction & much pleasure & which You will like the better the more You get used to it. Should in course of time anything turn up what You would like to have changed or altered—just let me know it please & I will have done it if by any means possible.

Wishing You good success & much pleasure with the new instrument, I remain

Yours very respectfully,

S. Berteling.

72. *Group of ocarinas by Alan Albright. San Francisco, Calif., 1981. Clockwise from top: Bass double, L. 9²¹/₃₂ in. (1981.217.2); alto triple, L. 6⁹/₁₆ in. (1981.217.3); soprano, L. 3⁵/₈ in. (1981.217.1); and tenor double, L. 5³¹/₃₂ in. (1981.137)*

The Museum's newest woodwinds are a group of four sleek-looking ocarinas (Fig. 72) made in 1981 by Alan Albright (b. Culver, Ind., March 16, 1941), a current resident of San Francisco. The ocarina (an Italian word meaning "goose-shaped") is a vessel-bodied instrument with whistle mouthpiece, improved from earlier vessel flutes of folk origin by Giuseppe Donati in Budrio, Italy, around 1860. Manufactured in huge quantities and various sizes around the turn of the century, especially by the Viennese firm of H. Fiehn, these popular earthenware instruments were sold by mail order in the United States, whereas in Europe they were played alone or in small ensembles. Later pushed off the market by cheap small harmonicas, ocarinas have made a comeback recently, executed in decorative forms in various materials. Alan Albright is one of the craftspeople who have given impetus to this little "renaissance."

Albright, who has a prep school background and a Harvard M.A. in French, taught for a year at Phillips Academy, then worked for child welfare agencies in New York City. Following military service in the Vietnam War, he returned to New York to continue welfare work and teaching in Chinatown. Influenced by the 1960s crafts movement, he sought a kind of cottage industry for himself, and in 1970 he and a friend began a small enterprise making bamboo flutes. Encouraged by this experience and by association with the Chardavogne Group of craftspeople in Warwick, New York, Albright experimented with other woodwind forms, including a novel four-hole chromatic ocarina developed in 1964 by the English mathematician and musician John Taylor and patented separately by Paul Johnson.

Albright wished to construct a chromatic ocarina capable of producing simple harmony in the manner of the obsolete double and triple flageolets, and while splitting firewood one day, he hit upon the idea of dividing the hollow vessel into two or three chambers, each with its own windway and finger holes. These polyphonic instruments, carved of carefully selected exotic hardwoods, now constitute much of Albright's output. The Museum's examples include a soprano ocarina of Mexican black poisonwood, a bass double of Andaman padauk, an alto triple ocarina also of padauk, and a tenor double of Mexican bocote.

Albright sells mainly through retail distributors, preferring to work quietly and avoid a rush of customers. In spring, 1982, he wrote to the Museum: "I am again confronted with a reluctance to continue production and a need to devote more energy to creativity. Part of my aim has always been to provide a catalyst (the folk instrument) for a person to realize his 'musicality.'" John Adams, an environmentalist who works in Alaska, composed nine songs for piccolo, ocarina, and percussion between 1974 and 1979; these have recently been recorded under the title *Songbird-songs* (Opus One records, Greenville, Maine) and give fresh impetus to the ocarina revival.

Unlike woodwinds, brasses were not manufactured in significant quantity in the United States before about 1825, except perhaps for signal horns made by tinsmiths. Many military brasses came from abroad as personal property or were captured in battle. The limited nonimportation act of 1806, the total embargo on foreign trade in 1807, the nonintercourse act against France and England in 1809, and President Madison's ban on British trade in 1811, followed by the War of 1812, all hindered the growth of brass-using precision industries by reducing availability of metals for nonmilitary purposes. Skilled sheet-metal workers were scarce also. Lacking zinc for making brass, resourceful Yankee clockmakers such as Asa Hopkins produced wooden mechanisms as late as 1837, when zinc finally became available; doubtless Hopkins's experience in woodworking paved the way for his entry into woodwind manufacture late in his career.

Mixed woodwind and brass bands were standard into the nineteenth century, but except for the soloist's keyed bugle, introduced to American ears around 1815, brasses generally played subsidiary parts. Moravian all-brass bands were a notable exception to the rule. By 1835, however, all-brass bands (with percussion) started becoming popular in the Northeast. Widespread application of keys and valve mechanisms greatly expanded the musical capabilities of earlier "natural" (unmechanized) brasses, and domestic manufacture was boosted in 1842 by an increase to 30 percent in tariffs on imported brasses. Foreign competition rose when the duty dropped to 20 percent in 1846, but demand continued to grow through the 1850s as an influx of Central Europeans brought a taste for the homogeneous, powerful all-brass sound earlier cultivated by the Moravians in Pennsylvania, Georgia, and North Carolina.

The Civil War fueled the brass band movement in North and South as towns, militia units, and patriotic societies competed in fielding the best (that is, loudest) volunteer bands. Retailers' catalogues illustrated formations and instrumentation appropriate for bands of six to upwards of twenty uniformed men and boys (Fig. 73). During the Reconstruction era, when valved cornets and saxhorns replaced outmoded keyed bugles and lower-pitched ophicleides, American manufacture increased dramatically, thanks in part to powered machinery. Still, imports dominated the market through the rest of the century.

Despite the band boom and the concurrent spate of new designs and patents, few basic features of nineteenth-century brass construction can be called peculiarly American. Important innovations were quickly copied by foreign manufacturers, many of whom supplied American dealers. Indeed, since nineteenth-century brasses

B♭ Bass.

1st Tenor.

2d Tenor.

Baritone.

3d B
Corne

73. *"How to March," showing a formation of cornets, backfiring horns, and percussion, from McCosh's Guide for Amateur Bands.* Illustrated in Lyon & Healy's New and Enlarged Catalogue, *Chicago, Ill., 1889*

HOW TO MARCH.

uba

Solo Alto.

1st Eb Cornet.

1st Alto.

2d Eb Cornet.

2d Alto.

1st Bb Cornet.

Snare Drum.

2d Bb Cornet.

Bass Drum.

Band of Fifteen.

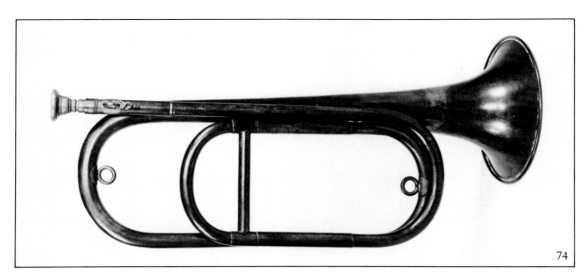

74

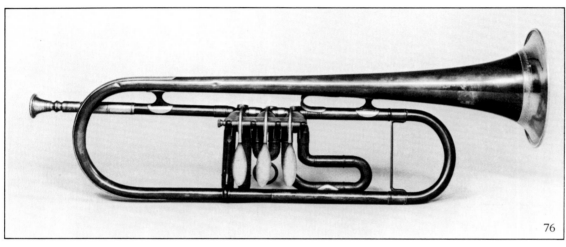

76

74. *Trumpet. Late 19th century. L. (without mouthpiece) 13²⁷/₃₂ in. (89.4.2278)*

75. *This mouthpiece, stamped* W. Seefeldt Phila., *is probably not original to the trumpet in Fig. 74*

76. *Trumpet. Late 19th century. L. 17⁵/₈ in. (89.4.3247)*

often lack a maker's mark or bear a seller's instead, it can be impossible to ascertain where and by whom a particular instrument was made.

The Museum's anonymous natural trumpet (Figs. 74, 75) is typical of the thousands that were made for field use here and abroad. It sounds in A-flat, but a tuning slide on the smaller of two loops can drop this pitch to G. The numeral *XXII* is scratched on the smaller loop. There are two sling eyes and a third ring holding a broken chain that once secured a mouthpiece. The present mouthpiece bears the stamp of William Seefeldt (b. Reading? Pa., 1829; d. Philadelphia, Pa., November 19, 1909), a manufacturer and seller active in Philadelphia after 1858. Seefeldt won medals for brasses exhibited at the Franklin Institute in 1874 and in Paris in 1878. Unfortunately, there is no way of telling whether this mouthpiece was sold by him with this trumpet or became associated with it later. However, the trumpet's tightly rolled bell rim, fine seam, and smoothly polished surface indicate late nineteenth-century manufacture.

A contemporary, more versatile B-flat trumpet (Fig. 76) is also anonymous, but its string-rotary valves are of a type common on known American

instruments. The wide bell garland of nickel silver (also called German silver, a hard copper-zinc-nickel alloy increasingly common after 1840) decorated with a band of Greek keys between rows of dots is as likely to be American as European. The trumpet's valves are individually numbered so that their rotors cannot be mistakenly interchanged. Where such close tolerances were involved, moving parts had to be individually fitted for reliable operation; this made valves fairly expensive. A dented instrument was usually worth fixing so long as its valves worked. To improve reliability, makers in the States and abroad introduced wear-resistant alloys and flexible linkages, lessening friction by reducing both the number of moving parts and the extent of their motion; these developments led to a quieter, faster, and ultimately cheaper mechanism.

This trumpet's valves have large touches at the ends of long levers that reach over the valves and are pivoted side by side on a rod mounted over the bottoms of the valves. This side-action arrangement means the trumpet must be held with the plane of its loops parallel, rather than perpendicular, to the ground. The system had only limited success.

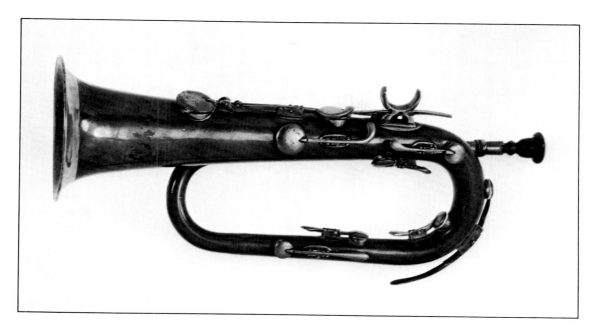

Although trumpets retained some of the prestige they had acquired long before through association with the aristocracy, Romantic composers preferred the less piercing sound of wider-bore bugles and cornets for solo work. The five-key Royal Kent bugle patented May 5, 1810, by Joseph Halliday of Dublin recalled earlier keyed trumpets in its use of tone holes, like those of a woodwind, to provide notes otherwise unobtainable or out of tune. Its fully chromatic scale allowed the keyed bugle to compete melodically with the clarinet and flute, and its commanding tone and agility appealed to American audiences right from the start. Richard Willis, whose performance on a double flageolet was noted above, offered solos on a keyed bugle in a New York concert of May 28, 1816, the year before he was appointed bandmaster at West Point. His subsequent tours as star soloist with the military academy's band quickly captured the interest of such renowned musicians as the Philadelphian Francis Johnson (c. 1792–1884), a famous black composer and bandmaster who became a virtuoso on the keyed bugle, and Edward ("Ned") Kendall (b. March 1, 1808; d. October 6, 1861), whose Boston Brass Band, founded in 1835, pioneered

the all-brass movement along with the Dodworth Band from New York.

Some keyed bugles were being made in America by 1825, but British imports ruled the market before the mid-1830s, when Londoner James Keat (b. May 7, 1813; d. Winchester, N. H., March 17, 1845) went to work for Graves & Co. Keat made B-flat bugles with seven and nine keys for Graves until 1837, when he evidently tried to start his own business. After Keat left the firm, Graves continued to produce B-flat models and the smaller E-flat type preferred by Kendall for solo use. Keyed bugles of gold and silver with up to twelve keys, costing as much as $480 by midcentury, were beautifully engraved as presentation pieces, but the Museum's plain copper example (Figs. 77, 78) with nine keys, marked *Graves & Co. Winchester, N.H.* (c. 1840), bears only an owner's name, *John W. Gaub*, engraved above the white brass garland. This bugle lacks its tuning shank. The unmarked mouthpiece is rimmed with composition material, probably to keep the player's lips from freezing in cold weather. The cupped keys (the lowest resting open) pivot in box mounts on oval footplates. A crescent-shaped finger rest straddles the third key.

79. *Cornet of nickel silver with three piston-rotary valves, pitched in B-flat, by Isaac Fiske. Worcester, Mass., c. 1875.*
L. 12⁷/₁₆ in. Mouthpiece is probably not original. Not shown: *Fitted wooden case inscribed* Stowe Band *(1983.119)*

80. *Maker's mark for the cornet in Fig. 79*

The gradual switch from many noisy keys to three quieter rotary valves was spurred by mechanical improvements such as the fast-acting eighth-turn rotors (patent 5919, November 14, 1848) invented by Thomas Dudley Paine of Woonsocket, Rhode Island, and the contributions of Isaac Fiske of Worcester, Massachusetts, which included an improved string linkage patented October 30, 1866 (59,204) (Fig. 79). Despite numerous innovations, however, it remained difficult to fit valves to a bugle without interrupting its rapidly expanding conical bore. The cornet's more gradual expansion was better suited to valves. A legendary contest at Salem, Massachusetts, in December 1856, pitting Kendall, the veteran bugler, against a twenty-seven-year-old E-flat cornettist, Patrick S. Gilmore (whose song "When Johnny Comes Marching Home" was published in 1864), showed why the valved cornet was superseding the keyed bugle: Gilmore's cornet supposedly fingered more quickly, was easier to blow, and had a more consistent tone quality throughout its range. Sweet-sounding yet brilliant and agile, the cornet remained the favorite soprano brass instrument well into the jazz era.

Two of the Museum's string-rotary-valved

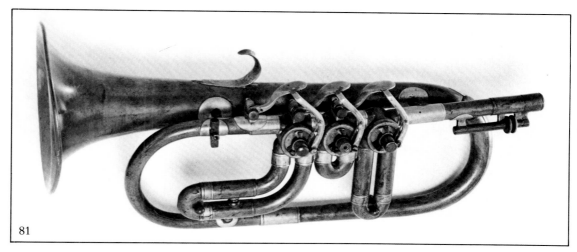

81

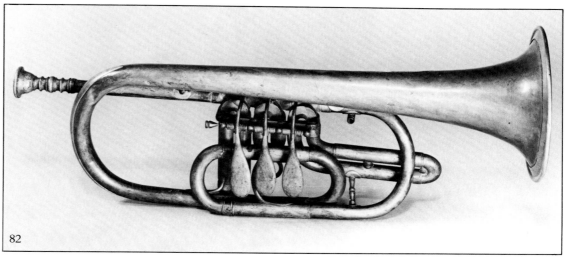

82

cornets from the third quarter of the nineteenth century differ significantly. The smaller (Fig. 81), in E-flat, was made by Henry G. Lehnert, winner of a silver medal at the Massachusetts Charitable Mechanic Association fair in 1865 and listed in Philadelphia directories from 1867 to 1914. This cornet's telescoping tuning shank is operated by a knurled nut on a threaded rod. The first (whole-step) and third (one-and-one-half-steps) valves have tuning slides on their descending tubes, but the shortest (half-step) center valve does not; nor is there a general slide on the main loop. The ferrules and oval touches are nickel silver, and the bell rim is rolled.

The larger, unmarked B-flat cornet (Fig. 82) has a yellower, more brittle brass tube too rich in zinc, a cheap stiffener that promotes tonal brilliance. Its seam is unattractively conspicuous, but the rods supporting both tube and mouthpiece socket are handsomely formed. The narrow nickel silver garland is undecorated. All three rotary valves and the secondary loop have tuning slides. A socket for a music holder indicates that this cornet was a parade instrument. Its long side-action touches require a horizontal playing position.

81. *Cornet in E-flat by Henry G. Lehnert. Philadelphia, Pa., 1867–80. L. 13⅛ in. (89.4.2183)*

82. *Cornet in B-flat. 1855–75. L. 14¼ in. (89.4.2182)*

83. *The maker's mark* Lehnert Phila. *is stamped on the bell of the cornet in Fig. 81*

84. Cornet with maker's mark of J. W. Pepper on bell, but possibly only imported or distributed by that firm. C. 1900. L. (without tuning shank and mouthpiece) 12¹³/₃₂ in. (1977.246.1). See also Colorplate 8

85. Engraved mark of J. W. Pepper on the cornet in Fig. 84

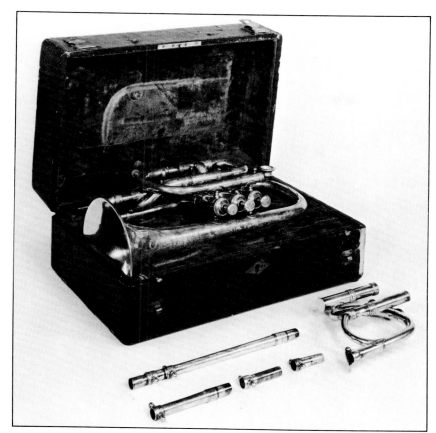

Far more attractive, a silver-plated cornet (Figs. 84, 85, and Colorplate 8) with engraved leaf ornaments and gold-plated bell interior is marked *Superior First Class J. W. Pepper Maker Philadelphia and Chicago No. 7554.* The owner's name, Frank R. Mintram, appears on the bell. Dating from around 1900, this richly appointed cornet has the long, narrow Périnet light-action piston valves reportedly introduced to this country by Henry J. Distin. Distin (b. London, England, July 22, 1819; d. Philadelphia, Pa., October 11, 1903), holder of thirteen instrument-related patents, worked for Moses Slater in New York around 1880 and later set up shop in Philadelphia. James W. Pepper started out as a music teacher and commercial engraver around 1876 and was soon printing sheet music. Much of Pepper's business after 1880 was importing French instruments for sale through outlets in several cities. Little is known of the firm's early history, but Pepper became a major supplier of band instruments to the army and navy after 1891 and won an award at the 1893 World's Columbian Exposition in Chicago.

Of special interest are this cornet's numerous accessories, fitted in the original plush-lined case (Fig. 86); five tuning bits of varying lengths, a separate shank that changes the pitch from B-flat to C by substituting a shorter length of tubing with its own water key (the longer B-flat section has a double water key that drains condensation at two bends), and a contemporary mouthpiece.

Pepper was an agent for Peter Thomsen of Philadelphia, who patented another cornet mouthpiece, an adjustable one, on June 7, 1881 (242,487). The Museum's gold-plated example (Fig. 87) has a sharp-edged inner cup and a separate rimmed outer shell encircled by a knurled band. The two parts are lightly threaded together, so that by turning its outer shell, the player can adjust the cup's depth. Numbers stamped on the exterior gauge this depth.

Allan Dodworth, the first leader of New York's famed Dodworth Band, is credited with having introduced in 1838 a distinctive brass instrument shape that appeared in American parade bands for over fifty years. These novel backfiring or over-shoulder cornets and saxhorns had the bell facing straight back over the player's left shoulder to project sound to the rear. Marchers who paraded behind their own hired band naturally wanted to enjoy its music, but they had trouble even keeping in step when the band following them sounded louder than their own in front. Backfiring instruments solved this problem but obviously were not useful on stage or in combination with bell-up or bell-forward models. One liability was that the long over-shoulder section, out of the player's sight, was particularly susceptible to damage. In the Civil War era American dealers ordered many backfiring horns from European subsidiaries or contractors, but the type never became popular abroad and was obsolete in the States by 1900.

86. *J. W. Pepper cornet in Fig. 84 in its original case with accessories; the rope handles are missing*

87. *Cornet mouthpiece by Peter Thomsen, distributed by J. W. Pepper. Philadelphia, Pa., after 1881. Diam. 31/32 in. (1980.332)*

THE J. W. P. CELEBRATED BAND INSTRUMENTS.

MAGNIFICENT MODEL.   **SHORT AND FREE ACTION.**   **LARGE BORE.**   **PERFECT IN EVERY DETAIL.**

FULLY WARRANTED. WE INVITE AND WELCOME COMPARISONS.

Will be Shipped, with Complete Outfit, to any Address, C. O. D., Subject to Six Days' Trial.

BEST IN THE WORLD.

The J. W. P. Celebrated Band Instruments are manufactured from the raw materials at our extensive factory in Philadelphia. They are the best in the world—thousands of musicians in every State and Territory in the United States, and in every Province of Canada, who have purchased and are constantly using these instruments, will cheerfully add their testimony in support of our claim. Our confidence in their superiority, is shown by the fact that we cheerfully place them in competition with any make—welcome the opportunity of doing so—ask nothing better than to allow a purchaser all the chance of comparison that he may desire. If others have sufficient confidence in their goods to place them in competition with ours and will ship on the same plan, an intending purchaser can select that which, in his opinion, represents the greatest value for the money and return the others. We ask no better method for the thorough introduction of our goods.

Our prices are extremely low and net—are so close to actual cost that we cannot make any discount. After taking off all discounts from the catalogue prices of other American Manufacturers, we venture the assertion that our prices will be found considerably less than theirs. Of course we do not claim to sell American Made Instruments as low as those of Foreign Make. To meet the latter, we refer to our two Imported Grades: Perfected Grade—Improved French Piston and the Improved French Piston.

Free Outfit. With this instrument we include, free of charge: Magnificent Leather Covered, Plush Lined, Square Case, with Nickel Plated Lock and Trimmings, J. W. P. Latest All Steel Music Stand, Specialty Mute, Piston Cleaner, Mouthpiece Box and Music Folio, which are worth and have never been sold for less than $9.10. In other words, for $35.90 we offer an instrument which is worth double that amount and which we will cheerfully place in competition with any cornet selling for $75.00 and at the same time present the six articles mentioned above, which cannot be purchased at any music store for less than $9.10. This is practically offering the instrument for $26.80.

NOTE.—This instrument is sold only with the outfit—in other words, prices named are net and *include* the six articles.

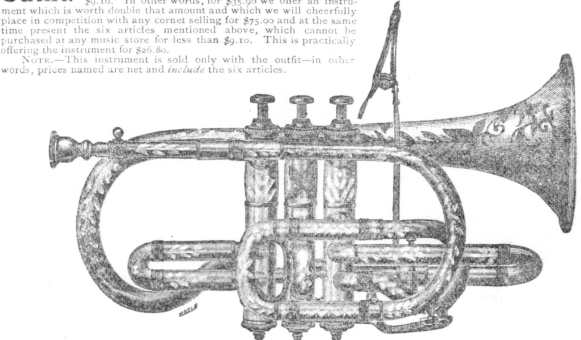

THE "ARTIST'S SOLO"—Bb CORNET—DOUBLE WATER KEY.

A and Bb Shanks furnished with each Instrument.

Exact Length, 12½ Inches;   Exact Width (top to bottom of pistons), 5¾ Inches;   Diameter of Bell, 4⅞ Inches.

No. 1000   Brass, elaborately engraved, engraved metal trimmings, highly polished, tuning bit, silver plated mouthpiece, improved adjustable music lyre, magnificent leather covered, plush lined case, J. W. P. latest all steel music stand, specialty mute, piston cleaner, nickel plated mouthpiece box and music folio.(A) **$35 90**

No. 1001   Elaborately engraved, engraved metal trimmings, silver plated, burnished, tuning bit, our perfected mouthpiece, improved adjustable music lyre, magnificent leather covered, plush lined case, J. W. P. latest all steel music stand, silver plated specialty mute, silver plated piston cleaner, nickel plated mouthpiece box and music folio.(A) **46 90**

No. 1002   Elaborately engraved, engraved metal trimmings, silver plated, burnished, gold mounted, tuning bit, our perfected mouthpiece, improved adjustable music lyre, magnificent leather covered, plush lined case, J. W. P. latest all steel music stand, silver plated specialty mute, silver plated piston cleaner, nickel plated mouthpiece box and music folio.(A) **48 30**

No. 1003   Elaborately engraved, engraved metal trimmings, gold plated, burnished, tuning bit, our perfected mouthpiece, improved adjustable music lyre, magnificent leather covered, plush lined case, J. W. P. latest all steel music stand, gold plated specialty mute, gold plated piston cleaner, nickel plated mouthpiece box and music folio.(A) **64 00**

The name *John F. Stratton* is engraved on a shield affixed to the bell of a nickel silver E-flat soprano cornet (Fig. 90) that is typical of smaller, rotary-valved, backfiring brasses made around 1860–75. A narrow bell garland and spiraled, tapered support rods are its only decorative features. John Franklin Stratton (Fig. 89) (b. West Swanzey, N. H., September 14, 1832; d. Brooklyn, N. Y., October 23, 1912), a major New York manufacturer and dealer, was introduced to music by his father, a well-to-do farmer who played violin and keyed bugle. Young Stratton started playing the slide trombone when he was six and within a year had joined his father's small band. Soon he learned to play the E-flat bugle and formed his own five-piece band (bugle, E-flat clarinet, trombone, snare and bass drums) that hired out for musters and entertainments. At the age of fourteen he moved to Lowell, Massachusetts, but was quickly apprenticed to a machinist in North Chelmsford because his talents were needed in the North Chelmsford Brass Band.

By seventeen years of age Stratton, then leader of the Worcester Brass Band, had learned to play the clarinet and cornet. These skills he put to use in 1851 as new leader of the Hartford (Connecticut) Cornet Band. He remained in Hartford for eight years, studying the violin and opening a music shop that failed in the 1857 crash. Thereafter Stratton came to New York to earn success

as a performer and arranger and ultimately as conductor of the Staten Island Philharmonic Society and of "Stratton's Palace Garden Orchestra." Privately he played arrangements of classical chamber music in an informal wind ensemble that included the brothers Allen, Harvey, and Jefferson Dodworth.

In 1859 Stratton started a factory for rotary-valved brasses on the corner of Centre and White Streets. This enterprise was fueled by Civil War demand for band instruments; Stratton added imports to his line and in 1864 became associated with another importer and later competitor, John Howard Foote. By 1868 Stratton had a factory in Markneukirchen, Germany; it was moved to Gohlis, near Leipzig, in 1870 and employed over 250 people, many of whom made violins for export. Stratton personally supervised this factory, providing machinery and designs while studying piano, composition, and music theory at the Leipzig Conservatory. Finally Stratton returned to New York in August, 1883. His business (Fig. 91)—which now included music publishing— had grown enormously, and though he claimed to be intimately familiar with every practical aspect of instrument manufacture, he had long since left the actual production to others. George W. Stratton, his elder brother, achieved independent renown as a composer and music merchant in Boston after 1866.

The Museum's Stratton E-flat cornet is the

89. *John F. Stratton, 1832–1912. Anonymous engraving reproduced in Stratton's trade catalogues*

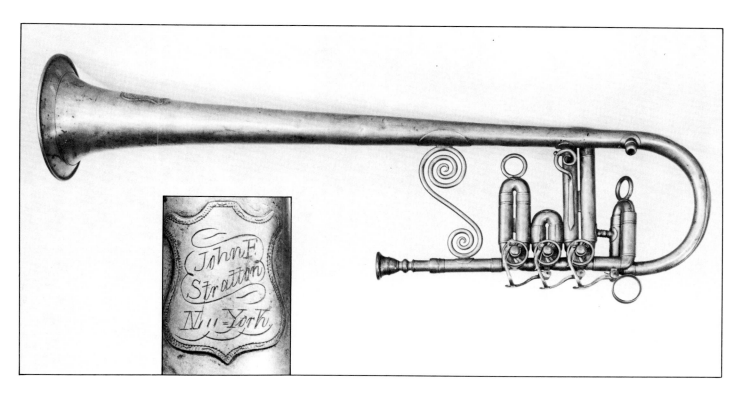

88. *Advertisement for J. W. Pepper cornet like that in Figs. 84 and 86, from Pepper's* Musical Times and Band Journal *10/112 (1889)*

90. *Backfiring cornet in E-flat by John F. Stratton. New York, N. Y., 1860–75. L. 21³¹⁄₃₂ in. (89.4.2295)* Inset: *Engraved shield affixed to bell of cornet*

JOHN F. STRATTON & CO.

IMPORTERS OF AND WHOLESALE DEALERS IN

Musical Instruments OF EVERY DESCRIPTION.

Musical Merchandise AND TOYS.

JOHN F. STRATTON & CO

VIOLINS

49

MUSICAL MERCHANDISE

JOHN F. STRATTON & CO.

SPECIAL NOTICE TO OUR CUSTOMERS.

Owing to the steady and continual growth of our business, we have found the four floors heretofore occupied by us at No. 55 Maiden Lane, entirely inadequate to the requirements of our business, and we have been compelled this year to look for more extensive and convenient quarters.

We have been fortunate in securing the needed accommodation within four doors of our present location, and take pleasure therefore in announcing to our friends and customers that we have leased for a term of years the commodious premises,

No. 49 MAIDEN LANE

(4 doors west of our present store)

to which we shall remove on April 1st, 1881.

In providing for our own necessities we have also endeavored to consult the convenience of our customers, and have no doubt but that those who are in the habit of visiting us will be pleased with the change. Our new building gives us not only ample accommodation in our lofts and basement for our large stock, but affords us a salesroom

On the street floor of twenty-five by one hundred and thirty-nine feet !

The only salesroom of the kind in this line of business in New York.

We take this opportunity to thank our many friends and customers for their long continued patronage of our house, and for the congratulations with which we know they will receive this new evidence of our prosperity. We shall hope to have the pleasure of meeting many of them in our new quarters at No. 49 Maiden Lane, and those who do not find it convenient to visit the city, will, we trust, continue to favor us with their orders per mail as heretofore.

Respectfully,

JOHN F. STRATTON & CO.,

No. 49 (formerly 55) Maiden Lane, New York City.

91. *John F. Stratton & Co. catalogue of musical instruments, musical merchandise, and toys, showing premises at 49 Maiden Lane, New York, late 1880–early 1881*

92. *Otto Bötticher*. Seventh Regiment Drilling in Washington Square, New York, *1851. (54.90.295)*

93. *"Over-the-shoulder Instruments" from Moses Slater's* Illustrated Catalogue of Brass and German Silver Musical Instruments, *New York, N. Y., 1874*

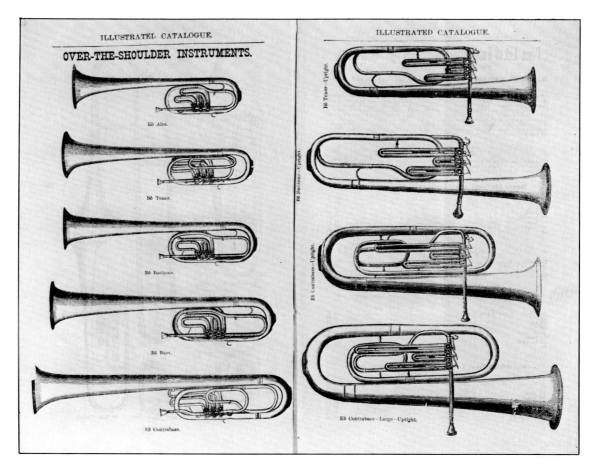

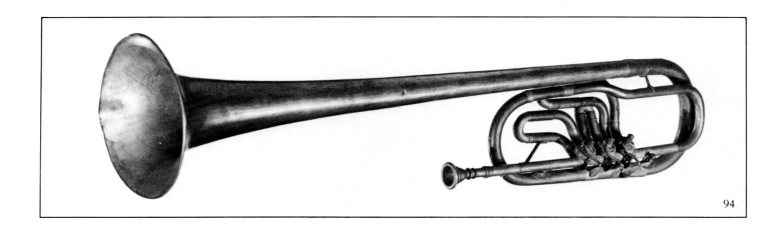

94

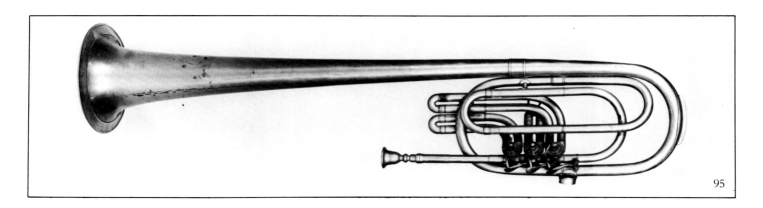

95

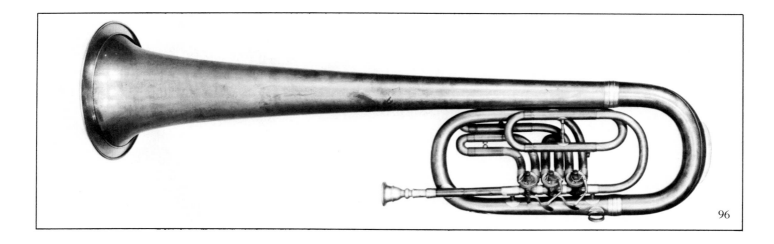

96

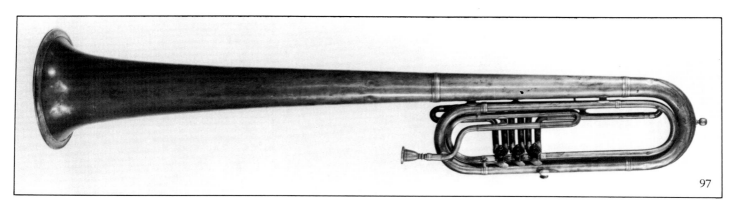

97

soprano member of a set of five backfiring sax-horns of various sizes. The nomenclature of such instruments, like their place of manufacture, is hard to pin down. The four lower-pitched ones shown here (Figs. 94–97) are called today simply E-flat alto, B-flat tenor, B-flat baritone, and E-flat bass or tuba, of which only the last was marked by its maker. Dating from around 1870, it is at low pitch, has top-action rotary valves, and bears the stamp *E. Seltmann* (Fig. 98). Ernst Seltmann was a Philadelphia manufacturer who occupied premises at 811 Callow Hill from 1864 to 1887. For a decade after his death his widow and son continued in business, probably import-ing and selling rather than manufacturing instru-ments.

Complementing the backfiring brasses and a set of European bell-forward helicons in the Mu-seum's collection is a family of bell-up brasses designed for indoor and outdoor use. The E-flat alto (Fig. 99) has the insignia of John Howard Foote on an oval brass plate soldered to the nickel silver tube. This tube has been rather casually patched in several places with brass, a common practice. Foote (b. Canton, Conn., November 11, 1833; d. Brooklyn, N. Y., May 17, 1896) was trained as a clockmaker in Bristol, Connecticut, and entered the music business in 1853 as a clerk for Rohe & Leavitt at 31 Maiden Lane in New

94. *Alto saxhorn. Possibly a German import. 1860–75. L. 33 1/16 in. (89.4.2296)*

95. *Tenor saxhorn. 1855–75. L. 35 1/8 in. (89.4.2297)*

96. *Baritone saxhorn. Possibly a German import. 1855–75. L. 35 1/16 in. (89.4.2298)*

97. *Tuba by Ernest Seltmann. Philadelphia, Pa., 1864–75. L. 57 11/16 in. (89.4.2301)*

98. *Stamp of Ernest Seltmann on bell of tuba in Fig. 97*

99. *Alto saxhorn by John Howard Foote. New York, N.Y., c. 1860. L. 29 1/16 in. (89.4.3127). Inset: Maker's stamp with initials J. H. F. and NYC monogram affixed to saxhorn*

99

100. *Bass saxhorn or euphonium by W. Seefeldt, or imported and sold by him. Philadelphia, Pa., 1860–80. L. 29¹¹/₃₂ in. The mouthpiece is not original. (89.4.2180).* Inset: *Stamp of W. Seefeldt on saxhorn*

101. *Baritone saxhorn by Moses Slater, or imported and sold by him. New York, N. Y., after 1865. L. 30⅛ in. (89.4.2179)*

102. *Label of M. Slater engraved on shield affixed to baritone saxhorn in Fig. 101*

York. He took over these premises and was listed as an independent maker from 1857 to 1863, but he joined Stratton briefly the following year and was thereafter primarily a seller and designer of instruments made for him by others.

Among Foote's and Stratton's competitors was Moses Slater (b. England, November, 1826; d. New York, N.Y., October 11, 1899), whose mark *M. Slater, Maker, N. Y.* is engraved on a plate fastened to the upright B-flat baritone (Figs. 101, 102). Slater's firm operated at various addresses from 1865 until at least twenty years after his death, and during the 1870s the business was managed by Henry Distin. The American Institute of the City of New York awarded Slater a medal at their 1881 fair, but by that time he was listed in city directories as an importer. This baritone, with three short, wide piston valves known as *Berlin pumpen*, might well be a French import despite its identifying mark.

Also possibly French, the upright B-flat bass or euphonium (Fig. 100) has a serial number 2683 and the stamp *W. Seefeldt Philad.* This bass also has Berlin valves. The E-flat contrabass (Fig. 103) is more likely of American origin, its rotary valves and overall style indicating a date before 1875. A nickel silver plate on its bell is engraved *C. A. Zoebisch & Sons, New York* (Fig. 104), a firm started by Charles A. Zoebisch in Lancaster, Pennsylvania, before 1846. Zoebisch was honored at the American Institute fair of 1847 and the business continued until 1905, the last twenty-five years chiefly as importers. He was probably the same Zoebisch who made brasses in Neukirchen, Germany, in the first half of the century.

A brass orchestral horn in F (Fig. 105) has a small oval stamp, *J. L. Allen N-Y Maker.* Joseph Lathrop Allen (b. Holland, Mass., September 24, 1815; d. New York? c. 1897) opened a shop in Sturbridge, Massachusetts, around 1838. He moved to Boston in 1842 and again a few years later to Norwich, Connecticut, where in 1847 he was distributing Farley & Pearson's reed organs as well as "Doct. Fontaine's Balm of a Thousand Flowers, warranted to prevent the Hair from Falling Off." No common salesman, Allen invented around 1850 an improved rotary valve incorporating the string linkage first proposed by Paine in 1848; Allen's version was widely adopted.

After returning to Boston in 1852, Allen quickly became a leading brass manufacturer, and his business flourished through the Civil War. After the war he lived in New York until 1872; his name appears in Boston listings in 1877 and again in New York from 1880 to 1897. Though the Museum's horn bears his mark—it is apparently the only extant horn that does—its short, fat Berlin piston valves are not of his design. This horn may have been produced by Allen's German workmen or imported. Its mouthpipe and nickel silver crook are replacements.

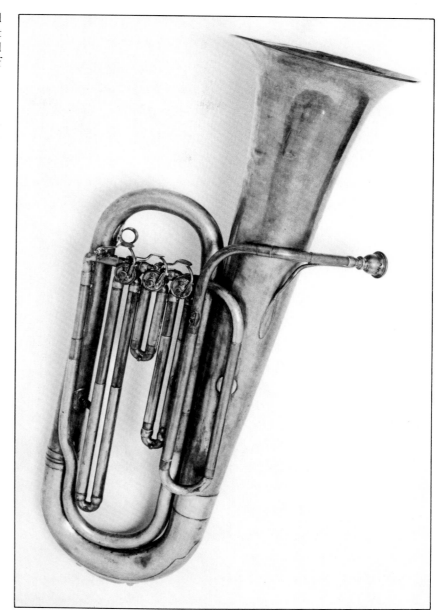

103. *Contrabass saxhorn by C. A. Zoebisch & Sons. New York, N. Y., 1860–75. L. 35³¹/₃₂ in. (89.4.2188)*

104. *Label of C. A. Zoebisch & Sons engraved on oval plate affixed to contrabass saxhorn in Fig. 103*

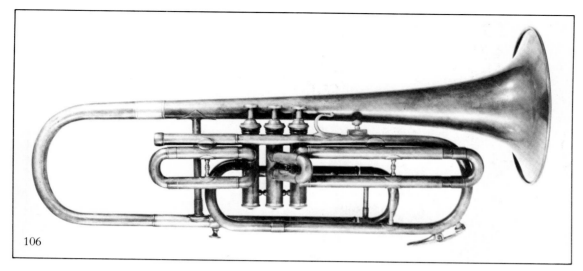

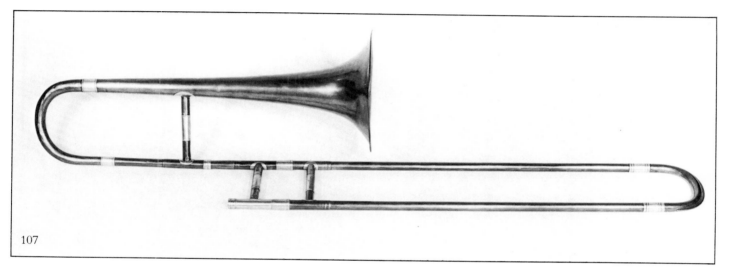

105. *French horn by J. L. Allen, or imported and sold by him. New York, N. Y., late 19th century. L. perpendicular to bell 16⁵/₃₂ in. The mouthpiece is not original. (89.4.2198). Inset: Stamp of J. Allen*

106. *Valved alto trombone (Italian?) imported and sold by August Pollmann. New York, N. Y., 1879–1905. L. 21¼ in. (89.4.2337)*

107. *Tenor slide trombone marked C. A. Zoebisch &*

Sons. New York, N. Y., late 19th century. L. 44⁹/₁₆ in. (89.4.2072)

108. *Engraved and impressed floral decoration and mark of August Pollmann on trombone in Fig. 106*

109. *Valved brass trombone imported by Henry Distin for J. W. Pepper, serial number 1766. Late 19th century. L. 46²⁷/₃₂ in. (89.4.2325). Inset: Mark of Henry Distin and J. W. Pepper on trombone*

Of three trombones (Figs. 106, 107, 109) with American marks (an E-flat valved alto engraved *August Pollmann's Light Action New York*, a B-flat slide tenor from C. A. Zoebisch & Sons, New York, and an imported E-flat valved bass marked *Henry Distin importer for J. W. Pepper, Phila. and New York N° 1766)*, the first (c. 1880–1900) deserves mention for its unusual size and mechanism. Valved trombones are most useful in situations where limited space makes extension of the more common long slide inconvenient. Though a bit heavier than slide models, valved trombones balance easily and are less taxing to play on parade because the player's right arm remains stationary. Pollmann's alto sounds in the same register as an E-flat alto saxhorn, but its narrow bore gives a brighter, more prominent sonority. Its yellow brass alloy contains much zinc. In addition to a main tuning slide, the three Périnet valves have individual slides. Other conveniences include a water key, a music-holder socket, and a removable bell section that unclamps for compact storage. Pollmann himself was not principally a manufacturer (Fig. 110); he may have imported this trombone from Italy. He was active in New York City from 1879 to 1905.

110. *Advertisement of August Pollmann, importer of trombone in Fig. 106*

William Harnett. Music and Good Luck, *1888. (63.85)*

98

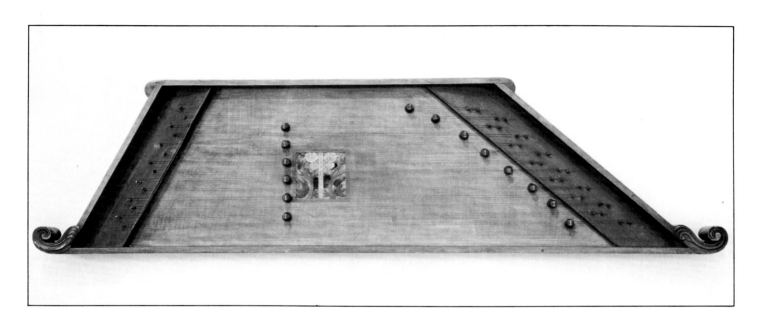

111. *Top view of hammer dulcimer, Fig. 112, showing alternating "chessman" bridges and square paper-and-cloth sound-hole decoration*

112. *Hammer dulcimer on table case with beater at left. Ohio?, c. 1815. W. 57¾ in. (1978.369). See also Colorplate 4*

Strings

American folk and popular musicians have usually relied on domestic makers for stringed instruments. In contrast, until a few years ago classical string players in the United States preferred to play imported European instruments almost exclusively. An exception is the concert harp, which (like the modern piano) was mechanically and tonally exalted by American builders. Although fine plucked instruments have long been manufactured in this country, few first-rate violin makers were active in the United States until fairly recently. Even the distinguished Gemünder brothers, August Martin (1814–1895) and George (1816–1899), German luthiers who settled in New York, imported many of the violins they sold. One reason may have been the difficulty of obtaining enough good wood for their own production; another was the strong professional bias toward owning an antique instrument. Today the long-standing prejudice against recent and American-made bowed strings is rapidly being overcome, due to the scarcity of old European violins as well as the excellent quality and reasonable price of many current domestic ones. The craft of violin making is now being taught in this country to growing numbers of serious apprentices.

Many hobbyists and mechanics have also taken up the challenge of making stringed instruments, from kits or from scratch. Some amateur craftsmen have produced amusing, unorthodox designs that seem to have little relevance to musical values. Folk makers, on the other hand, normally strive to follow traditional lines but may have limited access to customary materials, tools, and models; hence, they, too, have come up with many variations on standard designs. Commercial manufacture, especially of plucked instruments, has deliberately stressed novelty in form and materials; the American market is particularly fashion-conscious, and guitar styles, for example, change almost yearly. Avant-garde electric guitars as well as attractive vintage fretted instruments are now prized by collectors, and strong interest has also developed in preserving the less abundant relics of nearly forgotten folk and amateur makers who themselves gave little thought to posterity.

The hammer dulcimer, a zither with multiple courses of wire strings struck by light, flexible beaters, occurs from the Far East across to Europe where, known as the *cimbalom*, it is the national instrument of Hungary. Though occasionally written for in modern orchestral works, the hammer dulcimer is essentially a folk instrument, little changed since the Middle Ages. Common in middle-class households in seventeenth-century Britain, it was first mentioned in America in 1717 by Samuel Sewall of Salem, Massachusetts. Dulcimers followed the frontier to the upper Midwest, where they were widely played into the 1920s, long after their popularity had waned in England and on the urban eastern seaboard. In Chicago around 1900, Sears, Roebuck & Co. and Montgomery Ward & Co. sold trapezoidal dulcimers of "neatly decorated" simulated rosewood, probably mass produced by Lyon & Healy. Among smaller manufacturers' and homemade dulcimers there is considerable variety of size and form. Models patented after 1860, particularly those of James A. MacKenzie of Minneapolis,

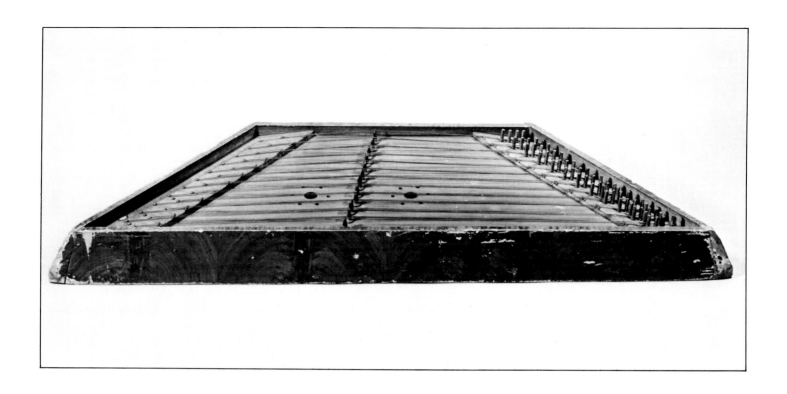

113. *Hammer dulcimer,
style of Perry Wight.
South Alabama, N. Y.,
mid-19th century. W.
45%⁄32 in. (1979.522.3)*

show increasing weight and complexity of structure.

What appears to be the oldest extant American hammer dulcimer (Figs. 111, 112, and Colorplate 4) was found around 1925 in Darrtown, Ohio, where chickens were roosting in its Sheraton-style crossbanded mahogany case. Unfortunately the cherry lid has lost its veneer. The case rests on rope-turned cherry legs, the front pair inset from the corners, where there are drop finials. This somewhat provincial cabinetry recalls New England card tables made around 1815, but it more likely came from the Western Reserve district around Cleveland. The wide, quite asymmetrical dulcimer of stained cherry has undercut, scrolled front corners and an unusual square sound hole outlined by green and red stripes and backed with gauze that holds cutout, painted cardboard flowers.

Fourteen tall, movable "chessman" bridges, each marked with its pitch letter and having a wire across the top bevel, support thin strings that stretch over wire-topped nuts to slender, flathead tuning and hitch pins driven into elevated sloping blocks. The fourteen pairs of strings cross one another alternately in diagonal planes, leaving the pairs farthest separated and easiest to hit near their respective bridges. The left-hand, treble row of bridges, placed closer to the center of the soundboard, divides its strings so that they can be struck on either side of the apex, drawing two pitches a fifth apart from each pair; thus the dulcimer has a twenty-one-note range. The soundboard is less than one-quarter inch thick and the bottom only slightly over half an inch; this light construction characterizes instruments

of little string tension and gentle tone. A padded whalebone beater and the shaft of another were found in the case. The family that owned this dulcimer since the 1920s refused Henry Ford's offer to purchase it; another dulcimer, perhaps Ford's favorite instrument, was featured in his Early American Orchestra (1924–47) at Dearborn, Michigan.

Another, heavier trapezoidal dulcimer (Fig. 113) dates from after the middle of the nineteenth century. Encased in poplar with painted orange graining, the instrument resembles those made in South Alabama, New York (northeast of Buffalo), by Perry Wight (1825–1900), some of whose dulcimers have his name stenciled inside the lid. This example has no lid, but the slanted outer walls, roundhead screws in place of hitch pins, and two cloth-backed sound holes, each surrounded by six smaller holes, are found on similarly painted instruments by Wight and other western New York State builders. The strings (of equal gauge) bend around the screws, passing over short individual rods of varying diameter, which act as nuts, to thick, squarehead tuning pins. The pin blocks slant down toward the sides, the better to resist the strings' pull. Presently the partly strung dulcimer has a single row of chessman bridges, but marks on the soundboard indicate that other bridges to the far right raised three double-strung bass notes. The twelve treble courses are quadruple-strung. Strain is taken up by a bottom just under an inch thick.

Two midcentury dulcimers share features in addition to rectangular shape that distinguish them from the foregoing trapezoidal ones. In both examples the pin blocks are on the same plane as the soundboard; the tuning pins are of the oblong-head type used in contemporary pianos; the thick soundboards have high arcade bridges that distribute string pressure more evenly than do chessman bridges. These instruments are designed to withstand greater string tension and to sound louder than more lightly built dulcimers. They also aspire to a more imposing appearance. The smaller one (Fig. 114), with two circular sound holes cut around stars, is veneered with rosewood, even over the pin blocks. Formerly it had twelve triple and eleven double courses of strings that were bent around hitch pins in the pattern rather than being individually hitched. The nuts—thick metal rods—rise toward the treble side. The instrument is unsigned, but the tuning pins have raised letters *WW* and *A* on opposite faces. A paper fragment on the bottom is dated 1865, and an indecipherable inscription is scrawled across the bottom.

The larger, a bulky parlor dulcimer (Fig. 115) that stood on four legs (now missing), is partly veneered in rosewood with machine-carved scalloped moldings. This case is identical to those used around 1850 by upstate New York manufacturers of small melodeons. Its locking lid, hinged in two panels, is held open by a sheet metal prop at the left side. Within, velvet-covered lamp rests occupy the rear corners. Two circular sound holes are each surrounded by twelve smaller ones. The eleven treble and eleven bass courses of varying gauge each have one wire bent around a flathead screw; this system, used in contemporary pianos, works only when string tension is high enough to prevent the string from slipping around the bend during tuning. The

bass bridge is located atypically at the left side. The all-purpose case's bottom is reinforced inside by a perforated brace that crosses from front to back and also supports the quarter-inch-thick soundboard. Two yarn-padded beaters with flexible steel shafts and wooden handles appear to be original.

The graceful Appalachian dulcimer has no British counterpart and is unrelated to the hammer dulcimer. Rather, it apparently derived during the nineteenth century from plucked zithers brought here by northern Europeans. Along with other Germanic borrowings (house types, rifles), these folk zithers mutated and diffused into contiguous mountain regions of southern Pennsylvania, eastern Tennessee and Kentucky, Virginia and West Virginia, western North Carolina, and states farther south. Despite its frequent occurrence in folk-style music today, the Appalachian dulcimer was not yet well known around 1890. Unfamiliarity accounted for the misidentification of two examples that early entered the Museum's collection; one was catalogued as a German zither, the other, less reasonably, as a Burmese harp.

Two shapes are common among Appalachian dulcimers: an elongated hourglass or figure eight that resembles an emaciated guitar, and a stretched oval or teardrop. A raised, usually hollow fingerboard extends the length of the body and terminates in a violin-type pegbox that holds three or four lateral pegs. Near the opposite end, where the wire strings hitch to nails or through holes in a tailpiece, a concave "strum hollow" under the strings allows clearance for a plectrum—customarily a turkey quill—held in the right hand. The left hand "notes" the strings

114. Hammer dulcimer. Mid-19th century. W. 40¹⁵/₁₆ in. (1979.522.2)

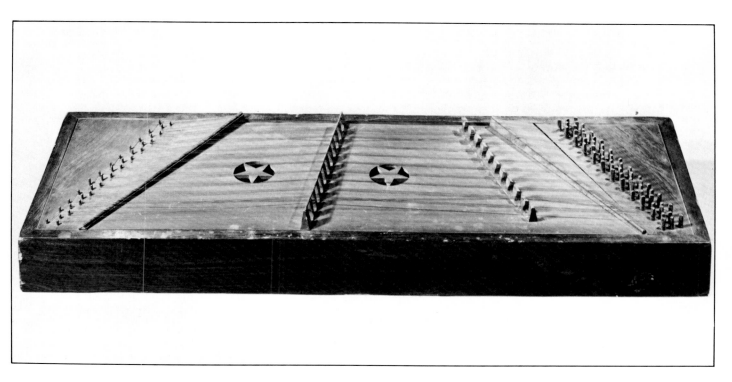

115. *Hammer dulcimer with legs and lid removed, beaters at left side. W. 41¹⁵/₁₆ in. (89.4.1440)*

against fixed frets with a stick, thumbnail, or fingertip, recalling bottleneck or Hawaiian guitar technique. The frets typically extend only partway across the fingerboard, and ordinarily only the highest string or double course is noted, the remaining strings serving as variable drones.

Normally the instrument lies sideways across the lap (hence "lap harp") or on a table with the melody strings closest to the player. When played with a fiddle bow (rarely), the instrument may be held perpendicular to the player with the peg end propped on a table. Sound holes are distributed along the top and sometimes, for added loudness, on the fingerboard; S-shaped holes were apparently borrowed from the violin, but hearts and circles are more traditional. The thin, flat top and bottom may overhang the sides as in a violin, and there may even be a violin-type sound post. Instead of the violin's quartered spruce top, though, many dulcimers have slab-sawn hardwood tops; their stiffness favors a bright sound. Often the surface is painted or lightly incised. The thick fingerboard provides rigidity; note letters or numbers sometimes occur between its frets. Variable tuning accommodates modal scales, but major is most common.

The Museum's most primitive example (Fig. 116) was acquired in poor condition from the United States National Museum around 1900. Its unglued walnut fingerboard, now secured only by a screw at the tail, has a thin-edged dado

underneath, interrupted by a bulge under the semicircular strum hollow. The pegbox, topped by a skimpy blank scroll incised with a line on each side, is simply an extension of the fingerboard; it holds three crude slotted pegs. The strings have bitten into the unprotected end grain of the fingerboard just above the hitching nails. There are no marks indicating where the two nuts might have been; these essential parts are absent. The seventeen frets, arranged along a scored line, are ordinary office staples that barely rise above the surface. The hourglass body of cherry or walnut is an entirely separate unit, its shallow sides, end blocks, and flush-edged top and bottom fastened by wire brads and glue. The crude S-holes have partly broken away. For all its sorry condition, the instrument shows no signs of wear from playing; perhaps it was never completed or was merely a model.

Of far superior workmanship, a second hourglass dulcimer (Fig. 117) of poplar has been painted to resemble rosewood. A multicolored spray of painted flowers fills the flat-bottomed strum hollow, and twinned heart sound holes pointing upward in traditional orientation are shaved on the inside edge to improve definition. Along the fingerboard a row of stamped numbers indicates degrees of a major scale, with the tonic (number 1) falling on the third, tenth, and seventeenth frets. The oak nuts, dovetailed into the fingerboard, fix the string length at 28³/₁₆ inches

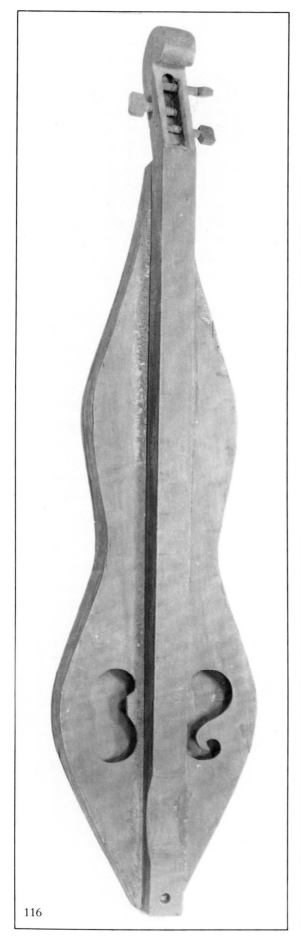

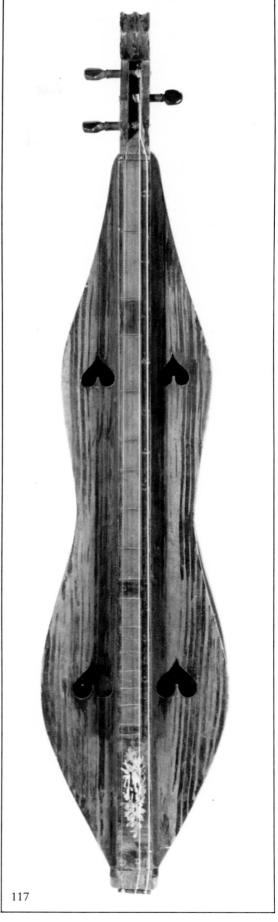

116. *Appalachian dulcimer. Late 19th century. L. 35³/₁₆ in. (89.4.2882)*

117. *Appalachian dulcimer. Huntington, W.Va., late 19th century. L.35⁹/₁₆ in. (89.4.988)*

116

117

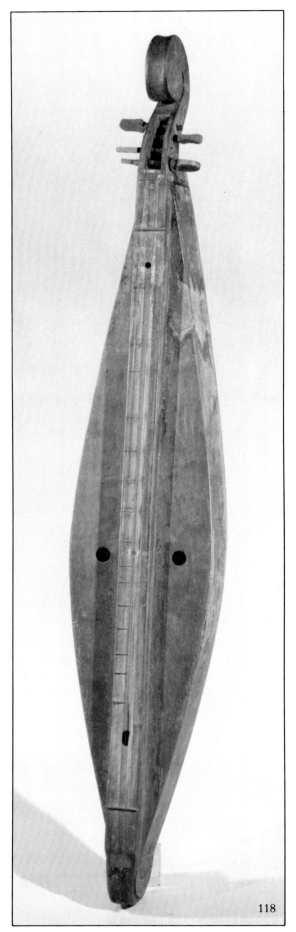

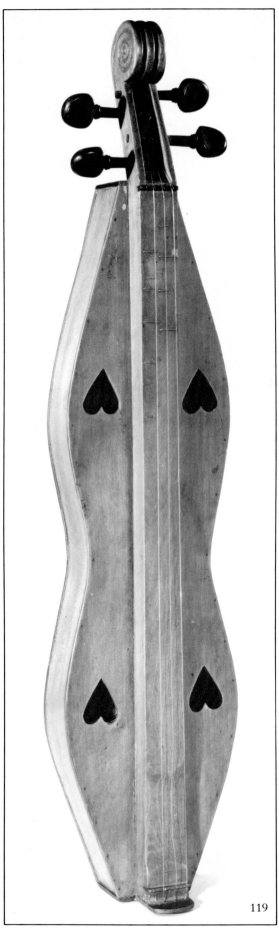

118. *Appalachian dulcimer. Late 19th century. L. 37²⁹/₃₂ in. (89.4.267)*

119. *Appalachian dulcimer by Nathan Hicks, after design by John Jacob Niles. Romanger, N. C., 1934. L. 36²¹/₃₂ in. (1975.122)*

118

119

and the third fret falls just at the spot (about 21³⁄₃₂ inches) required by equal temperament. Under the strings at the lower nut, the letters *D D G* define the tuning of the melody string (D) and drones (D G) a fifth apart. The strings fasten to a banjo tailpiece screwed to the end. The seventeen thick staple frets are worn from use. The pegbox, fitted with commercial violin pegs, terminates in a scroll with two deep flutes. Like the vertical tail block opposite, the pegbox is separate from the fingerboard. The back and thinner top far overhang the sides and are fastened by glue without nails. On the back, three low feet raise the body to increase resonance. The top is cut away in two long rectangles under the fingerboard so that the fingerboard's cavity forms part of the resonating chamber.

Within the lower right sound hole a light rectangle inside the back shows where a label has been removed. A very similar dulcimer, privately owned in Morgantown, West Virginia—one of seven apparently by the same maker—bears a fragmentary label reading

C. N. PR H RD
Manufacturer of the
AMERICAN DULCIMER
HUNTINGTON, W. VA.
STRINGS 15 cts. a set.
Sent Post-Paid by mai[l]

The manufacturer, whose identity has not been established, clearly made these instruments for commercial sale. West Virginia became a state in 1863, so this example cannot have been made before that but probably dates from the 1880s. Traveling salesmen took Huntington's wares to neighboring Kentucky and Ohio, where well-made instruments such as this may have served as models for homemade dulcimers.

Probably older, and of a shape less often seen, a lovingly made oval dulcimer (Fig. 118) with circular, shaved sound holes and pierced fingerboard is considerably worn from use. There is no strum hollow, so the plectrum has deeply scraped the area below the last fret. The short

strings (24¾ inches) offer room for only fifteen staple frets; as usual, the tonic falls on the third and tenth. Other frets have been moved to adjust intonation. While there are four tuning pegs and hitch pins (one has pulled out), the nuts have grooves for only three strings. The flat, undercut scroll with one wide flute, and the heel of the pegbox, are especially nicely shaped. Inlaid circles in the scroll eyes and inlaid crescents in the curved tail complement two decorative bands that extend the length of the fingerboard. The body is quite deep. Top and back end flush with the sides and are fastened with glue and wooden pegs. Despite its short strings the instrument is substantially longer and heavier than the foregoing hourglass ones. A quill plectrum was found inside the body.

An even more massive dulcimer of yellow poplar (Fig. 119) bears a typewritten label:

This four-string dulcimer was made by Nathan Hicks in the early spring 1934 at Romanger, North Carolina, for Miss Marion Issacs [sic], who lives in New York City. It was Pegged by Mr. Winterly and it was Strung Fretted and finished by John Jacob Niles. Mr. Niles wishes that this dulcimer with his fretting shall always be the property of Miss Issacs and the fretting shall not be copied by casual persons unless they have more than a commercial reason. The dulcimer was given to Miss Issacs by her mother to celebrate her birthday.

A small vignette of musical instruments is pasted below the label, and the signatures of Niles and Hicks are written across it. When this Depression-era dulcimer was made, the singer John Jacob Niles (b. Louisville, Ky., April 28, 1892) was well along in his career as a popularizer of American balladry. To accompany himself he designed a number of dulcimers loosely based on traditional models.

The ethnomusicologist Charles Seeger, writing to the Museum on June 5, 1953, referred to a pair of " 'dulcimoors' or 'whammadiddles' that were made for me by Nathan Hicks of Rominger [sic], North Carolina about twelve years ago. Hicks died soon after that. He was a shiftless, barely

120. *Appalachian dulcimer by Billy Reed Hampton. New York, N.Y., 1982. L. 33³⁄₁₆ in. (1982. 240)*

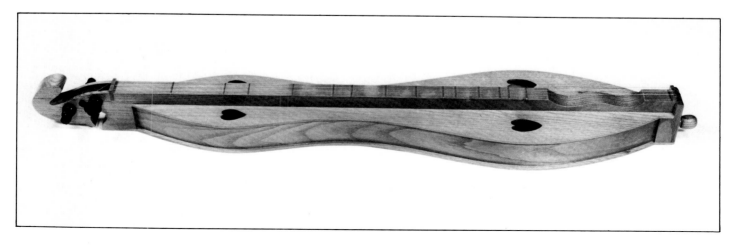

literate fellow. . . ." In a sketch appended to his letter Seeger shows an instrument with a pegbox integral to the fingerboard and a flat scroll decorated with an incised spiral on both sides; the body is squared off at both ends and has a vertical tailpiece that reaches well above the lower nut. The Museum's instrument shares these features but has in addition a complex arrangement of ten copper frets clustered near the top of the fingerboard. The advantage of this arrangement is unclear; it seems that the melody strings were noted without frets in the treble. The strum hollow is quite shallow, but the heart sound holes and tuning pegs are inordinately large. The slightly overhanging top and bottom are secured to the thick sides by brads and glue. Intended to be novel, this curious dulcimer breaks with folk tradition.

Although it was assembled in New York City in summer 1982, another dulcimer (Fig. 120) arises directly from the traditions of rural Kentucky. Made for the Museum's collection by Billy Reed Hampton (b. near Dongola, Ky., November 15, 1940), it utilizes heartwood from a four-year-old sassafras tree felled by a friend of the maker's in Whitesburg, Kentucky, as well as poplar cut from old furniture (for internal parts). The steambent sides are of unmatched grain because there was insufficient wood of one pattern. The fretting was copied from an old Kentucky banjo, with some "sharps" left out and the highest fret added; untypically, the fingerboard is solid. The heart and pegbox outlines are original. The three strings are tuned (by commercial nonslip pegs) do-sol-do, and the maker plucks them with a plastic pick or with his fingers, not using a left-hand noter. Hampton makes traditional instruments as a labor of love rather than for a living, and in true folk fashion he has learned solely from experience.

Banjos, sometimes called "the only indigenous American instruments," actually originated from African prototypes. Forbidden to use loud, provocative drums and winds, plantation slaves found comfort in playing quieter instruments made from local materials. Starting in 1678, many writers described the West Indian banza or bangil, made of half a calabash covered with skin and skewered on a long unfretted neck with, typically, four gut or fiber strings. In 1754 the banjer was first documented in Maryland; in 1774 the new spelling "banjo" occurred in Maryland and Virginia, where a traveling English merchant, Nicholas Cresswell, observed blacks dancing to a banjo "made of a Gourd something in imitation of a Guitar, with only four strings." Many cognate names probably derived from the Kimbundu *mbanza* ("stringed instrument") have been used simultaneously in the United States and West Indies, though "banjo" became the most common spelling after the mid-nineteenth century. In 1781 Thomas Jefferson called the Virginia banjar "The instrument proper to [the blacks] . . . which they

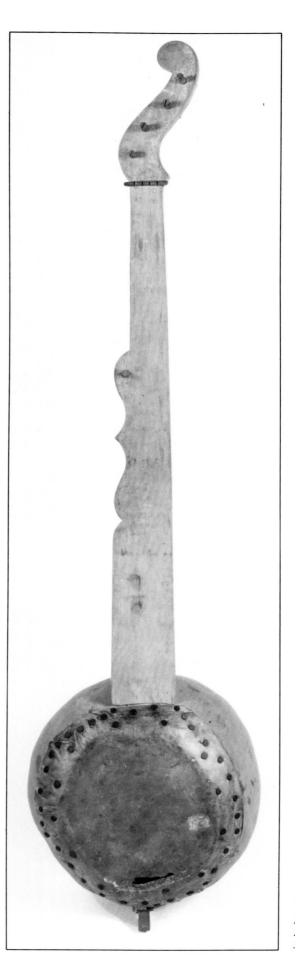

121. *Gourd-body banjo by William Esperance Boucher, Jr. Baltimore, Md., mid-19th century. L. 36¹³/₁₆ in. (89.4.598)*

brought hither from Africa . . . its chords being precisely the four lower chords of the guitar." This observation confirms one possible tuning: E, A, d, g, the reverse of the violin's.

The slaves' banjo, played both by plucking and by strumming with a thimble, attracted northern white songsters in the 1820s. By 1850, thanks to urban minstrelsy, banjos had begun a rapid commercial development. Among whites banjos were at first "for men only," but by the 1880s short "piccolo" banjos were being played by ladies. By 1920 the five-string banjo was considered a "white" instrument, thoroughly assimilated into middle-class urban culture. But bourgeois respectability did not end the making of crude folk banjos. Among blacks and rural whites the homemade banjo remained a sort of poor man's fiddle, sharing the fiddle's repertoire and many features of musical style, including florid ornamentation, much use of open strings and drones, relatively stationary left hand position, and variable tunings.

Banjos, like related Asian and African skin-topped instruments, require rigid, nonvibrating bodies to resist both the pull of the strings (not countered by a wooden top as in the guitar) and the tautness of the head. Modern commercial banjo rims are often made especially heavy to anchor the clamps that secure and stretch the skin; the massive rim helps impart a bright tone by not "soaking up" the vibration of the head.

One of the oldest extant commercial banjos (Fig. 121), perhaps made around 1845, closely resembles the seventeenth-century banza. Its gourd body has a large circular sound hole in back and a head that may be of sheepskin. In damp weather the head, fastened by tacks, must be tightened by heating, since no adjustable clamps are provided. Five strings (missing, as are the bridge and leather tailpiece) ran along a fretless neck faintly stamped *W. Boucher, Jr. Baltimore*. The perchpole (an integral extension of the neck that protrudes through the gourd) is numbered *VI*. The flat tuning head imitates the sideways-scroll outline of contemporary parlor guitars, but it curves to the left rather than the conventional right. One tuning peg for a high drone string is inserted from the back partway up the neck on the bracket-shaped side. Introduction of this drone string, evidently during the 1830s, has been tenuously attributed to Joel Walker Sweeney (1813–60), a famous minstrel from Appomattox, Virginia, who toured the United States and England. Sweeney's fretless, left-handed, five-string banjo (preserved in the Los Angeles County Museum of Natural History) may have been made by his cousin Robert Miller Sweeney, or by the maker of the Museum's gourd banjo, William Esperance Boucher, Jr.

Boucher (b. Hanover, Germany, 1822; d. Baltimore, Md., March 1899) was certainly largely responsible for popularizing the fifth string

through his manufactures. According to family tradition, he was a grandnephew of the French painter François Boucher. Immigrating with his father from Germany to Baltimore before 1845, Boucher built such a lucrative trade (Fig. 122) that he was able to advance five thousand dollars to a brother-in-law whose drayage business became the Railway Express Company. Boucher's many descendants became prominent in Maryland society; he had twenty children, and one grandchild became Maryland's attorney general. Unfortunately, family documents that might have shed light on Boucher's early years were recently misplaced.

In 1851 Boucher won a diploma for one of two banjos he entered in the fourth Maryland Institute exhibition. He exhibited a banjo and a guitar at New York's Crystal Palace in 1853. Boucher's label affixed within a drum in the Maryland Historical Society claims medals for violins (1855, 1856) and drums (1856, 1857, 1858), awarded at unspecified competitions. Three Boucher banjos donated in 1890 to the United States National Museum supposedly represent styles made in 1845–47. These banjos, like drums, have a cylindrical nailed wood rim (which frees the banjo maker from the inconsistency and limited availability of gourds, and supports greater string tension) and clamps. Boucher is said to have introduced clamp tighteners to banjos, but if so he failed to patent the innovation.

Two fretless five-string banjos, probably made around 1900 by the same "old plantation Negro" in northern Georgia who provided a fiddle and two gourd mandolins discussed below, have thin rims of soft wood with overlapped, nailed ends. These nearly circular rims resemble the shallow cylindrical cheeseboxes or sieves from which folk

122. *Advertisement of William Esperance Boucher, Jr., listing stock in trade, 1855–60*

WM. BOUCHER, JR.
38 EAST BALTIMORE STREET, one door from High St., BALTIMORE, Md.

Importer and Manufacturer of all kinds of

Musical Instruments,

Keeps constantly on hand an extensive assortment of

Italian, English, German and French Violin, Guitar, Banjo and Double Bass

STRINGS.

ALSO,

Flutes, Clarionetts, Flageoletts, Accordions, Guitars, Violins, Banjos, Tamborines, Bass and Side Drums, (Brass and Wood) Fifes, and in fact *every* variety of

MUSICAL INSTRUMENTS.

Bands supplied with all styles of Brass Instruments on reasonable terms.
The trade will find it to their advantage to give me a call.

110

banjos were sometimes made. The shorter banjo (Fig. 124) has a goatskin head sewn around a wire ring, which is permanently secured by a larger wooden hoop tacked over it. The whittled walnut neck has a separate perchpole holding a sheet copper tailpiece. The end of the neck is notched to clear the hoop. About halfway along the neck the fifth peg is inserted from the side; its string passes over a tiny protruding stud. The longer banjo (Fig. 125) of this pair is quite similar except for the method of attaching the head. The skin wraps around a wire ring held by a sheet iron hoop that is clamped by threaded rods to six handmade copper L-brackets. The brackets are screwed through the rim to walnut blocks that hold another iron hoop against the top of the rim within, for reinforcement.

Four low-priced banjos illustrate some typical sizes offered by catalogue merchants in their heyday. The circular parts of these factory-made instruments are made of metal, which provides the strength required by high-tension steel strings, introduced widely after the 1880s. The shortest (Fig. 127) is a "piccolo" banjo, which has a laminated maple rim banded with nickel silver. The head (missing) was held by a brass wire and a nickel-plated hoop tightened by sixteen clamps; a seventeenth holds the tailpiece. The cherry neck, secured against the rim by wedges, has an ebony fingerboard with four position marks and fifteen raised metal frets; like steel strings, these guitar-type frets and marks became common after the 1880s. This parlor banjo, marked *Bay State 301*, retailed for about fifteen dollars. The model 301 appeared in John C. Haynes & Co.'s 1896 catalogue with an eleven-inch rim, but the Museum's example, though marked *8* on the rim, has approximately a seven-inch outer diameter. Bay State was a well-known brand owned by Haynes, a major Boston distributor.

A cheaper, somewhat longer banjo (Fig. 128) has a nickel-banded maple rim and a brass hoop clamped to six "stars and stripes" shield brackets of a pattern illustrated in C. Bruno & Son's turn-of-the-century catalogues. The stained maple neck, deeply notched at the rim end, lacks a separate fingerboard but has twelve scratched lines in place of frets. The instrument is unsigned.

124

125

124. *Banjo with sievelike rim and tacked head. Georgia, c. 1900. L. 27¹⁵/₁₆ in. (89.4.3296)*

125. *Banjo similar to that in Fig. 124 but with clamped head. Georgia, c. 1900. L. 32¹¹/₁₆ in. (89.4.2820)*

123. *William Sidney Mount.* The Banjo Player, *1856. The banjo neck is strikingly similar to that of the Boucher banjo, Fig. 121. The conical metal object suspended from the player's neck appears to be a mouthpiece for a small brass instrument. In the vest pocket is a packet of G. B. Miller's fine-cut tobacco. Mount's attention to realistic detail extends to the player's correct hand position. The Museums at Stony Brook, N. Y., Gift of Mr. and Mrs. Ward Melville, 1955*

127

126. *Thomas Eakins*. Negro Boy Dancing, *1878. The banjo appears to be a commercial model with clamped head and inlaid position marks on the fingerboard; frets are not indicated in this watercolor drawing. The oval picture at upper left represents Abraham Lincoln and his son. (25.97.1)*

127. *Banjo sold by John C. Haynes & Co. Boston, Mass., c. 1900. L. 22⁷⁄₁₆ in. The head has been removed to show the perchpole secured by a wedge in a metal bracket and bolts that fasten the clamp brackets to the interior rim. (89.4.2887)*

128. *Banjo with scratched lines in place of frets. C. 1900. L. 26 in. (89.4.602)*

129. *Tenor banjo. C. 1900. L. 34⁵⁄₈ in. (89.4.2851)*

Also of modest workmanship, a much longer tenor banjo (Fig. 129) has fifteen raised frets on its stained birch neck. The ash rim is banded with nickel. The sixteen clamps with slotted nuts resemble those made in Chicago by one Cubley, who invented clamps that could be tightened with a screwdriver. The brass hoop is stamped *Pat 12¹* [Patent 1912?].

A later (c. 1920) tenor banjo (Fig. 130) of better construction has a rim prettily veneered with bird's-eye maple and a steel hoop with twenty clamps. The maple neck is wedged in place and has an ebony fingerboard with seventeen frets and four position marks of plastic. The tuning pegs (one does not match the others) all have synthetic ivory grips and metal shanks tightened by a screw; they are of the type advertised as The Champion, patented May 8, 1888 (382,465), by L. L. Filstrup and G. van Vant. An uneven striped inlay decorates the back of the neck and the circumference of the rim. Scratched inside the rim is the name *Richards*. Alone among the Museum's banjos, this one has an enclosed back with two **S**-shaped sound holes. Although it has a five-string tailpiece, this banjo carries only four steel strings. Four-string banjos were normally strummed with a plectrum rather than played

129

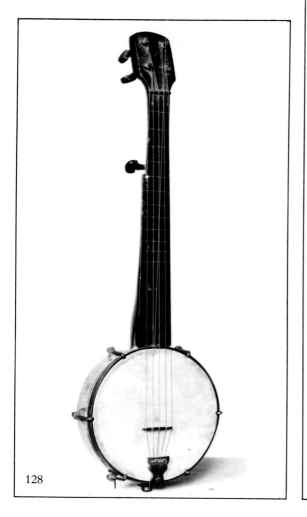

128

113

with the independent finger technique characteristic of the standard five-string banjo.

Two extraordinary concert banjos by the important St. Louis, Missouri, maker Hercules McCord exemplify the level of sophistication reached in the 1880s. A very long model (Fig. 131) with deep hickory rim and sixteen clamps on a notched, nickel-plated brass hoop displays many unusual features. The rim is partially enclosed on the back by a pine ring, burned and colored to resemble hickory. A heavy iron ring reinforces the top of the rim. The brackets fasten through the rim to brass braces that are held to the rim by copper rivets. A viola pegbox grafted atop the neck is modified by the addition of a socket holding the fifth peg; its string passes through a groove alongside the fingerboard to a tunnel through which it emerges. The ebony fingerboard has sixteen ivory inlays in place of raised frets, and dots in place of two higher inlays (McCord's long banjo necks accommodated as many as twenty-two frets or marks). The neck is secured by a wooden wedge through a stub that takes the place of a perchpole, and by a metal wedge through a brass fitting attached to the heel of the neck. A leather forearm shield covers part of the rim, and a hard rubber knob on the opposite side prevents the heavy rim from slipping off the player's lap; McCord patented a nonslip flange on June 12, 1883 (279,172). According to McCord's friend Clarence L. Partee, this particular banjo was made around 1859, but this date seems too early, in view of the complex construction.

McCord's ultimate design, patented August 14, 1883 (283,352), and April 8, 1884 (296,596), produced a very heavy banjo (Fig. 132) with an exceptionally loud sound. Said to be the first model with an all-metal rim, it has a nickel-plated brass frame marked *Pat*[ent], fitted with a screw mechanism that regulates the head's tension by pulling simultaneously on twenty-eight cables concealed by ribs on the back, in lieu of separate clamps. The system resembles that used in pedal-tuned kettledrums. There is no perchpole. The walnut neck has a rosewood fingerboard with nineteen inlaid ivory lines and six mother-of-pearl position marks. The instrument has rubber buttons on both sides of the rim, probably to prevent slipping.

According to Partee, himself a professional banjoist and composer, McCord's banjos were

130. *Plectrum banjo with four strings. C. 1920. L. 30¹⁵/₁₆ in. (1975.357.3)*

131. *Concert banjo with viola-style scroll and pegbox by Hercules McCord. St. Louis, Mo., c. 1880. L. 36¹³/₁₆ in. (89.4.2676)*

132. *Concert banjo with patented cable-tension device and protruding nonslip buttons by Hercules McCord. St. Louis, Mo., c. 1884. L. 36 in. (89.4.2677)*

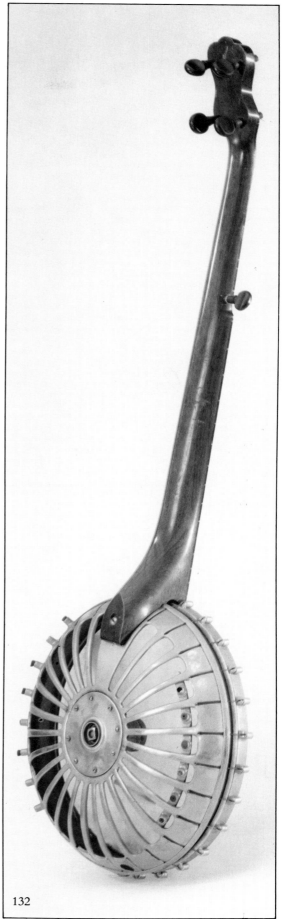

131

132

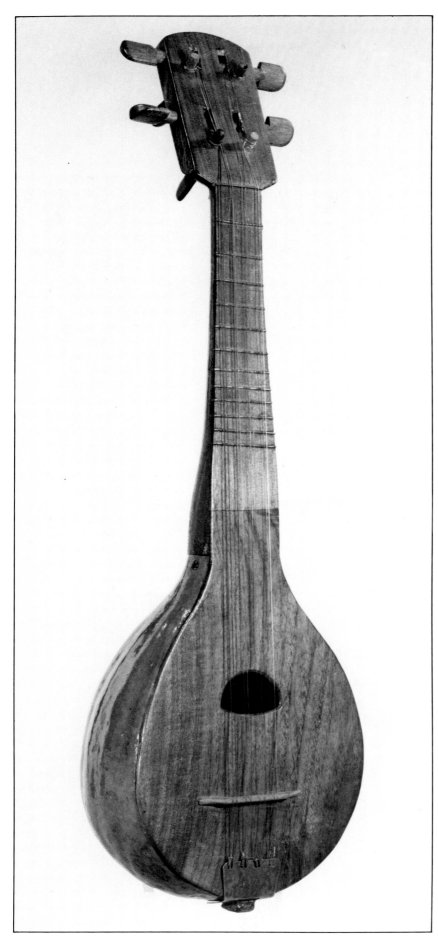

favored by such artists as Charles E. Latshaw, Joe Hart, and Charles C. Bertholdt. Instruments like these, and their repertoire, were far removed from rusticity; in the 1880s and 1890s a banjoist named Farland is said to have performed Bach's unaccompanied violin sonatas in concert.

Judging by their workmanship and materials, a pair of gourd-body mandolins were fashioned by the same person who made the two Georgia folk banjos mentioned above. These mandolins share distinctive features: The open side of the hard shell is covered by a thick walnut soundboard pierced by an irregularly shaped sound hole; the whittled walnut neck screwed to the gourd terminates in a slotted, angled head with four walnut pegs inserted from the back and two more in either side; a sheet copper tailpiece bent over the bottom of the gourd holds eight paired metal strings. The smaller mandolin (Fig. 133) has a low, loose, footed bridge and twelve sharp-edged frets made of the same thin brass stock used for the nut on both instruments. The longer mandolin (Fig. 134) is unfretted, and its bridge is glued on. Both are thickly varnished, and neither shows any sign of use. A third instrument of this style was given by Mrs. John Crosby Brown to the United States National Museum.

Although Handel, Mozart, and Beethoven occasionally wrote for the mandolin, it is usually associated with Italian popular music. In the eighteenth century mandolins were commonly played by women amateurs. They were known in this country by 1767, when Jacob Trippel advertised that he would make them in New York. In the same year John (Giovanni) Gualdo offered to teach the mandolin in Virginia, and in 1769 Gualdo, then in Philadelphia, advertised to sell and teach the instrument. Little serious attention was paid to the mandolin or its music, however, until the 1880s, when Italian immigrants began arriving in large numbers. A novelty of sorts, the mandolin was popularized during this decade by a professional touring ensemble from California known as the Spanish Students. Their success led to the formation of other ensembles such as Boston's Ideal Banjo, Mandolin, and Guitar Club, which gave concerts in every state; two members even played with the Boston Symphony.

Soon "potato bug" mandolins (so called because of their rounded, striped backs), the mainstay of innumerable music clubs, percolated through American society. Montgomery Ward's 1885 mail-order catalogue offered no mandolins, but in 1890 the Chicago company reported that "sales have more than doubled during the last year,"

133. *Gourd mandolin. Georgia, c. 1900. L. 23¼ in.* *(89.4.2767)*

and in 1897 Ward's boasted a "phenomenal growth of our Mandolin trade." Sears devoted two pages to mandolins in their 1896 catalogue; by 1905 there were six pages. By the early 1920s a potato bug mandolin had turned up in the remote Dungannon, Virginia, string band of Fiddlin' John Powers and Family.

American mandolin production began to increase as the annual number of Italian immigrants swelled from fewer than 3,000 in 1870, to 43,542 in 1885, reaching 221,479 in 1905. The newcomers, mostly poor refugees from depressed southern Italy, included many mandolin players and makers. Settling in urban Italian communities, these makers at first provided instruments only for their compatriots, who by 1900 numbered 175,000 in New York alone—more Italians than in Rome. As mandolins (but not their Italian music) became popular outside Italian neighborhoods, individual craftsmen faced stiff competition from factories run by Anglo-Saxons. Though a few of these makers entered commercial production to supply wholesalers, others made mandolins as a sideline while seeking more lucrative employment during the recession that followed the panic of 1893. Pushing into America's mainstream, Italian fathers discouraged sons from pursuing a handicraft so strongly identified with humble status. Some parents prohibited children from speaking the mother tongue. When individual mandolin makers probably earned even less than the average wage (1900) of twenty-two cents per hour, enforced Americanization was viewed as an economic necessity.

Confronted by great barriers to social adjustment outside their crowded tenements, the industrious but in many cases illiterate immigrants left little record of their work. Jealous of hard-earned skills, few older makers taught apprentices; fewer still bothered to advertise, claim patents, or modernize their methods. They had trouble raising capital for expansion; successful enterprise invited underworld interference. Meanwhile, Sears "discarded all imported mandolins on account of their worthlessness as a musical instrument" and marketed cut-rate domestic instruments by the carload. In 1896 Sears's cheap five-rib mandolin cost $3.45; in 1905 a better nine-rib instrument sold for only $1.95, while their forty-one-rib confection The Campanello brought just $19.95. (Price was determined by number of ribs, extent of inlay, and type of wood, which were irrelevant to musical quality.)

In order to compete with these mail-order bargains, independent makers had to offer something extraordinary. Two men who did so in New

134. *Gourd mandolin by the same maker as that in Fig. 133. Georgia, c. 1900. L. 31⁷/₁₆ in. (89.4.2821)*

135. *Nicòla Turturro (1872–1953)*

136. *Lyre-mandolin or Mandolira by Nicòla Turturro. New York, N.Y., c. 1904. L. 25½ in. (1975.357.1). See also Colorplate 5*

York were Nicòla Turturro and Angelo Mannello.

Nicòla Turturro (b. Bitonto, Italy, April 25, 1872; d. New York, June 30, 1953) (Fig. 135), son of a government forester, was apprenticed to a cabinetmaker in Rome. He married Frances Caiati and emigrated to America around 1900, the first of his family to do so. Settling in the Italian enclave of Mount Vernon, just north of New York City, Turturro may have been among the workers who produced the Vernon mandolins, mandolinettos, and guitars that C. Bruno & Son sold as "our own make." But he proceeded along independent lines, patenting a lyre-shaped mandolin on August 9, 1904 (767,023). His supplemental bass string attachment for plucked instruments received a patent on October 19, 1909 (937,121). Turturro moved to lower Manhattan's Little Italy around 1917 and north again to East 156th Street in the Bronx in 1924. There he

developed three more patents: a ukulele with peanut-shaped back (March 20, 1928; design patent 74, 766) produced for C. Bruno, whose stamp appears along with Turturro's on a privately owned example; a combined mandolin-ukulele with strings on both sides of the body (August 6, 1929; 1,723,751); and a complicated accordion mechanism (March 22, 1938; 2,111,953). The 1928 and 1929 patents evolved in response to the ukulele craze of 1916–30, during which the more expensive round-back mandolin lost favor.

Around 1940 Turturro moved for the last time, to Coney Island. Semiretired, he devoted himself to less taxing repair work, music teaching (mandolin, guitar, violin), and cabinetry projects. An enterprising performer, he and seven female relatives had formed a mandolin band, which entertained at the New York Athletic Club in Pelham, New York, and at nearby Glen Island.

137. *Mandolin band. Probably American, c. 1900. The central player holds a lyre-mandolin similar to Turturro's*

As an inventor he was concerned with making familiar instruments more versatile; consequently his innovations were not merely cosmetic but structural. His children—five of thirteen reached adulthood—assisted in the workshop, and for a while the close-knit family made instruments for resale under the trade names Tritone and Roma. Ukuleles were manufactured as a sideline in Turturro's final business venture in 1940–41, but World War II drew the sons into other paths. One became an experimental machinist, a wartime trade that attracted many instrument makers who were accustomed to precision work. None of Turturro's sons resumed instrument making after the war, and upon his death his tools and patterns were dispersed.

Turturro's lyre-mandolin (Fig. 138), called by him a Mandolira, imitates a French neoclassic form introduced to Italy in the Napoleonic era and seen most often in parlor guitars. The style faded after 1815 but was revived late in the century. Lyre-shaped mandolins were hard-to-make specialty items not sold through dealers' catalogues. As shown in the Museum's unique surviving example (Fig. 136 and Colorplate 5), Turturro solved the problem of combining the mandolin's ribbed, rounded back with the lyre's extended body by forming a domed rather than pear-shaped back, set off from the flat rosewood sides and tapered arms by celluloid strips. The dome comprises twenty-four flat rosewood ribs separated by light-colored wood stringing radiating from a mother-of-pearl disk. Embossed green paper lines the interior, reinforcing the many joints.

The deep back and hollow arms enclose a large resonating space. To let sound out, twin oval sound holes extending under the outer strings are supplemented by diamond-shaped holes at the tips of the arms. The oval holes open a larger area than the usual single hole. Between the ovals a longitudinal brace reinforces the wide, two-piece spruce top, varnished and edged with white celluloid outside five inlaid strips. Below the pick guard the top's receding angle causes the strings to exert firm pressure on the movable bridge. The sound holes are surrounded by conventional ornaments set in mastic, but the tortoiseshell pick guard has delicate mother-of-pearl floral inlays. The neck is mahogany, the front of the tuning head veneered with rosewood. A curved aluminum yoke serves more for ornament than for strengthening the tips of the arms. Behind the head the stamp *N. Turturro N.Y.C. Manufacturer* repeats the wording of a circular label inside the bowl. Twenty frets are interspersed with circular and diamond-shaped position marks. A mahogany base that allows the mandolin to sit upright reflects the curves that terminate the arms. A scalloped sleeve protector covers the tailpiece; like the bridge and other fittings, this was purchased ready-made.

The career of Angelo Mannello (Fig. 139) (b.

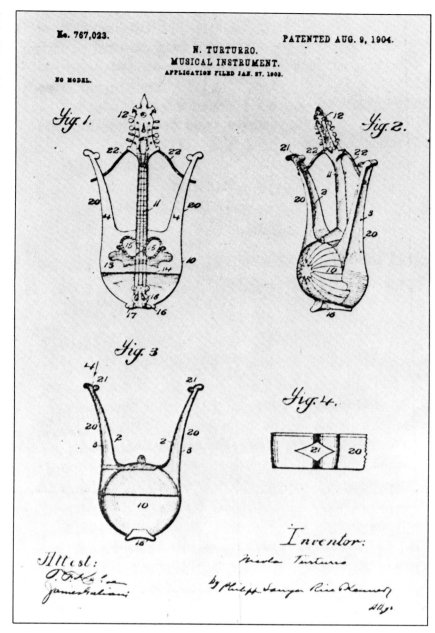

Morcone, Italy, December 11, 1858; d. New York, July 4, 1922) took a different and more expansive turn. The son of a carpenter, Mannello was apprenticed to a woodworker in Naples. Two brothers also worked with wood, one as a finisher, the other as a polisher. In 1885 Mannello came to New York, like Turturro the first of his family to emigrate. Within a month after his arrival he opened a shop that quickly prospered. By 1887 he had sent for and married Filomena Buccini, his roommate's sister, and had begun hiring helpers from his native village, probably providing some of them with the twelve-dollar boat fare from Italy. Before 1900 Mannello's shop occupied several premises in Little Italy; on Elizabeth Street between Grand and Broome, at 18 Spring Street, and at 355½ and 360 Bowery, all within a few blocks of one another.

138. *Patent drawing of lyre-mandolin invented by Nicòla Turturro*

139. *Angelo Mannello (1858–1922)*

140. *Mandolin by Angelo Mannello. New York, N.Y., c. 1900. L. 24⁹⁄₁₆ in. (1972.111.1). See also Colorplate 6*

140

Mannello created stunningly ornate mandolins for display at international expositions. Leaving his family at home, the entrepreneur traveled widely to pose with his prize products. Just eight years after arriving in America, he captured a bronze medal and certificate at the 1893 World's Columbian Exposition in Chicago. A mandolin with Mannello's label in Italian, dated 1893 and now in the Milwaukee Public Museum, shows that by then he already had a Chicago sales agent, Cesare Valisi. A certificate from the 1897 Tennessee Centennial Exposition was succeeded by a string of gold medals from the Paris Exposition Universelle Internationale and the San Francisco Midwinter International Exposition, both in 1900; the Pan-American Exposition in Buffalo in 1901; and the 1904 Louisiana Purchase Exposition at St. Louis. These fairs were not so rigorously competitive as might be imagined; the point being to encourage commerce, nearly everyone won some formal recognition. The Pan-American Exposition program lists only three exhibitors of plucked instruments (and, incidentally, misspells Mannello's name). Nevertheless his awards were well deserved (see insets, Fig. 145).

For all his talent, Mannello never learned to perform as a musician. Only one of his seven children was musical, a daughter who died of tuberculosis at nineteen. Three sons went to work sanding, varnishing, and stringing finished instruments, but the domineering father deliberately withheld from them the experience of making instruments from scratch.

Mannello's production line grew rapidly. By 1903 up to seventy-five employees in his brick factory at 630 Eagle Avenue in the South Bronx were turning out mandolins, guitars, and banjos by the score. These common instruments went at wholesale prices of three to five dollars each to C. Bruno & Son for exclusive resale under Bruno's name. Mannello himself continued to make beautiful mandolins for special customers such as Signor Perara's mandolin band in Minneapolis. Outfitting professional ensembles was an effective means of advertising and of garnering grateful testimonials. Realizing the value of reflected prestige, Mannello presented a mandolin to the soprano Adelina Patti.

Mannello's practice of hiring workers from Morcone involved him in founding the Società Morconese around 1917–18. This fellowship became a lodge of the Sons of Italy, and Mannello served as its powerful president until his death. In 1918 a suspicious fire destroyed his factory; taking this as a warning not to overstep himself, Mannello retrenched to 149th Street and Courtlandt Avenue, where his family assembled instruments on a reduced scale. A few years later Mannello died intestate, and his sons, deprived of his authority and knowledge, carried on as best they could until the Depression closed their shop forever.

141. *Detail of sound-hole decoration and pick guard on mandolin in Fig. 140*

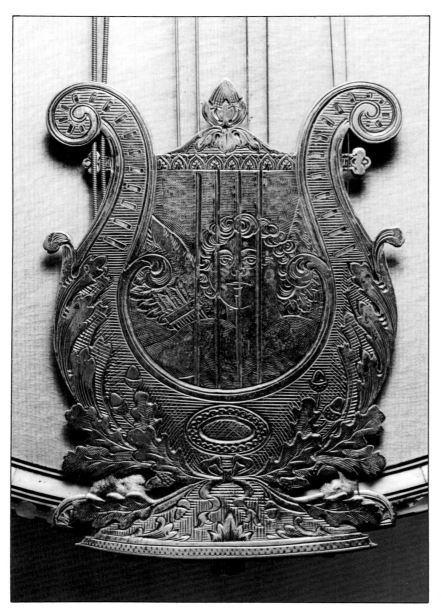

142. *Detail of sleeve protector in form of a lyre on mandolin in Fig. 140*

143. *Back of mandolin in Fig. 140*

144. *Fingerboard of mandolin in Fig. 140*

Mannello's early showpieces rival the richest of his Neapolitan models, notably instruments of the Vinaccia dynasty, who set the fashion for gorgeous mandolins from the mid-eighteenth century to the 1830s. Mannello was very likely inspired by magnificently decorated Neapolitan mandolins during his period of apprenticeship, and probably he sold instruments in Naples before emigrating; otherwise it is hard to fathom how he accumulated the capital to open his first workshop in New York. Certainly nothing sold through dealers' catalogues compared with Mannello's custom-designed masterpieces. These commanded prices above one hundred dollars, five times the cost of Sears's top models. Unlike Turturro, Mannello was not concerned with innovation. Instead, he expended his creative energies on lavish ornamentation, keeping to a standard structural pattern.

The two breathtaking mandolins in the Museum's collection are of special interest because they were cherished by Mannello's family as examples of his finest work. These two mandolins were made in 1900 or soon thereafter; their labels reproduce medals Mannello won at the San Francisco and Paris expositions that year.

The heavier and more ornate of the pair (Fig. 140, Colorplate 6), with a checkerboard back of ivory and tortoiseshell separated by metal stripes, is probably the earlier, since on its label the maker's name is misspelled "Manello," an oversight corrected in printing the second label. As though to make up for the error, on the earlier mandolin MANNELLO is spelled out on an ivory oval around the sound hole. The decoration of this instrument includes fourteen engraved human faces and figures (Fig. 141), most of them putti except for a partly clothed Columbia or Venus standing on a pair of scallop shells below a grotesque face on the back (Fig. 143).

Two putti, one surrounded by emblems of wisdom and power, the other sitting amidst panpipe, lyre, and lute, embellish the broad bottom strip or cap, flanking a framed, blank plaque. On the exquisite pearl-inlaid fingerboard three cherubic faces serve as position marks. A leafy motif rises around them to enclose a Cupid on the tuning head, surmounted by a classical broken pediment and urn (Fig. 144). Another Cupid peers from behind the imprisoning strings of an engraved lyre that forms the tailpiece's sleeve protector (Fig. 142); this imaginary lyre has an oval sound hole surrounded by beading that copies the beaded edging of the mandolin's top and sound hole. The lyre motif is repeated in inlay on the pick guard and appears again, this time paired with a guitar, engraved on the back plate of the geared tuners.

The second mandolin (Fig. 145) has a back composed of thirty concave bird's-eye maple ribs separated by metal stripes, encompassed by broad side bands and cap of ebony inlaid with ivory.

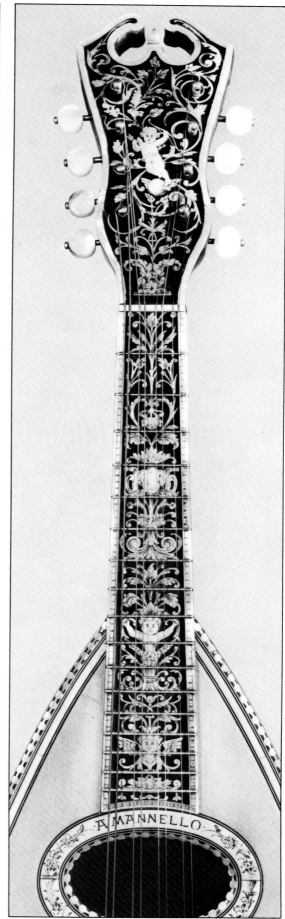

Again, classical figures and foliation dominate the decor; similar designs in mother-of-pearl enliven the fingerboard, head, and pick guard. The tuners and tailpiece are identical to those on the other mandolin, but a stamped golden lyre-and-wreath sleeve protector (not original) replaces the lyre-and-Cupid one.

Both instruments have one-piece fine-grained spruce tops and seventeen thin frets identically spaced on the fingerboards. The shapes of the heads and proportions of the bodies are also identical, but the separate bridges are not the same size. Neither instrument shows much sign of use, nor would instruments of this quality have been casually handled and exposed to normal wear and tear.

While Mannello advertised himself in 1894–95 as "the best maker in the country," a commercial George Washburn mandolin (Fig. 146) manufactured in Chicago around 1900 claims to be "Best in the World." Its label further guarantees materials and workmanship for one year and boasts awards from the 1893 World's Columbian Exposition and an 1894 fair in Antwerp. The mandolin even has a handwritten serial number, A-12953, indicating an extensive production run. Washburn was a top-of-the-line brand owned by Chicago's mammoth Lyon & Healy Company, for many years one of the country's largest music and instrument sellers. Lyon & Healy made everything from cheap dulcimers to pipe organs and world-famous harps. They employed more mandolin makers than any other firm, and claimed, "At any time you can find in our factories upwards of 10,000 Mandolins in various stages of construction." Their huge production rooms, equipped with belt-driven machinery, turned out over one hundred thousand instruments of various types in 1889 alone. Considering this rate, the quality of their better instruments was remarkably good.

In 1864 George Washburn Lyon (1833–94) and Patrick Joseph Healy (1840–1905) had come from Boston to Chicago to open a western branch of Oliver Ditson's thriving music publishing company. Expanding into instruments, Lyon & Healy kept up to date by introducing upright pianos to Chicago in 1871; but in that year the Chicago fire destroyed their store, along with most of the city's other businesses. Next year, though, the company reopened and for another century made or imported a large proportion of the instruments sold west of the Appalachians. At the time the Museum's Washburn mandolin was made, Lyon & Healy's customers included the Midwest's highest society: Cyrus H. Adams, Chauncy J.

145. *Mandolin by Angelo Mannello. New York, N. Y., c. 1900. L. 24⅝ in. (1972.111.2).* Insets: *Certificates of award to Angelo Mannello (1976.644.1–2)*

Blair, Mrs. Potter Palmer, Martin A. Ryerson, Robert Todd Lincoln. Their names appear on one page of a massive turn-of-the-century company ledger preserved in the library of the Museum's Department of Musical Instruments.

This mandolin, style 275, features a floral-engraved mother-of-pearl fingerboard with twenty frets extending over the sound hole, the finger positions subtly marked by horizontal designs. Mother-of-pearl bands outlined by red and white stripes with checkerboard wood inlays edge the two-piece fine-grain spruce top and oval sound hole. The top is only slightly angled below the pick guard, which is made of simulated tortoiseshell with conventional mother-of-pearl inlays. The crown-shaped, engraved sleeve protector is silver plated. Forty-four flat, narrow rosewood ribs separated by white celluloid stripes form the vaulted back.

After 1900 the mandolin's growing popularity gave rise to new body shapes that appealed to fashion-conscious eyes and were cheaper to make than the round-back model. Chief among these were the radical flat-back styles pronounced by the Gibson Mandolin-Guitar Company's 1921 catalogue to be "the first serious instruments of the mandolin family ever manufactured." Behind such ballyhoo lurked the unvoiced wish to Americanize a foreign object, to lessen its association with immigrant culture. Proud Americans had to do things better, but above all, differently.

William H. De Wick (b. New York, December 1869), a music teacher and sometime banjo maker in Brooklyn, patented a distinctive mandolin on February 27, 1912 (1,018,651). Intending to prevent the soundboard from sagging under pressure of the bridge and to render the treble strings loud and brilliant, De Wick adopted the familiar circular shape of the banjo, about which everyone could feel patriotic. He called his instrument the Bandonian (Fig. 147). Its body consists of two concentric wooden hoops fixed to a solid circular back. The inner hoop, to which the soundboard is glued, is perforated by sound holes around its circumference; thus the soundboard remains unholed and presumably therefore stiff, while the concealed sound holes make for an uncluttered banjo-head appearance. The thick outer rim is supposed to withstand, alone, the strain of the strings transmitted through the tailpiece. The fingerboard projects over the internally braced

146. *Mandolin by the Washburn Co. (Lyon & Healy). Chicago, Ill., c. 1900. L. 24 in. (1979.444)*

147. *Bandonian by William H. De Wick. Brooklyn, N.Y., c. 1912. L. 23 in. (1978.274). Insets: Mark of William H. De Wick and patent drawing of Bandonian showing internal construction*

146

top without touching it. The resulting structure doubtless produced a powerful ringing tone, probably lacking the sweetness offered by a top made more flexible by a large frontal sound hole.

Unfortunately, this cannot be verified by the Museum's Bandonian; its outer rim has deformed, making it unplayable. Ignoring the statics of the traditional mandolin, De Wick overlooked the effect of isolating the stress-bearing tailpiece from the soundboard, which would normally provide lateral reinforcement. He fell into the same trap as other eager patentees whose errant "improvements" mirrored their naive faith in progress.

While the rage for Italianate mandolins and ukuleles subsided after the Depression, the guitar's long-standing popularity shows no sign of abating. Spanish guitars, so called regardless of their origin, were imported to this country during the eighteenth century and made in New York by 1767. The somewhat misleading term "Spanish" reflects the distinction that arose abroad around 1760 between the familiar figure-eight Continental shape and the unwaisted "English guitar," actually a cittern with paired wire strings. The first guitar tutor published in America covered both types: *Complete Instructor for the Spanish and English Guitar, Harp, Lute, and Lyre* (Charleston, South Carolina: J. Siegling, 1820). But shortly after this tutor appeared, the English guitar became obsolete in the States and in Britain.

Spanish guitars—favorite parlor instruments of women amateurs and decorated to appeal to their taste—were extremely fashionable in German-speaking lands from about 1790 to 1830. Vienna in particular attracted renowned guitar players, composers, and builders. One of these builders, Christian Frederick Martin (b. Markneukirchen, Germany, January 31, 1797; d. Nazareth, Pa., February 16, 1873), was to achieve lasting fame in America. After having been trained in guitar making by his father, Johann Georg, a member of the cabinetmakers' guild, Christian was employed in Vienna by Karl Kuhle (whose daughter, Ottilie Lucia, he married) and by Johann Georg Stauffer, for whose novel bowed guitar (arpeggione) Franz Schubert composed a famous sonata with piano accompaniment (1824). Martin became Stauffer's foreman but returned to Saxony after the birth of his son Christian Jr. (b. October 2, 1825; d. November 15, 1888).

148. *Guitar by Christian Frederick Martin. New York, N. Y., 1835–38. L. 36¹³/₁₆ in. (1979.380). Insets: Label of guitar and stamp inside showing double image caused by reimpression*

149. *Guitar by C. F. Martin & Co., style 27. Nazareth, Pa., 1867–98. L. 37 in. Rosewood back and sides (1983.348)*

150. *Guitar by C. F. Martin & Co., serial number 39598. Nazareth, Pa., 1929. L. 36¾ in. Spanish cedar back and sides, pick guard of synthetic tortoiseshell (1984.130)*

148

149

150

At home a bitter dispute between the violin-makers' and cabinetmakers' guilds over who had the right to make guitars was finally resolved in the cabinetmakers' favor in 1832, but by then Martin was fed up. He departed for New York on September 9, 1833, and first appears in New York directories in 1834 as a violin and guitar maker at 196 Hudson Street. Though Martin is not known to have made any violins in New York, his wholesale and retail shop sold imported instruments and accessories as well as his own guitars. He also advertised instrument repairs and piano tuning. After a brief association with one Heinrich Schatz, Martin entered partnership with Charles Bruno (founder of C. Bruno & Son) on May 1, 1838, at 212 Fulton Street. Bruno, who had come from Germany to Macon, Georgia, in 1832 and had moved two years later to New York, continued to distribute Martin's guitars even after May 29, 1839, when Martin sold his stock to Ludecus & Wolter. Martin followed Schatz to the Moravian community at Nazareth, Pennsylvania, where the family-owned Martin company still flourishes.

Martin's guitars bore New York labels until 1898; they were sold in New York by John Coupa, among others, in the 1840s, and later by a number of dealers, including Bruno and C. A. Zoebisch, whose names appear sporadically with Martin's on labels and in directory listings. The Museum's oldest Martin guitar (Fig. 148) is branded *C. F. Martin New-York* on the back; inside, a pink paper label probably engraved by W. F. Harrison includes the Fulton Street address but has *196 Hudson Street* added by hand. Since this label displays Martin's name alone, the guitar it identifies was probably made before the Martin-Bruno partnership took effect.

This early Martin guitar is of typical Italo-Austrian pattern. The curvaceous body tapers in thickness from tail to waist, then reduces more sharply toward the neck. The sides and one-piece, slightly arched back, laminated inside with mahogany veneer for strength, are of bird's-eye maple. The fine-grain spruce top bears a dark brown edging and diagonal checked purfling banded by green, light, and dark stripes; the back purfling is a simpler inlay of light and dark stripes. The purflings and the mother-of-pearl and abalone inlays around the sound hole may have been imported from Germany, where their manufacture was a specialty. The ebony fingerboard with twenty-one frets extends over the top but does not touch it. The ebonized neck is fitted at the heel (of so-called ice-cream cone shape) with a keyed screw that can change the neck angle and string height, a device said to have been invented by Stauffer; it appears on instruments by him, by his son, and by E. N. Scherr in the Museum's collection.

This guitar's tuning head follows a pattern popular abroad, resembling a flattened violin scroll turned sideways, the strings being secured in a diagonal line. A silver-plated panel engraved with a sunburst encloses the back of the geared tuners. The pin bridge has a saddle made of fret wire, below which is a separate inlaid birdlike ornament of ivory and abalone. The braces within are carefully notched into the liners. A compartment in the blue-wool-lined case holds a wooden capo (an adjustable nut for altering the guitar's pitch) faced with leather and equipped with a gut string wound around a peg to secure it around the guitar's neck. The guitar was of course strung with low-tension gut, the lowest strings being wound with wire.

It is tempting to speculate that Martin might have known and perhaps influenced another immigrant guitar maker, Emilius Nicolai Scherr (b. Copenhagen, Denmark, May 5, 1794; d. Philadelphia, Pa., August 14, 1874), whose work was more varied but is less remembered than Martin's. Third son of the organ and piano builder Johan Nicolai Scherr (c. 1751–1804), Emilius was apprenticed at A. Marschall's, Denmark's major piano manufactory, before being emancipated in 1819. In that year and the next he received a total of 1200 *rigsdaler* from the authorities to go abroad, as was the custom, for further training. This he sought in Germany, where he worked for an organ builder in Linz. Although his request for 600 *rigsdaler* for a trip to Italy was refused, on March 6, 1821, Scherr was granted a further 300 *rigsdaler* to finish his training. On May 25, 1822, the king gave him leave to find employment outside Denmark, and on October 17 of that year he arrived in Philadelphia on the brig *Minerva* out of Hamburg, accompanied by his German wife, Catherine, as well as by the piano builder C. F. L. Albrecht.

Scherr first appeared in Philadelphia directories of 1825 as a pianoforte and organ builder, his name misspelled "Cornelius N. Sheer." He joined the Musical Fund Society in 1828 while living on High Street, but moved successively to Pine, Chestnut, Green, and Broad Streets in later years. Scherr apparently had retired by 1861, when his occupation was listed as "gentleman." In 1860 his son E. N. Scherr, Jr., appeared in directories ("pianos") at the Green Street address along with another son, Philip R. Scherr. The next year Emilius Jr. was listed as "secretary U.S. Navy," but military archives do not record him. Others living in the Green Street house in 1861 included Adolf (Rudolf?) Scherr, distiller, and William Scherr, gentleman. The 1850 census mentioned two daughters who died in childhood.

Scherr's lineage continued in New York, where in 1909 an Emilius William and an Emilius W. Jr. had separate residences on Seventh Avenue. The father was an agent for the Atlas Silk Hosiery Company; the son was a patent attorney who by 1933 had a Wall Street office. Finally, the *New York Times* of February 14, 1959, carried the obituary of the attorney's widow, Amy Lay Hull, a well-known storyteller and portrayer of historical personages. She lived quite near the Metropolitan Museum, and one cannot help wondering whether she knew of the Museum's two Scherr harp-guitars. Whether or not Emilius W. Jr. was familiar with his forebear's accomplishments, a strain of musical inventiveness ran in his blood; on September 17, 1918, he received a patent himself (1,279,013) for a means of illuminating perforated player-piano rolls so that expression marks could be more easily read. He assigned this patent to the Aeolian Company of Connecticut.

Emilius Nicolai the elder contracted in 1825 to install an organ of twelve stops in Philadelphia's First Moravian Church at a price of twelve hundred dollars plus the previous organ. Scherr's organ, with two manuals and pedals, was described by his friend Abraham Ritter (1857) as "of very heavy tone . . . with nothing to elasticize it." This organ was replaced around 1858 with an organ built by J. C. B. Standbridge, organist of the church. Coincidentally, Ritter (who, despite his criticism of Scherr's organ, composed a hymn in his honor) and Standbridge were judges at the seventh exhibition of the Franklin Institute (1832), at which Scherr was awarded two premiums but no medal for his three entries (the only medal went to Francis Hopkinson Smith). The judges reported as follows:

No. 343. A square piano, made by E. N. Scherr, is a good instrument, possessing brilliancy of tone, of good action, and remarkable for the superior finish of the internal mechanism. The fine open tone of this instrument, is, (perhaps) injured by the useless, but splendid, heavy exterior cabinet work.

No. 345, is a harp guitar, a new invention, made and patented by E. N. Scherr, to whose ingenuity the public is indebted for the production of so good and sweet an instrument, *which well deserves a premium.*

No. 344, is an harmonica, made by E. N. Scherr, that especially deserves commendation; this instrument is well adapted for the parlor or hall, of sweet, yet powerful tone, of most splendid workmanship in each and every particular, and in the opinion of the committee richly *merits a premium.*

No example of Scherr's "harmonica," perhaps a set of musical glasses, is known today. He advertised this instrument, together with the ordinary Spanish guitar, as a product of his manufactory in *Poulson's Daily Advertiser* for July 31, 1835 (Fig. 153).

Scherr's pianos were justly admired, judging from a beautifully veneered and decorated square example in the Chicago Historical Society, supposedly purchased by Agustín de Iturbide, emperor of Mexico in 1822–23, for his daughter. It is marked *New Patent E. N. Scherr Philadelphia* (no piano patent is recorded for Scherr). Another

151. *Emilius N. Scherr and family in the living room of their Pine Street home, Philadelphia, Pa., c. 1830. Unknown artist, possibly German or Scandinavian. Collection of the Pierce family, New Haven, Conn.*

152. *Letterhead of Emilius N. Scherr, showing (from left, not to scale) a square piano, a chamber organ with female player, and an upright piano. From a letter of 1828 to W. D. Lewis. Lewis Nielson Papers, courtesy The Historical Society of Pennsylvania, Philadelphia, Pa.*

153. *Advertisement of E. N. Scherr from* Poulson's American Daily Advertiser, *Philadelphia, Pa., July 31, 1835*

square piano, in the Smithsonian's collection, is marked *Emelius* [*sic*] *N. Scherr, Fecit Philadelphia* and may date from the mid-1820s. According to Smithsonian archives, Scherr sometimes added "Late Maker to their Majesties, the King and Princess of Denmark" to his name, but the validity of this assertion has not been confirmed. Nevertheless, Scherr was an innovative and respected builder—he supplied a piano for the White House in 1841—whose opinions on piano construction engaged him in controversy. Around 1855 he sold his business to Birgfeld & Ramm, whose square pianos made "strictly . . . in the style formerly adopted by MR. E. N. SCHERR" won enthusiastic praise from the celebrated Louis Moreau Gottschalk in 1856.

Scherr's interest in piano design was shared by his Norwegian friend Ole Bull, the most renowned and influential violinist to visit America in the nineteenth century. Three letters from Bull to Scherr, part of the Dreer collection at The Historical Society of Pennsylvania, date from May and October 1844, and December 1845, when Bull was touring in the East; these letters deal with personal and compositional matters, not with instruments. Scherr did, however, supply pianos to other touring virtuosi, and was in touch with such luminaries as Leopold de Meyer, Alfred Jaell, and Henriette Rossi Sontag in the early 1850s.

Significantly, Scherr's letterhead (Fig. 152) showed pictures of square and upright pianos and a chamber organ, but no grand piano; like many contemporary makers he is not known to have built any grands at all. Though piano making probably accounted for most of Scherr's wealth (the 1850 census valued his real estate holdings at forty thousand dollars, and he employed two Irish chambermaids), most of his surviving instruments are harp-guitars. The unique feature for which the harp-guitar's patent was granted (October 6, 1831) was an elongated body that rested at one end on the floor; this is the instrument's only harplike aspect. The harp-guitar used the same technique and tuning as the ordinary Spanish guitar, so no special training was needed to play it. Though all extant examples have the shape shown in a contemporary lithograph (Fig. 155) by Lehman and Duval, Scherr's patent covered any such instrument that reached the floor, regardless of shape. However, the official image reconstructed from Scherr's description after the 1834 Patent Office fire destroyed the original drawing was pure fantasy.

That Scherr's floor-supported design was not an isolated quirk is shown by another patent, July 22, 1834, awarded to Filippo Trajetta, for a family of bowed instruments—violin to contrabass—each having a foot upon which it stood vertically on the floor. Trajetta's object, expressed in the patent, was to provide a bowed instrument "which should yet be free from those objections

which exist to the violin in the hands of females, from the awkward manner in which it is intended to be held." Called Plettro Lyra, his instrument was suited especially to performance in church by women accompanying the choir; it was "from the manner of holding it, more congenial to the dignity of the place of performance than . . . the violin, even in the hands of male performers." Trajetta (1777–1854; also known as Philip Traetta), it must be noted, was no crackpot, but a highly distinguished composer from Venice who arrived in Boston in 1799 and lived in New York and Charleston before settling in Philadelphia, where he founded the American Conservatorio.

One of the Museum's two Scherr harp-guitars (Fig. 154) has had its original tuning head replaced. Screwed over the lower of two sound holes, a convex metal fixture of unknown function, marked *Jos. Beckhaus Phila.*, seems not to be an integral part of the instrument. Joseph Beckhaus (1811–89), a German immigrant who established an important carriage factory in Philadelphia in 1853, may have been acquainted with Scherr through the German Lutheran church; Scherr's daughters were buried in the cemetery

154. *Harp-guitar by E. N. Scherr. Philadelphia, Pa., after 1831. "Moustache" shows below damaged bridge; head replaced. L. 57½ in. (89.4.1519)*

155. The Patent Harp Guitar Invented by E. N. Scherr. *Lithograph by Lehman and Duval. Philadelphia, Pa., c. 1836. Courtesy The New-York Historical Society, New York, N. Y.*

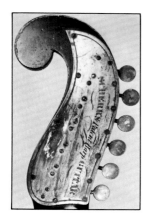

156. *Harp-guitar by E. N. Scherr. Philadelphia, Pa., after 1831. Bridge replaced. L. 58¹¹⁄₁₆ in. (55.48)*

157. *Engraved mark of E. N. Scherr on plate enclosing tuning mechanism of harp-guitar in Fig. 156*

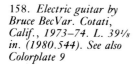

158. *Electric guitar by Bruce BecVar. Cotati, Calif., 1973–74. L. 39⅛ in. (1980.544). See also Colorplate 9*

156

there. This harp-guitar has nineteen frets, and sides, neck, and arched back of rosewood. Its bridge is badly damaged.

The other instrument (Fig. 156) retains its original sideways-scroll head, containing geared tuners marked *Schrader Philadᵉ. Patent*. John H. Schrader was listed as a turner and machinist from 1822 to 1855. In 1828 he advertised to instruct gentlemen in the art of turning and mentioned his stock in trade: lathes, drills, milling tools, billiard balls, and so on. Musical instrument hardware is not mentioned, but Scherr may have relied on Schrader for tuners and also for the key-turned screw with which the guitar's neck angle can be adjusted—a device, similar to C. F. Martin's, useful only on instruments with low-tension gut strings. This harp-guitar, engraved *Scherr's Patent Harp Guitar* (Fig. 157) on the plate behind the tuners, has twenty frets, and back and sides of curly maple. As late as the 1950s this instrument was played professionally by folk singer Edith Allaire, in whose memory it was donated to the Museum by her mother.

By the middle of this century, when Scherr's guitar had become a curious anachronism, many popular performers had already turned to amplified instruments for greater dynamic impact and expressive range. The "electric" guitar, certainly the most widely exploited amplified instrument, was developed for pop music in this country chiefly by Les Paul, the composer, performer, and electrical engineer whose fame arose in association with the late singer and actress Mary Ford. Following Les Paul's path, inventive younger Americans have designed electric guitars with contours that run from the conventional to the bizarre and even outrageous. It is interesting to observe how fashions in guitar design have changed as the instrument's social image has evolved from that of a lady's demure parlor-song companion to an aggressive rock lead with strong phallic implications. This gradual shift from feminine to masculine associations seems to have begun sometime after the Spanish-American War, when guitars became more common in folk music of the United States. Compact magnetic pickups used in modern electric guitars have transformed the traditional hollow, figure-eight resonator into a solid body shaped according to the maker's fancy rather than acoustical dictates.

Bruce BecVar (b. Louisville, Ky., June 22, 1953), who currently resides in San Rafael, California, is a largely self-taught guitar maker and player of remarkable talent. For the rock guitar (Fig. 158 and Colorplate 9) first displayed controversially in the Museum's André Mertens Galleries for Musical Instruments in 1974, BecVar united elaborate traditional designs with a modern body structure and advanced electronic components. His decorative materials, chosen for varied color and texture, include Benen wood and Brazilian rosewood, with a carved, stained bone grotesque, for the tuning head (brass Schaller tuning machines are used); maple and mahogany veneers and flamed Hawaiian koa wood for the neck; ebony for the fretboard, accented with abalone and bone within a geometric pattern of silver wire; flamed koa and flamed and bird's-eye maple with rosewood and maple binding on the solid body, which features a depiction of David and Goliath in bone, abalone, and rosewood and includes ornaments of dyed maple marquetry and mother-of-pearl.

Two three-dimensional snakes carved of bird's-eye maple with bone teeth and turquoise eyes flank the body, preserving a vestige of figure-eight form. The bridge and tailpiece are handmade of brass. Monolithic ceramic-magnet pickups set into the body are connected to volume, gain, hum-balancing, and tone controls. These last operate continuously variable active low-pass filters; a three-position switch selects the resonant characteristics of the filters, allowing imitation of other guitars' timbres. All components are shielded against electrostatic noise. Exclusive of connecting cords, the guitar weighs almost seven pounds.

Because Eastern European immigrants were relative latecomers to the United States, their characteristic instruments have not been completely assimilated into America's musical mainstream. The balalaika had accompanied peasant songs and dances in north and central Russia for almost two centuries before 1888, when musical reformer Vassil Vassilyevitch Andreyev and his associates presented an ensemble of balalaikas of several sizes adapted for playing popular and patriotic music. Balalaika bands were subsequently adopted by the Imperial Guard, and in the aftermath of the 1905 and 1917 revolutions Russian émigrés spread the modern balalaika wherever they settled. Andreyev's Russian National Balalaika Orchestra appeared at Carnegie Hall in 1910, and New York's present Balalaika Symphony Orchestra was founded in 1937. Though most balalaika players employed in restaurants and vaudeville houses bought instruments made abroad, at least one Russian maker, Ustin Smolensky (b. October 29, 1891), was active in New York before World War II.

One of six children reared on a poor farm near Grodno, in White Russia, Smolensky loved gypsy violin music but could never afford an instrument or lessons. From 1909 to 1912 he worked on the building of the Siberian railway, saving enough to bring himself to the United States. He arrived in Philadelphia on December 12, 1913. Smolensky's first job in America was at Bethlehem Steel's open hearth furnaces. During World War I he operated a drill press, but after the war he switched briefly to coal mining in Mt. Carmel. Around 1919 he sought work unsuccessfully in Philadelphia; in 1920 he moved to New York and occupied one room in an East Fifth Street tenement, where he lives today.

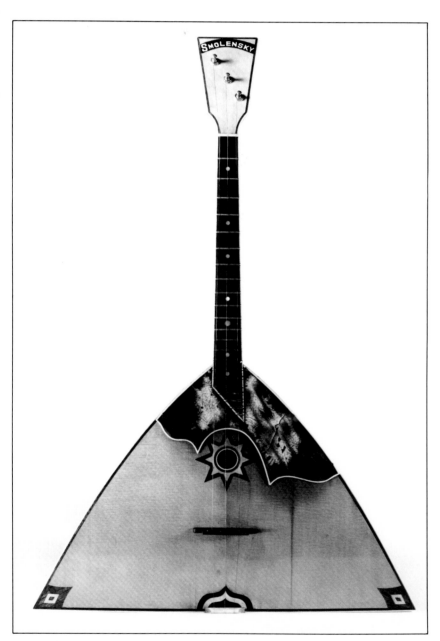

159. *Balalaika by Ustin Smolensky. New York, N. Y., 1939. L. 28½ in. (48.146)*

135

160. *John George Brown.* The Music Lesson, *1870 (21.115.3)*

murder his wife in the American Museum of Natural History and commit suicide with acid.

The Museum's Smolensky balalaika (Fig. 159) is signed inside and dated April 4, 1939. It was intended for the 1939 World's Fair in New York, where officials had agreed to display it—but only among Polish artifacts, since Poland then occupied Smolensky's birthplace. He therefore refused the opportunity and later gave the balalaika to the Metropolitan Museum.

This instrument represents the modern type, with three wire strings, twenty-two frets, and mother-of-pearl position marks on an ebony fingerboard. A raised shield of synthetic tortoiseshell fits around the end of the fingerboard at the apex of the triangular body. Smolensky bought the three Grover tuners but made all the wooden parts. The vaulted back is built of seven walnut ribs separated by light stripes. The neck and flat bottom are likewise of walnut, bound at the edges with white celluloid. The typical small sound hole, lower corners, and saddle area are inlaid with bold geometric patterns in walnut and limba woods. The craftsmanship is remarkably professional. Yet in his approach, methods, and self-sufficiency, Ustin Smolensky belongs to a distinctive folk culture that has withstood the urban melting pot.

Though occasionally played by buskers in city streets, harps are among the most staid instruments, expensive and difficult to maintain and transport. During the nineteenth century harps were produced for a limited market, predominantly professional musicians and female amateurs in wealthy households (Figs. 160, 161). Before the Chicago factories of Lyon & Healy and Rudolph Wurlitzer began to dominate the field (the former after 1889, the latter starting in 1909), Americans relied mainly on French and English firms for concert harps. There were, however, some notable New York manufacturers who built harps along standard European lines.

Among the best of these makers was John F. Browne (d. c. 1871), who had worked in London for the distinguished Erard house before setting up shop in New York in 1841. Browne exhibited at New York's Crystal Palace in 1853 and won gold and silver medals at American Institute fairs in 1856 and 1857. He was succeeded by his son Edgar J. (d. 1878) in 1872; the business was carried on by George Buckwell after Edgar's death.

In an undated price list of around 1845 John Browne and his partner J. Delveau extolled their "improved double-action harps," which "are constructed on the most approved principles, with all modern improvements, are unequalled in brilliancy of tone, fineness of touch, and perfection of mechanism. Particular care is taken to fit them for the extremes of climate in this country, in which respect they will be found far superior to any of European manufacture, imported in the usual way. Price $500–750. . . ." Browne also

While employed by the National Biscuit Company in New York, Smolensky fulfilled a dream by taking violin and cello lessons, a pursuit ended by an arm injury. Previously, though, when fixing a crack in his violin, he had become interested in instrument repair and construction. Leaving Nabisco in 1932, he devoted himself to this craft and made his first balalaika in that year, copying one he had seen in a Second Avenue shop window. This initial effort was ruined when its owner left it in the sun. As instruments were brought to him by friends for repair, Smolensky studied their structure and copied them, using wood salvaged from razed buildings and, later, wood ordered from Europe. On a small table in his room, using only a few tools, Smolensky has made altogether about a dozen violins, three violas, two cellos (one awaiting completion), some bows, three or four mandolins, a couple of guitars, one small and one large dombra, and three balalaikas. Many of these instruments he still owns. A man of astonishing independence, he prefers not to sell his own products; consequently he remains virtually unknown outside his ethnic neighborhood. Smolensky is proud of being self-taught and self-employed. He refused an offer of employment from the luthier Dmytro Didtschenko, perhaps wisely, since Didtschenko went on to

sold imported harps, notwithstanding their purported unsuitability for the American climate: "His arrangements are such as to enable him to transact business at European prices, thereby saving the purchasers the high duties imposed by Tariff on these Instruments."

A gothic-style concert harp (Figs. 162, 163) engraved *J. F. Browne & Co. Makers New York 709 Broadway* on the brass plate that reinforces the neck, can be dated to about 1859–66 on the basis of the address. The mechanism has a stamped serial number 3103. Seven pedals at the base, one for each different note of the diatonic scale, raise their strings' pitch successively by a half and a whole step (hence "double action"), allowing a complete chromatic compass on forty-four diatonically tuned strings. The pitch is altered by pairs of disks at the top that rotate slightly to pinch the strings between projecting "forks." Within the neck and hollow hexagonal pillar, veneered with bird's-eye maple, rods and levers connect the disks to the pedals. An eighth pedal opens louvers on the back of the harp for a tonal change. The soundboard has painted and gilt floral designs on a white background, while the pillar's gilt capital supports plaster angels playing instruments below a pierced canopy. When the harp made its first known orchestral appearance in America, in a New York concert conducted by Theodore Thomas on May 13, 1862, an instrument like this was probably played.

The costly and delicate modern pedal harp requires precise hand-and-foot coordination and constant retuning due to repeated mechanical stretching and relaxing of the strings. From time to time makers seeking economy and ease have eliminated the pedal mechanism and increased the number of strings to twelve per octave, one for every chromatic pitch. This expedient results in crowded strings and greatly increased strain on the frame and soundboard.

In 1845 the French piano builder Henri Pape designed a novel chromatic harp in which the strings were arranged in two planes that crossed near their centers, distributing the pull more widely and separating the neighboring strings sufficiently for convenience in playing. Pape's design lay dormant in France until Pleyel, Wolff & Cie. revived it late in the nineteenth century. The harpist Mme. La Roche (Fig. 164) is believed to have introduced the chromatic harp to America around 1895, but its impact on American makers was limited.

Only two chromatic harps of domestic manufacture are known to exist from the turn of the century; each is identified by an engraved oval plaque reading *H. Greenway Inventor Sole Manufacturer Brooklyn, NY Chromatic Harp.* One of them is in the Museum's collection (Figs. 165, 166). The strings of this somewhat ungainly instrument descend from two metal-reinforced necks supported by two octagonal pillars crossed in an **X**.

161. *Kenyon Cox.* The Harp Player, *1888 (12.40)*

The pillars are capped with gilt plaster floral castings; the intersection of the pillars is ornamented by gilt grapevines. The left-hand neck (the player's left) holds forty-five strings corresponding to the naturals of a piano, while the right-hand neck holds thirty-three accidentals grouped like a piano's black keys. The divided soundboard, decorated like the necks with gilt and black vegetal swirls, forms an angle of about thirty-five degrees descending from a central ridge. The three-sided back has eight oblong sound holes. The tuning pins are very much like a piano's.

This harp requires the player's hands to operate on two widely separated planes and to move up and down to reach both sets of strings. This variation in plucking points makes the tone uneven. Further, with this arrangement it is impossible to perform the fast glissandos in different keys that are so idiomatic in nineteenth-century harp music. Consequently Greenway's chromatic harp has a severely limited repertoire, although it is well adapted to playing simple piano music without transcription.

The nineteenth century's triumphant technology and belief in progress brought many experiments with bowed string instruments. Some innovations bore little resemblance to the classic

violin family; the more extreme the shape, the less likely it was to have been produced by a practical musician.

Among the more serious American inventors was William Sidney Mount (1807–68), a Long Island painter who depicted many scenes of folk and domestic music and was himself a talented country fiddler. His instrumental accomplishments culminated in an 1852 patent for the Cradle of Harmony, a concave-back, guitar-shaped violin, the outgrowth of his experiments going back to 1837. Though the novel violin was unsuccessful, Mount's paintings, diaries, and correspondence with his brother (a dancing teacher) give insight into the vital role instruments had in this artist's life. William Harnett was another American painter whose interest in music led him to collect instruments, which often figured centrally in his works.

Many less remarkable men sought immortality in designing bowed instruments, to no avail. The little that is known of the life and works of Sylvanus J. Talbott outlines a typically dead-ended career. Talbott (b. Brookline, Mass., February 13, 1838) set up as a "manufacturer" in Milford, New Hampshire, at the age of twenty-six. In 1863 he married Abbie J. Brooks; their son, Edgar Forest, was born in 1865. For thirty years Talbott labored in Milford before moving in 1891 to Lynn, Massachusetts, where he entered the town's 1893 directory as "Sylvanus J. Talbott & Co. wood-

162

162. *Harp by J. F. Browne & Co. New York, N. Y., 1859–66. H. 67½ in. (1971.152.2)*

163. *Engraved mark of J. F. Browne & Co. on neck-plate of harp in Fig. 162*

164. *Poster showing Mme La Roche posed before a Greenway chromatic harp. New York, N. Y., c. 1895. Courtesy The Richard Stoelzer Collection of Musical Instruments, Adelphi University, Garden City, N. Y.*

165. *Chromatic harp by Henry Greenway. Brooklyn, N. Y., c. 1895. H. 66³⁄₁₆ in. (89.4.1235)*

166. *Nameplate of harp in Fig. 165*

165

167. *Harp by Lyon &*
Healy, serial number
3351. Chicago, Ill., 1929.
H. 74¼ in. Formerly the
property of Salvation
Army General Evangeline
Booth (1983.346)

workers," in partnership with E. C. Burdick, who earlier had been a surveyor. This listing continues until 1912, when the word "novelties" replaced "woodworkers." In 1913 Talbott moved to Egg Harbor, New Jersey, northwest of Atlantic City, but he returned to Lynn the next year and remained there (no occupation was listed) through 1922. He vacated his residence to live with another family in 1923 and thereafter is heard of no more.

Talbott's sole musical accomplishment seems to have been his invention of the "Alexander violin," patented December 20, 1887 (375,224). This instrument (Fig. 169), a bowed zither made of pine resembling in its truncated half-cone shape the Japanese koto, has sixteen wire strings and two slit sound holes on the arched front, and knob handles on the flat back and larger end. The patent drawing (Fig. 168) shows a curved bridge behind which the strings were stapled to the body. The Museum's example, one of only three located so far, lacks staples and curved bridge and instead had a separate movable bridge for each string, much like a koto's; these are now missing. An ordinary violin bow was employed.

Talbott saw his advantage in avoiding fingering altogether by having each string produce one note only. The soundboard's curvature spaces the strings so that they can be bowed individually. A paper strip beneath the strings near the zither-type tuning pins identifies the pitches: diatonic from C to D two octaves above. What music Talbott had in mind for his instrument is unknown. So is the identity of "Alexander," who is not named in the patent (which Talbott assigned to his son, who predeceased him in 1896). The Museum's instrument is marked *Alexander Violin* on the back, along with the patent date. Quite possibly its design was inspired by an Oriental model seen at a trade fair or exposition.

Another curious stringed instrument of the late nineteenth century is a hybrid bowed mandolin (Fig. 171). Its label reads *Hand made by Joseph Collingwood The Famous Violin Maker, for H.J. Weckwerth sole patentee, Germania, Wisconsin*, with a handwritten addition *Daniel Nolan 1900*. Weckwerth may have been among the German immigrants who settled Germania, a village in Marquette County. Nothing is known of his life. Joseph Collingwood (b. Pittsburgh, Pa., 1853; d. 1928), however, was a highly regarded and prolific violin maker, possibly descended from a mid-eighteenth-century London luthier of the same name. Collingwood settled in Ottumwa, Iowa, in 1882. His usual label bears no resemblance to the one in this instrument, probably supplied by Weckwerth.

The design patent (June 27, 1899; 31,077) covers only the instrument's appearance (Fig. 170). The pear-shaped body, with flat tail and D-shaped sound holes, amplifies four pairs of mandolin strings that stretch from a steel tailpiece over a crude bridge and commercial fingerboard to a flat

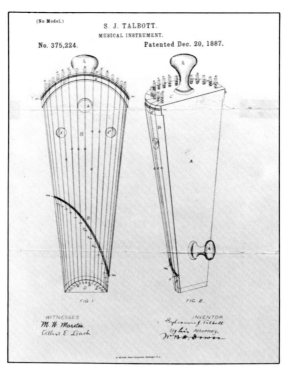

168. *Patent drawing of Alexander Violin (bowed zither) invented by Sylvanus J. Talbott*

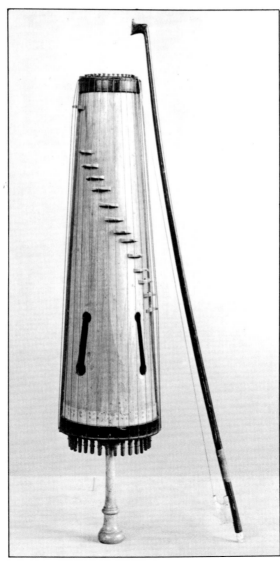

169. *Alexander Violin by Sylvanus J. Talbott. Milford, N. H., after 1887. Bridges replaced. L. 21⅛ in. The bow is a standard commercial violin model (89.4.51)*

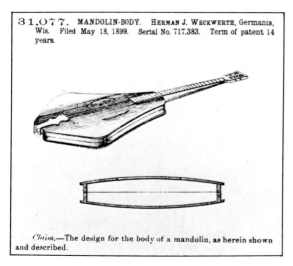

170. *Patent drawing of mandolin body invented by Herman J. Weckwerth*

171. *Bowed mandolin by Joseph Collingwood for the patentee, Herman J. Weckwerth. Ottumwa, Ia., c. 1900. L. 26 in. (89.4.2909)*

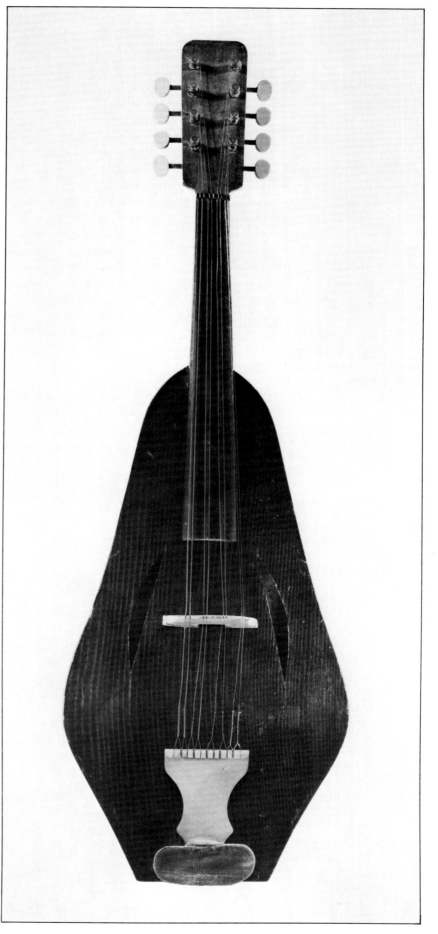

head bearing geared tuners. The patent drawing does not include a bridge and shows a flat fretted fingerboard more like a mandolin's; the present example's high arched bridge and violin-type fingerboard indicate that its strings were bowed rather than plucked. This model also has a violin's sound post and bass bar and a padded chin rest on the tailpiece. The one-piece arched maple back and pine top are varnished dark brown. The only apparent virtue of Weckwerth's design is that the body would have been easy to construct because it contains no complex curves and joints. Daniel Nolan must not have found it very useful, since he gave it away after affixing a handwritten note: "This is presented to the Museum of Arts by Daniel Nolan musician Brooklyn N.Y. November 1902." Why it was accepted will remain forever a mystery.

Ever since the Middle Ages attempts have been made to build a practical keyboard instrument capable of sustaining tone through bowing strings; the hurdy-gurdy, bowed by a rotating wheel, is the earliest and most successful type. Leonardo da Vinci sketched a keyed, bowed *viola organista* around 1488, and in the late sixteenth century Hans Hayden of Nuremberg built harpsichord-shaped instruments with treadle-operated circular bows. The nineteenth century saw its share of bowed keyboard innovations, and one example, bearing the name Claviola, is in the Museum's collection (Fig. 173). Because this name has been applied to several different instruments, confusion has arisen regarding the origin of this example. The Museum's 1903 catalogue of keyboard instruments mistakenly credited the Claviola's invention to the ingenious engineer John Isaac Hawkins of Bordentown, New Jersey (later of

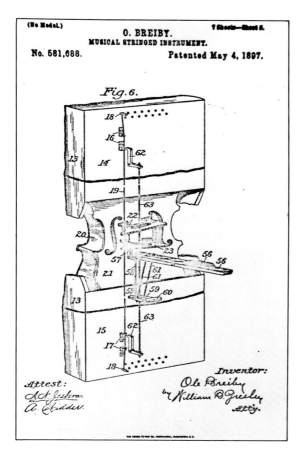

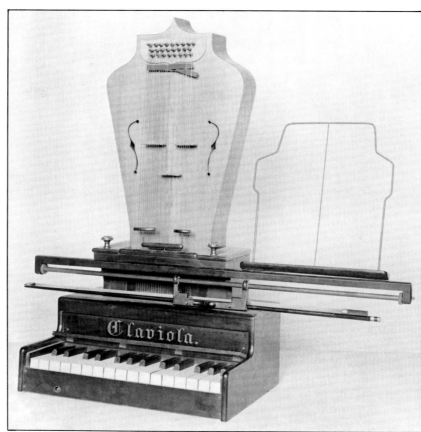

172. *Patent drawing of Claviola invented by Ole Breiby, showing detail of key mechanism. The drawing differs significantly from the actual instrument*

173. *Claviola (bowed zither) by Ole Breiby. Jersey City, N. J., after 1897. H. 23³/₈ in. (89.4.2404)*

Philadelphia). Hawkins, an English immigrant noted for novel piano designs, did invent a keyboard instrument with bowed strings. A Philadelphia newspaper's announcement of its debut was reprinted in the New York *Commercial Advertiser* for June 12, 1802:

> CLAVIOL.—We are informed the lovers of Music will have a grand treat in the course of the ensuing week. Mr. John I. Hawkins, has just completed a Musical instrument, on a construction entirely new; he calls it a Clavial [*sic*], from Clavis, a key and Viol. The Music is produced from gut strings by horse hair bows rosined, it is played on with finger keys like the organ or Piano Forte. This instrument, we are told, produces the sweet enchanting tones of the [glass] harmonica, the rich sounds of the Violin, and the full grand chords of the Organ.

Hawkins's Claviol, which intrigued Thomas Jefferson (who tried unsuccessfully to obtain one), has not survived. Several scholars inadvertently assumed that Hawkins invented the Museum's much later Claviola, and in discussing Hawkins's instrument printed the description of this later instrument.

A patent date of May 4, 1897, recently discovered inside the dilapidated framework of the Museum's instrument, led to identification of Ole

Breiby as its inventor. Local records do not mention Breiby, a subject of the King of Sweden and Norway who lived in Jersey City, New Jersey, at the time the patent was recorded. Perhaps he was inspired by accounts of Hawkins's model. The patent documents (581,688) express the ambitious intent behind the instrument's now inoperable mechanism:

> I am aware that various forms of violin-pianos have been devised hitherto, but they have been of such cumbersome and clumsy construction as to render it impossible to use them as musical instruments or they have been of extremely limited compass. . . . In other words, the forms devised hitherto have been mere machines or toys, while it is my object to produce a musical instrument fitted for the rendition of musical compositions with all the effect of ordinary violins. This result I am enabled to secure by the use of the improved features of construction herein described.

In its existing form, which differs from the patent drawings (Fig. 172) but operates on the same principle, Breiby's instrument is essentially an upright zither. Twenty-five metal strings run vertically along the face of the sound box, over a sectional bridge, to tuning pins at top and bottom, the lower tuning pins serving simply to hitch the

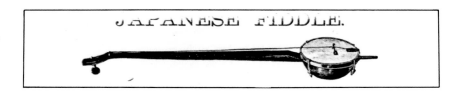

174. *C. Bruno & Son wholesale catalogue advertisement for Japanese fiddle. New York, N. Y., c. 1898*

175. *Japanese fiddle. C. 1900. L. 31⁵/₁₆ in. Tailpiece, bridge, and tuning peg not original (89.4.1537)*

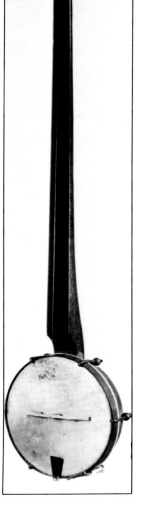

strings. A short distance in front of the strings an ordinary violin bow slides from side to side along a metal track, the frame of which supports a wire music rack. Below, a twenty-nine-note keyboard operates notched levers that push individual strings forward against the bow. The topmost four keys produce their notes by pushing strings one octave below while these strings are stopped at their midpoints by a device that gives octave harmonics—or so the description states.

It is hard to perceive the value of Breiby's complicated system. Very possibly the full-blown design illustrated in the patent drawings was never constructed; it looks like a cello trapped inside an upright piano. The Museum's smaller tabletop version represents a compromise. Breiby's patent calls for two foot-operated reciprocating bows, but the Museum's instrument requires the player's right hand to move the bow, leaving only the left hand free for the keyboard. Similarly, on the violin the right hand moves the bow while the left fingers the notes.

To avoid confusion, it should be noted that the Claviola for which Ludwig & Company of New York (founded 1889) received an award at the 1901 Pan-American Exposition in Buffalo was an unrelated coin-operated automatic piano player.

More conventional violin-family instruments have occupied American makers from all social strata. Folk craftsmen, undeterred by classic for-

malism, often depart from standard violin models in exuberant ways arising out of untrammeled imagination. Their works sometimes recall the fantastic violins depicted in Renaissance art. Like experimental violins of the early sixteenth century, homemade country fiddles fit no fixed pattern; even their number of strings varies. Similarly, many rural fiddlers today adopt relaxed postures like those of players hundreds of years ago, who held the instrument loosely against the shoulder or chest rather than clamped under the chin. Another retrospective feature of modern fiddles is a flattish bridge that favors drones and chords. Finally, the provincial suspicion that fiddles are somehow diabolical has its roots in the distant past. The slang expressions "fiddling around" (meddlesome puttering), "fiddle-faddle" or "fiddlesticks" (nonsense), "fiddling" (trivial), "to fiddle" (to cheat), and "a fiddle" (an arrest warrant) still convey disdain and reproach.

The name "Japanese fiddle" for a one-stringed instrument that only distantly resembles any real Oriental type reflects the Western fascination with Japanese culture that arose after Commodore Matthew Perry opened Japan to trade in 1854. The Japanese fiddle enjoyed a popular vogue lasting from the 1880s to the 1930s both in England (where George Chirgwin promoted it in music halls after 1878) and in the United States, where one-stringed banjo-like instruments already had a long history among Southern blacks. The Mu-

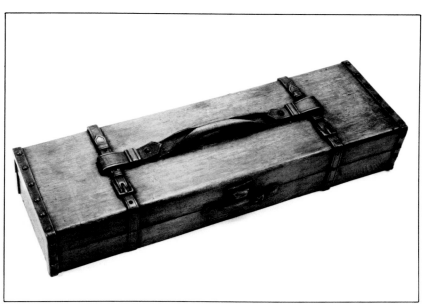

176. *Fiddle case entirely carved of walnut, including straps and tacks. Georgia, late 19th century. W. 30¹⁵/₁₆ in. (1980.215.2)*

177. *Folk fiddle. Georgia, c. 1900. L. 22⁹/₁₆ in. (89.4.1312)*

seum's example (Fig. 175) obviously derives its structure from the banjo, although it may have been held vertically on the knee and bowed. Its unfretted mahogany neck pierces a small hemispherical brass body, which has an air hole in back and a six-inch calfskin head held by six clamps. The long, slender neck terminates in a flat, angled head that presently holds a tuning peg of Japanese design, but this peg is probably not original.

A rare illustration of such an instrument (priced at $6.25) in the 1887 C. Bruno & Son catalogue (Fig. 174) shows a conventional peg as well as the original string and fittings that are missing from the Museum's example, believed to be the only one of its type in a museum collection. Doubtless other types masquerade elsewhere under mistaken identities, for many Japanese fiddles were manufactured with crude wooden bodies or with sophisticated diaphragmatic sound boxes coupled to amplifying horns of aluminum or brass, copied from the Strohviol and Phonofiddle (especially loud "violins" adapted for use in early phonograph recording studios). Scarcely encountered after World War II ended the vaudeville age and brought things Japanese into disrepute, the musically limited Japanese fiddle could not compete in the long run with more versatile conventional instruments.

Around 1900 the same Georgian who made two banjos and two gourd mandolins discussed above also fashioned a sprightly fiddle (Fig. 177) with a bright yellow maple neck and poplar body. The petite body has narrow F-holes through which a bass bar and sound post can be seen. The bridge is so high, though, that the strings can hardly be pressed to the over-length walnut fingerboard. The highly figured front and back are barely arched, have no purfling, and stop flush with the sides. The pegbox has a projecting lower end and an asymmetric scroll. The shape of the walnut tuning pegs and the curious use of a small copper plate to join the neck and back are characteristic of this craftsman. A light, short walnut bow accompanies the fiddle. Its outward curvature and thin band of horsehair (fewer than fifty strands) seem primitive. The shape of the bow's tip comes from nineteenth-century models, while the double-pointed grip ("frog"), adjusted by a screw turned by a yellow button, is a personal conceit. Neither fiddle nor bow shows much sign of use.

An unrelated but equally whimsical violin case (Fig. 176) also came from Georgia. It was found in a pawnshop in Milledgeville, formerly the state capital. A quick glance reveals nothing remarkable about the rectangular case, reinforced at the ends with tacked leather bands and secured with leather belts, one of which forms a grip across the top. A flap on the front protects the lock. Appearances, however, are deceiving. The bands and belts, tacks and buckles, strap handle and flap are all

177

178

carved of solid walnut. The curled handle, cut in full relief with rows of stitch marks simulating a seam, particularly expresses the unknown whittler's joy in duping the eye, somewhat in the manner of William Harnett's trompe l'oeil paintings. The interior, with red cloth lining and compartments for accessories, is fitted out to hold a regular violin and bow. Incised gilt designs on inside surfaces reflect the Eastlake furniture style of the 1870s. Perhaps the case's proud owner carried it to country music conventions in the South, where fiddling contests have been held since the 1740s; there, its humor and virtuosity would have been applauded.

Altogether more austere, a large, boxy fiddle (Fig. 178) of hemlock and maple was found in a cottage near the Shaker community of New Lebanon, New York. It was obviously intended for practical use and has been repaired with wooden plates on the sides of the cracked pegbox. The bridge and tailpiece are replacements, as is one commercial tuning peg. The top and back far overhang the sides, and the projecting points have suffered some damage. Purfling is merely suggested by score lines on top and back, but the off-center scroll has uncommonly fancy fluting. There is nothing coy or delicate about the broad-beamed upper and lower bouts and ample waist; in fact the proportions are almost those of a small viola. The Georgia fiddle flaunts bright color and exotic grain; this wood is somberly covered with dark brown varnish.

The possibility that this may be a Shaker instrument is interesting. The New Lebanon Shakers, descended from an English Quaker sect that settled near Albany in 1776, accepted "worldly" instruments only in 1874 to make the declining sect more appealing to outsiders (celibate, the Shakers depended on conversion). Previously they had feared that skill in instrumental performance would breed sinful pride, but in 1870 in response to dwindling membership a melodeon was introduced to accompany vocal music among the Shakers of Canterbury, New Hampshire, and gradually instruments were adopted in other communities. In view of the long-standing antagonism between advocates and enemies of instrumental music in the Northeast, the possibility that the Shaker convert "Father" Joseph Meacham (1742–96) of Enfield, Connecticut, leader of the church from 1786 until his death, was related to the instrument makers John and Horace Meacham is intriguing.

Bearer of a wholly different tradition, Lars Jørgen Rudolf Olsen (b. Copenhagen, Denmark, December 11, 1889; d. Teaneck, N. J., March 5, 1978) was one of seven children. Their father, Hendrik Christian, was a master saddler, upholsterer, and sometime dresser and royal bodyguard at the Royal Danish Theater. After confirmation, in 1904 Lars Olsen began five years of unpaid apprenticeship with Emil Hjorth & Sønner, in-

178. *Folk fiddle. New York State, late 19th or early 20th century. L. 24¼ in. (1979.21)*

179. *Lars Jørgen Rudolf Olsen (1889–1978) in his workshop, c. 1914*

180. *Violin, Stradivari model, by L. J. R. Olsen. New York, N. Y., 1915. L. 23⅝ in. (1978.217)*

180

181. *View of Olsen's workshop at 651 Third Avenue, New York, c. 1914*

182. *Materials, tools, and documents from Olsen's workshop, displayed in the Metropolitan Museum's André Mertens Galleries for Musical Instruments*

strument repairers and suppliers to the Danish court. For Olsen, who came from a modest background and lived in a seamy neighborhood, to be accepted for this training was an impressive achievement. In 1909 he entered the prestigious atelier of Otto Möckel in Dresden and moved to the Berlin branch of that firm in 1912. Having earned his letter of mastery and a stipend for travel in France and Holland, Olsen spent the summer of 1913 in Amsterdam working for Karel van der Meer and studying bow making with yet another distinguished master, Max Möller. Despite discouraging reports of the lack of opportunities in America, that fall Olsen emigrated to New York, where he was briefly employed by the violin restorer John Markert. In 1914 he opened his own shop (Figs. 179, 181) at 651 Third Avenue near Forty-second Street, overlooking the noisy Third Avenue El.

Olsen married the granddaughter of the piano manufacturer George Steck in 1920 and became a naturalized citizen the next year. By 1942 Olsen had gained regard as "a craftsman of extraordinary experience and skill," according to a local journalist. When the Third Avenue building was vacated in 1957, Olsen moved operations to his house at 292 Cherry Lane, Teaneck, New Jersey, where the workshop was hidden in a back room to avoid the attention of municipal zoning authorities. There Olsen worked in increasing isolation until his eighty-ninth year, leaving work unfinished at his death. His wife died in 1959; they had no children, nor did Olsen train an apprentice.

Throughout his career Olsen was principally occupied with second-hand dealing, repairs, and adjustments, not new construction. His output by 1942 numbered some forty violins, three cellos, a viola, a viola d'amore, and a few bows; this total did not increase much in later years. In 1933, in fact, Olsen had been summoned before the New York Labor Board in an inquiry concerning "homework in tenements" and was prohibited from making new instruments in his shop. No doubt the experience led to his secrecy later.

Many testimonials preserved in Olsen's scrapbooks show the esteem in which he was held by his customers. His sensitive skill must have owed something to his musical ability. An accomplished violinist, Olsen played with amateur orchestras and at home where he and his wife, a pianist and cellist, assembled a library of standard chamber music. No mean draftsman, Olsen compiled a large sketchbook of full-scale working drawings

183. *Viola by John C. Harris. Albany, N. Y., 1884. L. 25⁷/₁₆ in. (06.185)*

of rare violins that he wished to reproduce: instruments by Stradivari, Amati, Guarneri, Lupot, and other masterpieces that passed through his hands until the 1930s. Other notebooks full of measurements and varnish recipes survive from his student days, and dated test panels preserve varnish experiments that continued into the 1960s.

Along with Olsen's Stradivari-model violin number 5 (Fig. 180) dated 1915 and perhaps kept for his own use, the Museum had the good fortune to acquire the contents of his workshop (Fig. 182), left undisturbed after his death. This fully furnished room in Olsen's otherwise derelict house would have felt like home to a north European luthier of two centuries earlier. Among Olsen's voluminous papers are many revealing snapshots of the workplace at different periods. Photos taken for publicity purposes more than half a century apart show that the shop's interior remained almost unchanged after 1914, even following the move to Teaneck. Frozen in time, the same tools (many of them made by Olsen according to traditional patterns), measuring instruments and templates, varnish bottles, even a spray of dried herbs seem rooted in the same spots, convenient to his hands. Old lucky coins, a rabbit's foot, and religious and family mementos further indicate the stasis that Olsen maintained almost superstitiously in his workplace, a tangible link with the grand tradition of his youth.

Unlike Olsen, John C. Harris (b. Salem, N. Y., October 21, 1824; d. Cambridge, N. Y., October 26, 1886) remains obscure, one of countless self-taught but serious makers whose reputations never extended far beyond their homes. Harris was a teacher of vocal and instrumental music, and a band leader, clarinetist, violinist, and part-time violin maker around Albany, where directories list him between 1871 and 1881. According to his widow, who presented his only known viola to the Museum in 1906 (Fig. 183), he was conversant with the history of Italian violins and much admired Paganini, Ole Bull, and other performers of the period. He wrote essays on various subjects for local newspapers, and must be considered a multitalented and literate man.

The printed label in this viola reads *J. C. Harris. Faciebat. Albany, N.Y., U.S., 1884 OP. 6.* (His name, the *84*, and the *6* are handwritten.) Another of Harris's rare instruments, a violin, opus 23, preserved at the New York State Museum in

184. *Alto violin by Louis Condax, after design by Carleen Hutchins. Buffalo, N. Y., 1966. L. 32½ in. Intended to be held vertically like a cello (1983.425)*

Albany, is dated 1872, suggesting that his violins and violas were numbered separately. The Museum's viola—which would have been called "tenor violin" by many Americans of its time—is not a distinguished instrument. The top is wormy, the uneven purfling is ill fitted, and scraper marks show beneath the murky varnish. The too-narrow fingerboard, tailpiece, and other fittings were commercially manufactured. Though unprepossessing in itself, the viola proudly displays Harris's monogram stamped on the back; a blank shield carved behind the scroll would have been inscribed with an owner's initials, had the instrument ever been sold.

Unlike Harris, William Darracott, Jr. (b. Milford, N. H., 1799; d. Milford, December 7, 1868), is still well regarded for instruments of strong design, born of regional tradition and intended for a native repertoire. The son of a cooper, Darracott became Milford's first dentist in 1843 and for some years remained the only one in the area; fortunately, as his obituary records, "his well-stored mind, unusual readiness in conversation, and sympathetic nature, mitigated the discomforts of the dentist's chair." In his youth he had put his hands to making violins and Yankee bass viols, called "church basses" after their customary use to accompany church choirs in New England. He also ran a shop where pianos were auctioned; there he was assisted by his son George L. (b. July 15, 1831; d. March 17, 1905). George, who played in one of the state's best militia bands, the Washingtonian, was a mechanic. He married his brother's widow. By 1861 he was an established piano action maker; as late as 1889 a music trade directory listed him as a piano key manufacturer. Perhaps George and his father were related to the George Darracott who served with Jonas Chickering on the Committee of Arrangements for the first Massachusetts Charitable Mechanic Association exhibition and fair in 1837.

A handsome, cello-like church bass (Fig. 186 and Colorplate 7) signed *G. L. D. Milford, N.H.* and partially dated *3ᵈ-61*, made by George or for him by his father, is among the most elegant of its type in conception and craftsmanship. It must have meant a lot to Darracott's descendants; it was carefully preserved in their house for years before it was given to a violinist across the street whose brother was a professional cellist in Boston. From that neighbor it was borrowed in 1975 by the Currier Gallery of Art in Manchester for an

185. *Yankee bass viol or "church bass" by William Green. Medway, Mass., 1807. L. 47¼ in. Inscribed within: "This cello was owned in Duxbury a great many years ago + was played in church. My father bought it of Seth Weston who lived near Duxbury Beach/Repaired by S. M. Briggs, South Hanson, Mass. in 1907."* (1982.101)

exhibition celebrating New Hampshire musical crafts.

The attractive spruce top and slab-sawn maple back have unusually fine five-stripe purfling and radiant varnish. The geared tuners and F-holes with closed ends are typical provincial features. Inside, the footed neck block extends a short distance along the back for strength, and the sides have interior liners and corner blocks. Body and string lengths exceed a cello's norm, so this husky instrument is unsuited to rapid playing in high hand positions. But for moderate bass lines such as the player would ordinarily encounter in church music, this size poses no technical difficulty and offers a powerful if unrefined sound. In function and form the instrument has much in common with earlier European string basses used to reinforce vocal bass parts at written pitch.

Sounding an octave lower, an enormous three-string double bass (Fig. 189) with a fragmentary label was almost certainly built by Abraham Prescott (b. Deerfield, N. H., July 5, 1789; d. Concord, N. H., May 1, 1858). Educated at the Atkinson Academy, Prescott farmed for several years before starting to make church basses in his spare time. He traveled about to sell these, and demand was such that around 1820 he employed a few helpers and expanded production to include other bowed instruments. In 1831 he opened a store in Concord. The date *1851* penciled inside this much-worn double bass probably records a repair; Prescott's firm stopped making stringed instruments when Abraham retired in 1850. More likely the bass dates from before 1829, by which time he had made 147 string basses in Deerfield. These are listed in a ledger covering the years 1820–43, preserved in the New Hampshire Historical Society.

Once inhabited by rodents and insects, this cavernous bass has many Yankee features, among them inner and outer side liners, corner blocks, a footed neck, and geared tuners. The buttermilk-finished body's lobed lower bouts and angled, flat back with fancy purfling (there is none on the front) are not uncommon in New England work. A massive scroll has been grafted atop the pegbox; one side of the scroll has fallen off, but the remaining side has an inlaid mother-of-pearl eye.

186. *Yankee bass viol or "church bass" by William Darracott, Jr., or George L. Darracott. Milford, N. H., 1861. L. 5¹⁄₁₆ in. (1979.204). See also Colorplate 7*

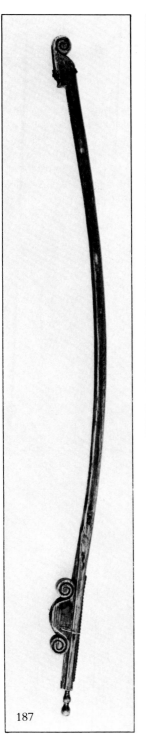

187

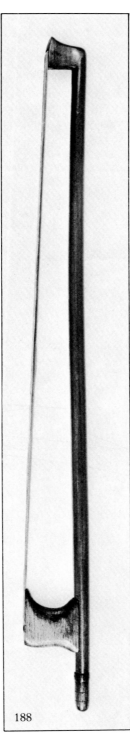

188

187. *Bass bow. Pennsylvania?, mid-19th century. L. 27¹⁷/₃₂ in. Chestnut stock with frog adjusted by wire loop over sawtooth ridge (hair absent). (1983.118)*

188. *Bass bow. New England?, 19th century. L. 27¹⁵/₃₂ in. Round maple stick with oak frog adjusted by screw terminating in an elongated acorn knob (1983.129)*

189. *Double bass by Abraham Prescott. Probably Deerfield, N. H., before 1829. L. 79 in. (1980.492)*

Before the Civil War many New Englanders produced and sold both string basses and keyboard instruments, especially reed organs. Like Prescott, a number of these craftsmen were deacons who intended their instruments to accompany singing in what were known as "catgut" churches (in reference, of course, to the bowed strings). Churches that eschewed instrumental accompaniment were called "anti-catgut." The pioneering piano builder Benjamin Crehore reportedly made bass viols as early as 1785, possibly with the encouragement of his cousin, the singing-master William Billings, who stressed the importance of a heavily reinforced choral bass line. When Prescott started making lap organs around 1837, at least eight of his employees were also making church basses on their own; three of them (John Pearson or Pierson, Nathan? Farley, Milton Morse) later moved to Worcester, Massachusetts, and were probably the trio who started a reed organ factory there in 1847. As we shall see below in reference to keyboard making, the close inter-relationships among New England instrument makers were personal as well as professional; many of these craftsmen enhanced their opportunities by marrying into established businesses.

Mather Brown. Portrait of a Young Girl. *1801.* *(65.235)*

154

KEYBOARDS AND AUTOMATA

190. *Bentside spinet by Johannes Clemm. Philadelphia, Pa., 1739. W. 74¼ in.*
The keyboard is a replacement. (44.149). Photograph by Richard Cheek

191. *Detail of nameboard of spinet in Fig. 190. Photograph by Richard Cheek*

Keyboards and Automata

Expensive and hard to construct, keyboard instruments of all types were scarce in the colonies. Graceful spinets (small harpsichords of a form introduced into England from Italy in the seventeenth century) were especially prized by well-to-do ladies. The first known advertisement for music lessons in America, printed in the *Pennsylvania Gazette* for March 5–13, 1730, offered lessons on the spinet as well as dancing and needlework taught by Thomas Ball's sister "lately arrived from London."

The oldest extant American spinet, in the Museum's collection, comes from the same era and place; it is inscribed *Johannes Clemm fecit Philadelvhia* [*sic*] *1739* (Figs. 190, 191). Johannes Gottlob Clemm (b. near Dresden, May 13, 1690; d. Bethlehem, Pa., May 5, 1762) was one of the few professional keyboard makers of his day in America. He had been destined for the ministry by his father, but after study in Freiburg and Leipzig and following his father's death, he took up instrument making. In 1724 he secured a commission for a harpsichord from Count Nicolaus Ludwig von Zinzendorf, protector of the persecuted Moravian Brethren. Soon Clemm became involved with Zinzendorf's new pietistic community of Herrnhut, but he was later mysteriously excommunicated. Seeking opportunities elsewhere, he took his family to Pennsylvania in company with a group of Schwenkfelders, and after a twenty-three-week journey via Rotterdam, he arrived on the *Pennsylvania Merchant* on September 18, 1733.

Clemm bought land for a house near Philadelphia and found ample work, some of it in association with the painter Gustav Hesselius. When New York's Trinity Parish voted to order their first organ, Clemm's scheme for one of eleven or twelve ranks came highly recommended. Clemm won the £520 commission and began work on the organ with his son William in 1739, the year the Museum's spinet was finished. Eventually this organ grew to twenty-six stops on three manuals, at that time the largest organ ever made in the colonies. In Philadelphia in 1740, according to Dr. Alexander Hamilton's diary (June 9, 1744), the preacher George Whitefield so inveighed against secular music as to curtail it severely for several years, no doubt driving some musicians to seek employment elsewhere. Clemm's situation in New York certainly led to his son Johann Jr. being engaged as Trinity's first organist in July, 1741; he served three years.

In 1744 the elder Clemm received £40 for further work on the Trinity instrument, and after his wife's death in 1745 or 1746 he moved to New York to be near this organ, which apparently was not working very well. In 1751 he had to overhaul the organ (which was finally offered for sale in 1762, the year he died, and replaced with a Snetzler organ imported from England). In 1752 he sold his four-acre Pennsylvania property to William, who remained in Philadelphia.

While living in New York, Clemm kept in touch with the Moravians, and in his old age he was reconciled with the communities at Bethlehem (founded 1741) and Nazareth. Settling in Bethlehem in 1757 and readmitted to communion,

Clemm taught his craft to the joiner David Tannenberg (1728–1804), another follower of Zinzendorf, who had immigrated in 1749. It must be said that neither Clemm nor the better-known Tannenberg was a superb craftsman; neither had served a formal apprenticeship in instrument making. For such men of modest skill from many parts of Europe, the lack of guild-regulated standards of quality in the colonies was, like religious freedom, a stimulus for immigration. The teacher and organist Gottlieb Mittelberger, who shepherded an organ from Heilbronn to Philadelphia in 1750, observed:

> In Pennsylvania no profession or craft needs to constitute itself into a guild. Everyone may engage in any commercial or speculative venture, according to choice and ability. And if someone wishes or is able to carry on ten occupations at one and the same time, then nobody is allowed to prevent it. And if, for example, a lad learns his skill or craft as an apprentice or even on his own, he can then pass for a master and may marry whomever he chooses. It is an admirable thing that young people born in this new country are easily taught, clever, and skillful. For many of them have only to look at and examine a work of skill or art a few times before being able to imitate it perfectly. Whereas in Germany it would take most people several years of study to do the same. But in America many have the ability to produce even the most elaborate objects in a short span of time.[5]

Clemm's spinet, somewhat slipshod in design and construction, looks as though it was rushed to completion to make way for the Trinity organ project; perhaps it was mainly William's work. The spinet, which suffered alterations to serve as a display case after it became musically obsolete, is typical of contemporary Philadelphia woodwork in that it is encased in solid black walnut. The case is lightly constructed, the right side being quite thin to facilitate bending. Molding is carved into the edge of the German-style frame-and-panel lid (a replacement modeled after the original's form) and is applied around the case's lower edge except along the spine, which was intended to stand against a wall. The side joints are weakly butted, not lapped or dovetailed. There is no sign of a hinged panel such as would normally enclose the keyboard, nor of old hinges along the spine. A lock has been removed from the top of the nameboard, where it secured the lid. The bent side begins very close to the key well and thus leaves too little soundboard area around the bridge at the treble end; this represents poor design. The fifty-six-note FF-c³ keyboard was replaced in the nineteenth century, but the slotted rack that guided the original keys remains in place. Many other interior parts have been removed, but the soundboard of Atlantic white cedar, a common wood in Pennsylvania, survives; it has an unevenly cut sound hole, colored red around the edge. The case rests on three baluster-turned maple legs, mortised and pegged to molded yellow pine stretchers.

Hundreds of better-made spinets were pro-

192. *Bentside spinet by John Harris. Boston, Mass., 1769. W. 79½ in. (1976.229). See also Colorplate 10*

duced in Britain by builders such as John Harris before the spinet's place there was usurped by the new square piano. Shortly before the piano made its solo debut in London, Harris sailed on Captain Robert Calef's London packet to Boston, where he arrived early in May 1768. Harris promptly announced his presence in the *Boston Chronicle* for May 16–23: "From London, JOHN HARRIS, who is just arrived in Capt. Calef, begs leave to inform the public, that he MAKES and SELLS all sorts of HARPSICHORDS and SPINNETS [*sic*]. Likewise mends, repairs, new strings, and tunes the said instruments, in the best and neatest manner. Any ladies or gentlemen that will honour him with their custom, shall be punctually waited upon. He lives at Mr. John Moore's, next door to Dr. Clarke's in the North-end." In June Harris moved to "Mr. Gavin Brown's Watchmaker North-side of KING-STREET" and the newspaper carried his revised advertisement until mid-November.

The Museum's Queen Anne–style spinet (Colorplate 10, Figs. 192, 193), inscribed on an inlaid maple plaque *John Harris Boston New England Fecit*, is believed to be the one mentioned in the *Boston Gazette* for September 18, 1769: "It is with Pleasure we inform the Publick, That a few Days since was ship'd for Newport, a very curious Spinnet [*sic*], being the first ever made in America; the performance of the ingenious Mr. John Harris, of Boston (Son to the late Mr. Joseph Harris, of London, Harpsichord and Spinnet Maker, de-

ceas'd) and in every Respect does Honour to that Artist, who now carries on said Business at his House a Few Doors Northward of Dr. Clarke's, North-End, Boston." This spinet was probably shipped to the family of the Newport, Rhode Island, merchant Francis Malbone and passed to his daughter Mary when she married in 1795.

The attractive instrument is "curious" only in the old sense of being elaborate and skillfully made; its design is typically British, as New England taste required. The case is handsomely veneered with figured mahogany panels set off from straight-grain mahogany banding by bold diagonal ("barber-pole") inlay. The mahogany plank lid, secured by tulip-shaped brass strap hinges, has a delicate molding added below its edge, complementing a similar molding around the lower edge of the case. Only the spine is left plain. The FF-f³ keyboard omits the little-used FF-sharp key for the sake of symmetry. The natural keys are covered with ivory scored with two lines and have gilt arcades on the fronts; the accidentals are of black-stained hardwood. The case sides vary in thickness, the spine and front of Eastern white pine being thicker than the white oak bent side that trails off to an angled piece adjoining the spine. Within, the case walls and jack rail are inlaid with a single light stripe in the mahogany veneer. The white cedar soundboard lacks a sound hole.

Two alternating rows of hand-forged iron tuning pins are driven into the maple pin block, on

193. *Plan view of spinet in Fig. 192*

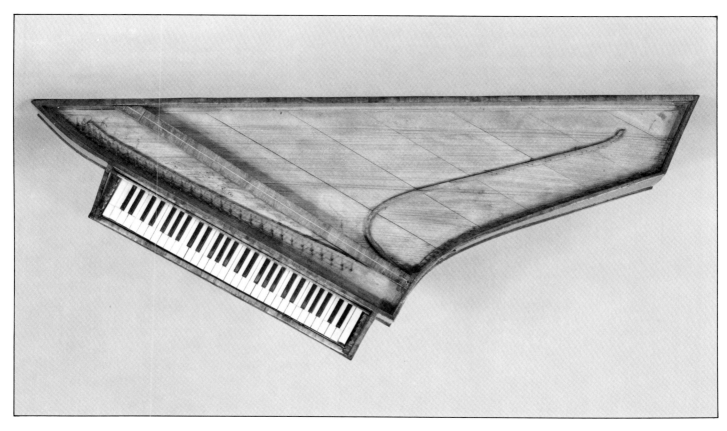

which a two-piece nut supports the strings, the lowest fourteen of which are brass. Gauge numbers 4-13 are inked on the nut. Probably Harris obtained these standard sizes of music wire from England. In comparison with Clemm's layout, Harris's design uses somewhat longer strings in the bass and shorter ones toward the treble, where there is ample room around the bridge.

The fruitwood jacks retain worn quills in bristle-sprung tongues and are weighted with rectangular leads. The jacks slide in a thick cherry guide under which a thin lower guide has been added. Two old replacement jacks were bushed with newspaper to assure a snug fit, evidence that the spinet was long kept in working order. The trestle stand, of typical New England design, has four baluster-turned supports squared to intersect horizontal braces and terminating in plain cabriole legs with pad feet. The stretchers have a small molding planed in the top front edges.

The cost of a spinet in the colonies could be high. A bill dated October 23, 1772, preserved in the Massachusetts Historical Society, records the purchase in Boston by Isaac Smith, Esq., of a new spinet from John Harris for £126, of which £57.15.0 was allowed in exchange for an old spinet; the bill was paid in two installments. This document in Harris's handwriting is our only record of his later activity. Most likely his trade was ruined by the Revolution. Harris's dates are unknown, and he has been confused with another John Harris (son of Renatus Harris, an organ builder) who received British patent 521 (1730) for a harpsichord mechanism; our Harris, however, seems not to have been an innovator, though he may have been the "Maker of the Armonica" who lived in Bloomsbury Market in 1763.

Among the papers of Gen. John Cadwalader (1742–86) in The Historical Society of Pennsylvania are three revealing accounts relating to harpsichords; their upkeep was a constant expense. A bill dated April 25, 1774, from carpenter William Evans has as its first item, "To making a Case for the Harpsichord £ -7..6." The same bill equates this sum with the cost of ten pounds of hand-wrought nails or half the cost of laying a stable floor, a substantial outlay. The same amount was "Reciv.ᵈ April.26.1774. from M.ʳ Wollide 7. Shillings and Six pens in full for tuning the Harpsichord" by Godfreed Welzell [Godfrey Welzel], who much later "Reced. 16 Nov.ʳ 1791 from Philemon Hiskins son Ex[ecu]tor: of John Cadwalader Esq. a check on the Bank for ten dollars & 60/100 for tuning the Instrument for 16 Months." (*Instrument* was the old German term for any small stringed keyboard.) Cadwalader was one of Philadelphia's richest men; it was in households such as his that harpsichords and spinets were chiefly found.

The chore of maintaining harpsichords led Francis Hopkinson to deliver four papers on improved quilling methods at the American Philosophical Society in Philadelphia between 1783 and 1787. Hopkinson, who played in Governor Penn's musical soirees in the late 1760s, discussed these methods with Thomas Jefferson and ordered a harpsichord quilled in his system from Burkat Shudi (the Younger) and John Broadwood of London in 1783. But still easier maintenance enticed many other buyers toward Broadwood's sturdy, inexpensive square pianos, which were louder and more expressive than old-fashioned spinets. On June 1, 1771, Jefferson canceled his order for an English "clavichord" (by which he must have meant a spinet, since clavichords were very rare in Britain) and requested a piano instead. Four years later, in Philadelphia, the German immigrant Johann Behrent built "an extraordinary instrument, by the name of the piano-forte . . . in the manner of a harpsichord"; this was the first known American-made piano.

So important was America's contribution to piano construction, and hence to the future of music, that some further consideration of the instrument's history is appropriate here.

Although the grand piano emerged at the Medici court in the late 1690s, Bartolommeo Cristofori's invention won only limited acceptance in Italy, where the more incisive-sounding harpsichord was firmly entrenched. Not until the middle third of the next century did the piano find more fertile ground, mainly in German towns where widespread domestic use of the clavichord had accustomed keyboard players to controlling dynamic nuances that transferred well to the more robust piano. During the 1730s and 1740s Gottfried Silbermann, J. G. Clemm's reputed master, copied Cristofori's complex scheme and sold several grand pianos to King Frederick the Great of Prussia. For common customers, though, builders sought merely to increase the clavichord's loudness by altering its mechanism without sacrificing its economical rectangular shape.

Two forms of piano action thus arose before 1750. In the Cristofori-Silbermann type, the hammer shanks, hinged to a rail above the keyboard, were treated as third-class levers set in motion by intermediate levers pushed by spring-assisted escapement jacks on the keys—a bulky but powerful system with four moving parts per note (not counting the damper). The cheaper clavichord-derived mechanism had at first only two moving parts, key and hammer shank, the latter a first-class lever mounted on the key itself and pinched into motion against a fixed rail. This simpler action was perfected during the lifetime of Mozart (1756–91), but even before his birth the vogue of the hammer dulcimer, which offered a broad dynamic range and tonal variety through use of soft and hard beaters, had encouraged development of small clavichord-shaped "table" or "square" pianos on which players could imitate the dulcimer's dazzling effects by using stops to control dampers, mutes, and other tonal devices.

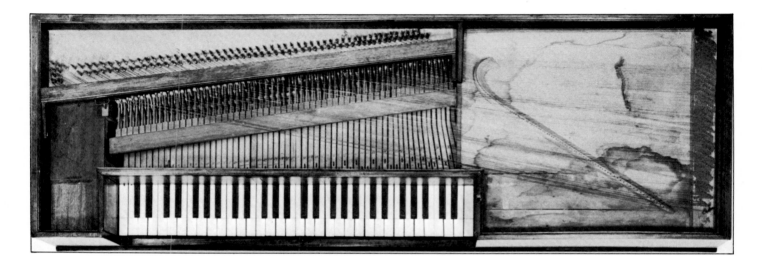

Around 1760 many Saxon craftsmen fleeing the Seven Years' War migrated to England, attracted by its stability and promising market. Led by Johann Christoph Zumpe, a Silbermann protégé hired by the harpsichord maker Burkat Shudi (the Elder), German piano makers set about producing square pianos for London's musical trend setters. The novel little pianos gained status when Queen Charlotte's music master, Johann Christian Bach, played on a Zumpe square, which he had purchased for £50, during a benefit concert on June 2, 1768. This occasion marked the first public solo piano performance in England. Zumpe's modest instruments had simple "single" actions that generally followed the Cristofori-Silbermann pattern but omitted the intermediate lever and escapement. As the market burgeoned, these parts were reintroduced in the better class of pianos.

On July 17, 1783, Shudi's Scottish son-in-law and successor, John Broadwood, received a patent that paved the way to larger square pianos. By moving the tuning pins from the far right side of the case (as in a clavichord) to a row along the back, Broadwood brought them within easy reach for tuning and more evenly distributed their stress; the redesigned structure could now be enlarged to accommodate longer strings, more treble keys, and a larger soundboard. Broadwood claimed that his new "underdampers," pivoted on brass arms beneath the strings, were quieter and caused less friction than overhead dampers; they were operated by a convenient pedal instead of a hand stop and could thus be raised while both hands were playing. Finally, Broadwood's patent called for a sound post to connect the soundboard with a second soundboard beneath, but this attempt to increase sonority was soon abandoned.

Equally seminal was a patent granted November 9, 1786, to John Geib, another German expatriate who like Zumpe had worked for Shudi and who later came to New York. Geib's patent involved a so-called double action with a short intermediate lever and an adjustable escapement jack or "grasshopper" hinged on the key, a return to Cristofori's principle. This double or "hopper" action, with its overhead dampers, fast repetition, and strong blow to the strings, was widely adopted in America alongside Broadwood's earlier improvements.

Quiescent during the Revolution, American

196. *Piano by Dodds & Claus. New York, N. Y., c. 1791. W. 62⅛ in. (1978.379)*

piano manufacture had resumed on a small scale in the 1780s as makers again congregated in Philadelphia, Boston, and New York, the nation's capital until August, 1790. The partnership of Dodds & Claus produced in 1791 or 1792 the instrument that may be the oldest extant New York piano, now in the Museum's collection (Fig. 196). If this example is typical, it suggests a general level of quality inferior to that of London pianos, though the influence of John Broadwood's innovations is apparent in the damper and tuning pin arrangement.

Thomas Dodds and Christian Claus arrived in New York separately. Dodds (d. 1799?) announced his arrival "in the last ship from London" in the *Independent Journal; or, the General Advertiser* of August 13, 1785. He claimed to be a builder and tuner of organs, harpsichords, and pianos and a repairer of all kinds of instruments with twenty years' experience. He also sold violins, cellos, fifes, flutes, oboes, clarinets, bassoons, horns, and aeolian harps from his house at 74 Queen Street (now Pearl Street), where his neighbor and competitor at number 81 was John Jacob Astor. On January 25, 1788, Dodds petitioned the State Senate's House of Assembly for naturalization and an end to imports of instruments; naturalization was granted on March 1, 1788.

During the next year, while Dodds was selling mahogany as well as instruments, he supplied a piano for Elenor [*sic*] Custis. The price of £29.17.4 (part being allowed in trade for an old spinet) was paid by her adoptive father, George Washington, on June 30, 1789, exactly two months after his inauguration. Nelly, age ten, started music lessons that fall at Mrs. Graham's school; she sometimes practiced four or five hours daily. In the year Nelly received her piano, Congress enacted protective tariffs to counter the influx of foreign goods that had begun after the peace of 1783. These tariffs proved a boon to American manufacturers and partly answered Dodds's plea for a halt to imports.

Christian Claus, believed to have been a native of Stuttgart, was living in London's Soho district when he obtained a patent on October 2, 1783, for a keyed striking mechanism that would fit inside an English guitar to make it playable "in the manner of a pianoforte" without damaging female fingernails. One such instrument made by Claus in New York survives at the Museo del Conservatorio Luigi Cherubini in Florence, Italy; it may date from around 1793, when Claus "[wished] to inform the ladies that he intends to manufacture piano fortes and common guittars [*sic*] *the same as he used to do in London*" (*Louden's Register*, June 10, 1793). Claus came to New York around 1788 and was listed as an instrument maker in a 1789 New York directory; he joined Dodds in 1791. Dr. Alexander Anderson, called "the father of American engraving," recorded in his diary on March 24, 1792, that he had purchased an old violin for five dollars and "put it into Mr. CLAUS'S hands to repair and varnish," for which Anderson paid $2.50.

On February 12, 1792, the partners proclaimed in *The Diary, or Louden's Register*, "The Forte-Piano is become so exceedingly fashionable in Europe that few polite families are without it. This much esteemed instrument forms an agreeable accompaniment for the female voice, takes up but little room, may be moved with ease, and consequently kept in tune with little attention—so that it is on that account supperior [*sic*] to the harpsichord." As an inducement Dodds & Claus guaranteed their pianos for two years, an optimistic gesture since the partnership seems to have terminated in 1793.

The Museum's piano (Figs. 194–96) was probably made in part by a journeyman. The carved *A W N° 7* on the bottom of the case corresponds to a pencil inscription *7 Whaitte* within, apparently identifying Archibald Whaite[s] (d. August 14, 1815). This English employee of Dodds arrived in New York in 1784. He advertised independently in *Louden's Register* of September 22, 1792, and became an important New York piano maker in his own right. This piano is the earliest evidence of his work. The mahogany case, veneered only on the front and inlaid with plain stringing, rests on a matching frame with four square tapered legs on casters; this stand, which has been altered, once held a shelf that extended between the legs and was indented in the front to make room for the player's shins. Above the keyboard, the light paneled nameboard (Fig. 194) stenciled *Dodds and Claus. N°. 66 Queen St New York.* appeals to national sentiment, displaying a Federal eagle and twelve stars.

To the left of the keyboard a relic of clavichord construction appears: a lidded compartment in which extra strings and tuning equipment were kept. The hand-forged tuning pins lie along the back as in a Broadwood instrument, but a spatial miscalculation caused displacement of the lowest two pins to the hitch pin rail at the far right side. The piano has two strings for each note. Gauge numbers 8-14 are inked by the tuning pins where layout marks show that the pins were repositioned during construction. The bass strings are loosely overspun; they have no gauge numbers, since such strings were not of standard diameters. For each note a crudely shaped pewter underdamper lever pivots precariously in a leather tab on a wooden post. The use of underdampers and short key levers allows the case to be quite short from front to back. The single action, without escapement, has oddly shaped mahogany hammer shanks with tiny striking blocks suited to the strings' close spacing. This mechanism may represent the "new invented hammers and dampers" touted in Dodds & Claus advertisements that first appeared in *Louden's Register* on September 19, 1792.

Originally there seem to have been two pedals at the left, operating the dampers and mute. A pedal toward the right raised a hinged flap over the front of the soundboard; when the lid was closed, raising this panel gave a swelling effect, and the panel could even be slammed to simulate cannon fire in programmatic battle pieces. In homes, pianos such as this commonly had objects placed on top and so were usually played with only the keyboard cover open; a ledge inside the cover forms a music rack. The whole lid was seldom opened except for tuning or on special occasions. Here, a prop stick for the lid is screwed to the right inside wall of the case. In better pianos a folding music rack was installed behind the nameboard, but none appears in this instrument. Since square pianos were normally placed with the undecorated long side against a wall, the player sat with her back to the room.

Dodds & Claus economized on their FF-f³ keyboard by omitting the FF-sharp key, as did John Harris in his spinet. The piano keyboard further resembles Harris's in having stained hardwood rather than ebony accidentals, and single-scored ivory natural heads; the natural key tails, however, are of cheaper bone. The key fronts are covered with decorative molded wooden slips.

In Philadelphia before 1800 the music trade attracted many astute businessmen and an affluent clientele. Michael Hillegas, later a treasurer of the United States, opened the colonies' earliest known music store in Philadelphia in 1759; John Adams and Thomas Jefferson were among his customers. After British occupation ended in 1780, Philadelphia became America's first piano-making center. One of the industry's pioneers, German-born Charles Albrecht was listed as a joiner in Clement Biddle's 1791 directory; he declared his allegiance to the United States on February 15, 1798, but the oldest of his extant pianos is dated 1789. It is instructive to compare that piano, preserved in The Historical Society of Pennsylvania, with a later, undated one in the

Museum's collection (Fig. 198), inscribed *Nº 24* behind its nameboard. Both pianos display the fine craftsmanship characteristic of Albrecht's work, but the two are quite different in construction.

The older piano, like the Dodds & Claus, follows Broadwood's model in having underdampers (with wooden arms), and tuning pins along the back. It employs a single action and once had two pedals controlling the dampers and an overhead mute. The Museum's piano has the same FF-f³ range but has a double action without escapement and overhead dampers on horizontal, whalebone-sprung arms hinged to a tilting panel in the back of the case. An old-fashioned hand stop to the left of the keyboard raises the dampers by tilting the panel. This system, used by Zumpe as early as 1767, was thought by some makers to weaken the case, and was generally abandoned toward the end of the century. A second retrospective feature of this piano is the placement of tuning pins on a pin block that runs diagonally across the soundboard, isolating a triangle at the right rear corner. Why Albrecht returned to this old-fashioned layout after having used Broadwood's in 1789 is unclear. He seems never to have settled into one pattern; he even made German actions on occasion.

The inscription *Charles Albrecht Maker Philadelphia.* (Fig. 197) is painted in gold on a pointed oval garlanded by flowers, centered on a crossbanded light panel that extends on the sides of the key well. The Hepplewhite exterior has mahogany panels separated from a contrasting light border by fine geometric stringing of typical New England pattern, unusual in Pennsylvania. The sturdy stand has four square tapered legs supported by stretchers on either side, and brass bolt covers at the corners. The crossbanded skirt is cut away in front to leave room for the player's knees. The legs, inlaid with stringing in normal Philadelphia fashion, are lacking their casters. The keyboard has unscored ivory naturals with deeply molded fronts, and solid ebony accidentals; they show little wear. A folding music rack once served to prop up the lid, but its lengthened vertical strut at the right has been cut down. A wooden panel once fit over the strings to keep out dust and mute the tone and action noise.

Street directories list Albrecht as an instrument maker from 1793 until his presumed retirement in 1825; thereafter he is cited as a "gentleman" until his death around 1833–34. Another piano maker, said to have been Charles's successor, was Christian F. L. Albrecht, who arrived from Germany on the same ship with Emilius N. Scherr and was active in Philadelphia from the mid-1820s to around 1842–43; the relationship, if any, between the Albrechts is uncertain. In 1824 Christian shared a business address with John G. Klemm, another German immigrant instrument dealer and music publisher who may well have been related to Johann Gottlob Clemm.

In contrast to Pennsylvania's music-loving German population, New England's puritanical society felt an aversion to secular performance. Still, music figured importantly in Boston's public entertainments during much of the later eighteenth century. A joint concert in Boston in 1771 by David Propert and James Joan (Juhan) may have introduced American audiences to the piano. The city's concert life declined during the Revolutionary era and was revived only around 1786. On April twenty-fifth of that year America's first known public concert featuring a piano concerto was played in Boston. At that time there may have been as few as thirty pianos, all probably imported, in the city, and the study of piano playing was, as in most places, largely confined to young women who had no professional aspirations.

Into this somewhat dilettantish milieu was born America's first known native piano maker, Benjamin Crehore (b. Milton, Mass., February 18, 1765; d. Milton, October 14, 1831). Descended from Pilgrim ancestors who had settled near Boston in the mid-seventeenth century, Crehore was a mechanic and cabinetmaker by training. He reportedly became intrigued by a bass viol he was repairing and began making string basses in the 1780s, probably for church use. In 1792, while in nearby Salem the painter and organist Samuel Blythe (1744–95) was still building old-fashioned spinets, Crehore exhibited a combined piano-harpsichord, perhaps similar to one patented the same year in London by John Geib. Crehore began manufacturing pianos seriously a few years later in a shop shared with Capt. Lewis Vose, a harness maker. Copying British pianos that he had tuned or repaired, Crehore made perhaps as many as a dozen a year, assisted by apprentices who included Alpheus and Lewis Babcock and John Osborn, later major figures among Boston's piano builders.

Between May 1798 and June 28, 1799, Crehore's partner was the prominent musician Peter Albrecht van Hagen, who had arrived in Charlestown from Rotterdam in 1774. Some Crehore pianos were finished and sold in van Hagen's music store. Others were sold in New York between 1797 and 1801 by the composer and music publisher James Hewitt, whose daughter was evidently the first pianist to play a Beethoven sonata publicly in America (in Boston on February 27, 1819). In the *Boston Gazette* of November 23, 1801, Messrs. Mallet and Graupner advertised "a large assortment of American Piano Fortes, manufactured by Mr. Benjamin Crehore, whose genius and experience, cannot fail of producing as correct and elegant work, in this line, as any imported from abroad; and it is hoped will insure him the patronage and encouragement of his fellow citizens. His instruments will be warranted by Messrs. M. & G. for six months."

197. *Detail of nameboard of piano in Fig. 198*

198. *Piano by Charles Albrecht. Philadelphia, Pa., c. 1798. W. 62¹³⁄₁₆ in. (89.2.185)*

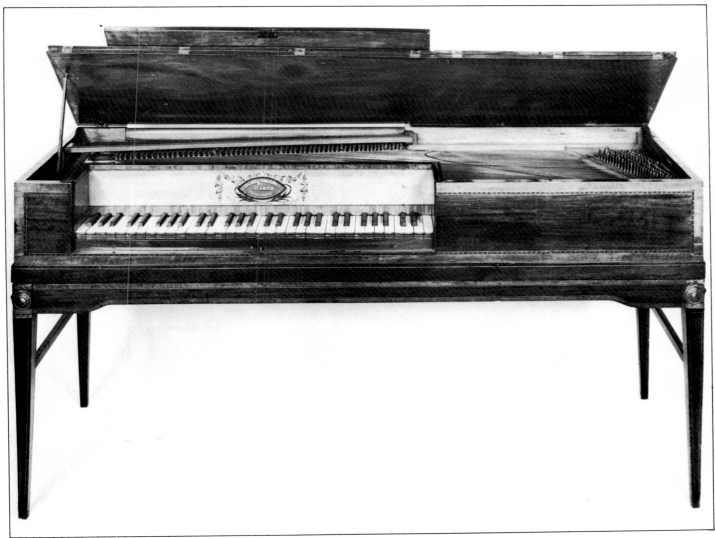

199. *Plan view of piano by Benjamin Crehore. Milton, Mass., c. 1800. W. 65¹³⁄₁₆ in. (89.4.2858)*

On July 11, 1804, Crehore entered into partnership with the organ builder and mechanic William Goodrich (1777–1833) to manufacture "organized Forte-Pianoes" (combined piano-organs) which, like the earlier piano-harpsichord, enjoyed only a brief vogue in England and the United States. None by Crehore and Goodrich survives, and the partners' venture was short-lived. A similarly ephemeral "improvement" was advertised in Boston's *Independent Chronicle* of March 23, 1807, wherein Johann Christian Graupner, the so-called father of American orchestral music, offered the public a transposing piano "made under his direction, after a plan of the Germans by Messrs. Crehore and Babcock of Milton. It is particularly convenient to accompany the voice on such an instrument as it may be put in one moment (by its movable key board) several notes above or below Concert pitch, as best suits the compass of the voice." Crehore's interest in mechanical inventions extended to his development of a veneer saw and of a jointed wooden leg; he also owned part interest in a chocolate mill.

Of Crehore's five or six extant pianos, all built along English lines, the Museum's (Fig. 199) is among the larger in compass (FF-c⁴) and probably dates from shortly after 1800. Although its condition is poor, it was never altered, and its essential parts are intact. English-style decorative scrollwork, perhaps intended to aid sound transmission when the lid was shut, pierces the nameboard, which is veneered in characteristic northeast New England fashion with bird's-eye maple. Painted flowers garland the inscription *Benjamin Crehore Musical Instrument Maker Milton* (Fig. 200). On three sides the case is veneered with a single broad mahogany band outlined by Boston-style geometric stringing and crossbanded with variegated rosewood above and below. The lid includes a pedal-operated swell flap. Another pedal (missing) raised the dampers by lifting the rear of the key levers, on which the damper wires are imbedded in posts that are flexibly mounted so as to remain vertical during the keys' arcing motion; this ingenious system may be Crehore's invention.

The heavily worn keyboard has unusually narrow accidentals topped with ebony slips. The normal double action includes ten extreme treble keys that run beneath the soundboard, striking undamped strings through a gap between the soundboard and the back of the case. This arrangement, introduced by William Southwell of London in 1794, allowed extension of the keyboard compass upward without widening the case or shortening the soundboard. As in Albrecht's piano the tuning pins are clustered toward the right side. A dust panel still lies over the strings, but two drawers formerly hung from the stand are missing. The square tapered legs with inlaid edging angle sharply at the foot, another New England feature.

Embargoes and warfare in the early nineteenth century kept luxury imports scarce, but after 1815 peace at home and depression abroad spurred domestic manufactures and imports to the point of overexpansion and collapse in the panic of 1819. Before this temporary setback the piano market had boomed, and many buyers still favored foreign products for the sake of snob appeal, if not for their musical superiority over American instruments. A normal mode of acquiring pianos and other large pieces of furniture from abroad was to purchase these from ship captains who had bought them to fill empty cargo space and bring a profit upon resale at dockside. Among the papers of the Philadelphia lawyer and banker William Meredith (1772–1844; in later years a member of the American Philosophical Society and a director of the Academy of Fine Arts) in The Historical Society of Pennsylvania, two letters express typical concerns in purchasing a piano, in this case perhaps a German or Austrian

grand, quieter and "more delicate" than an English model.

Baltimore June 22.ᵈ 1816

My dear Sir

On receiving your letter this morning, Mʳˢ W. & myself went in search of the Piano to which you refer, and had no hesitation about engaging it for you at the sum,—450,—which you mention. We consider it as well worth some hundred dollars more. It is not so sonorous or strong-toned as the English Grand-Pianos, but is in every other respect what you could wish. A more beautiful piece of furniture or an instrument of more curious mechanism could not be found. You will, I think, congratulate yourself on the acquisition. I will employ the best *packer* in this city, & I trust it will suffer no injury in the transportation. Will you have it sent round by sea, or committed to the New Castle packets? I have twice availed myself of the latter with impunity. Your piano is, however, of more delicate workmanship than the English. I feel happy that you have addressed yourself to me even for so trifling an office, & need not repeat that you must command me at all times to any extent.

ever, Dear Sir, truly your's

Robert Walsh Jr.

Baltimore June 27.ᵗʰ 1816

My dear Sir

I have had your Piano packed in such a manner, that, I think, it can suffer no injury. Mʳ Didier has undertaken to have it shipped as early as possible. I will myself have an eye to this matter. As the Piano was the property of a Sea-Captain to whom the money was desirable, I thought it well to pay it at once. You have but to re-imburse me *here* in the sum of $450. The Freight &c—we shall know hereafter. Take notice that we do not recommend the Piano as of the *very* highest excellence on the score of the musick. It is, nevertheless, a great bargain, & such as, I doubt not, you would have bought yourself without hesitation. You know that I have told you from time to time, that the only thing wanting in your house was a good instrument of the kind; *bien entendu que* even this deficiency would never have been felt especially by your hble servᵗ, had you not occasionally suspended interlocution for the sake of a sonata.

We tender our best respects to the ladies.

ever, your's faithfully,

Robert Walsh Jr.

After about 1820 square pianos grew in size and importance as furniture. Piano builders increasingly relied on cabinetmakers for tasteful cases and legs. In the absence of old-fashioned framed stands, legs or fancy trestle bases now attached directly to the case. Square tapered legs gave way to turned and fluted ones that became thicker and more numerous (up to eight) to support heavier instruments and withstand the sway occasioned by pedaling. To remain within reach, pedals had to be brought toward the center of the case; of necessity, though, the keyboard remained off center to the left. To draw attention from this asymmetry, the nameboard offered a decorative focal point. In keeping with tradition, piano builders almost always signed and very often numbered or even dated their products; therefore pianos are especially useful as stylistic guideposts to the history of furniture.

200. *Detail of nameboard of piano in Fig. 199*

201. *Piano by Gibson & Davis. New York, N. Y., c. 1815. W. 69¾ in. (63.205).* Inset: *Detail of nameboard of piano*

Two fashionable New York pianos by the rival firms of Gibson & Davis (Fig. 201) and John Geib & Son (Fig. 202) have cases reliably attributed to the workshop of Duncan Phyfe, whose brother or nephew Isaac Phyfe was identified as a piano maker in directories of the 1820s. John Geib, Jr., was himself associated with Duncan Phyfe's workshop in 1815, around the time both pianos were made. The cases are characteristically crossbanded with fine mahogany veneers and have stylish rounded front corners. The curved legs are carved with rippling waterleaves beneath fat urns. The backs of the cases are left plain save for handholds cut in to ease lifting. Parts of the bases intended to face the wall are also undecorated. Both pianos have double actions with FF-c^4 compass, standard for the period, but differ considerably in string lengths and internal details. The Gibson & Davis keyboard has an extra-wide FF key, a device occasionally used to fill space needed for sliding the action out for maintenance. Despite this piano's otherwise rich appearance, its keyboard has stained rather than solid ebony sharps and plain flat natural fronts instead of the normal molded fronts used by Geib.

Thomas Gibson (b. Scotland, 1763; d. Putnam, N. Y., 1858) and Morgan Davis, perhaps a native of Wales, immigrated from England around 1801 and began advertising in New York the following year. They were partners until about 1822 and remained neighbors for another two decades. Gibson's directory listings ceased in 1845 and Davis's in 1841. Their piano, serial number 22, has *Gibson & Davis New-York from London* written in gold on a dark blue tablet below a painted songbook and instruments resting on vine tendrils, the whole framed by blue sky and flanked at the ends of the flamed maple nameboard by cloth-backed scrollwork. A damper pedal (missing) was secured to the central reeded leg. The tuning pins are located along the back.

The Geib & Son piano is laid out with tuning pins at the right. Three brass pedals under a stylized gilt lyre, a favorite motif of the period, control (from the right) a swell flap, a mute, and the dampers. The pedals and splayed legs are awkwardly located for a pianist sitting at the middle of the keyboard, but the left foot was seldom called upon in pedaling so the player was spared an undignified stretch.

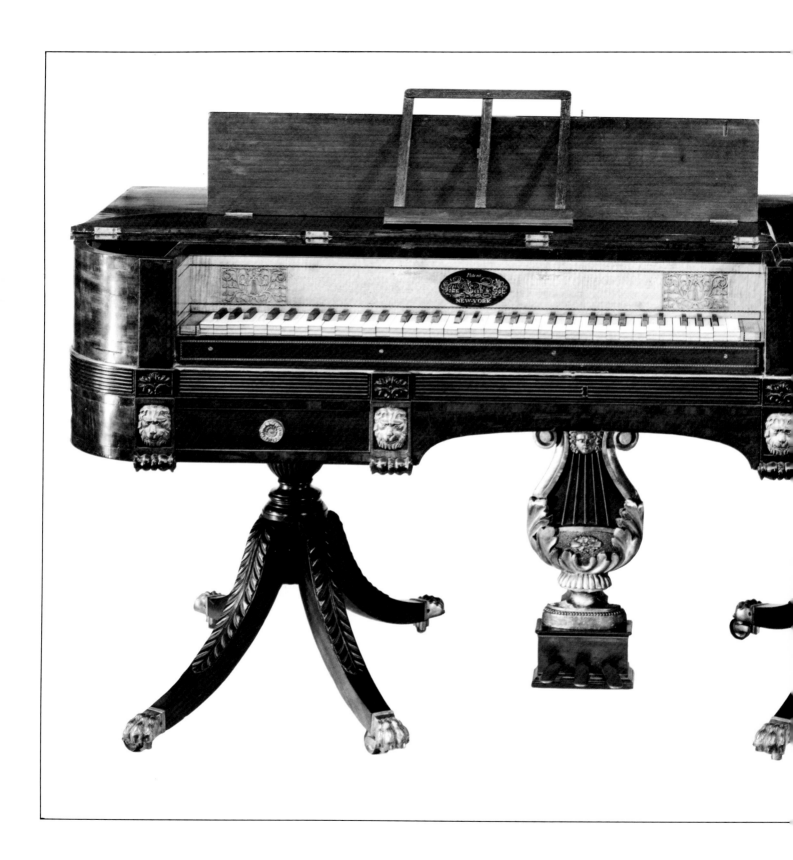

202. *Piano by John Geib & Son. New York, N. Y.,*
c. 1816. W. 72 in. (69.259)

203. *Detail of carved decoration on piano in Fig. 202*

204. *Detail of nameboard of piano in Fig. 202*

205. *John Wesley Jarvis.* John Geib *(1744–1819), 1815–20. Courtesy The New-York Historical Society, New York, N. Y.*

206. *John Wesley Jarvis.* John Geib, Jr. *(1780–1821), 1815–20. Courtesy The New-York Historical Society, New York, N. Y.*

207. *Advertisement of John and Adam Geib & Co., New York, 1816*

208. *Piano by Adam and William Geib. New York, N.Y., 1822–27. W. 68 in. (45.126).* Inset: *Detail of nameboard of piano*

Tombstone-shaped inlays in pilasters punctuate the richly figured veneers above a band of horizontal reeding, below which gilt lions' heads between rosettes and scrolls (Fig. 203) set off a drawer on either side of the arched center. The satinwood nameboard (Fig. 204) is inscribed *Patent. John Geib & Son. New-York* on a black oval (the patent referred to may be the famous British one), and a label on the bottom identifies a former owner, Elizabeth Henderson. The piano's serial number 5414 probably continues the series that had reached 4910 by the time Geib left England, where he had been making up to eight or ten pianos a week.

Geib pianos, often of exceptional elegance, were probably beyond the means of most professional musicians. A Geib & Son square piano with two pedals and drawers was sold in Flatbush, New York, for $270 on September 19, 1812, but that piano might well have been plainer than this one from the shop of Phyfe.

John (Johannes) Geib (b. Standerheim, Germany, February 27, 1744; d. near Newark, N. J., October 18, 1818), the youngest of sixteen children, was recorded as an organ builder when he received British denization on February 11, 1792. It is not known when Geib arrived in London, but he married there in 1779; the couple had eleven children. After a successful career involving employment or partnership with a succession of leading builders, Geib left for Philadelphia with his family on the ship *Factor*, departing July 24, 1797. His reputation preceded him; "Herr Geib, organ builder from London" is mentioned in a letter from New York's Trinity Church organist John Christopher Moller, received by the St. Michael's and Zion Corporation in Philadelphia before June 1, 1797.

After a brief stay in Philadelphia Geib established himself on Barclay Street in New York, not far from Gibson & Davis. In 1798 he built a thirteen-stop organ for the German Lutheran Church, played by Moller and by Frederick Rausch upon its completion in January, 1799. Around 1801 he erected an English organ in Trinity Parish's St. Paul's Chapel, and in 1802–03 he built a new organ for the parish's St. George's Chapel. He survived bankruptcy in 1802, maintained a Boston showroom in 1804, and went on to build organs for churches from Salem, Massachusetts, to Bethlehem, Pennsylvania. In 1810 he continued his close connection with Trinity Parish by building an instrument for its Grace Church.

Geib was buried in St. Paul's churchyard along with his son John Jr. and other members of the family. Portraits of Geib and John Jr. (Figs. 205, 206) by John Wesley Jarvis, now in the New-York Historical Society, depict confident and successful businessmen; indeed, Geib Sr. had invested about twenty-five thousand dollars in land between Vesey and Canal streets, and his descendants prospered in the music trade for another two generations.

Geib's sons published sheet music, including James Hewitt's setting of "The Star Spangled Banner" (published November, 1817); they sold other makers' instruments, including Clementi and Astor pianos (a John Gieb [sic] sold woodwinds to Boston merchant and music publisher John Rowe Parker around 1817–18); and they manufactured pianos under their own names. John Jr. made instruments independently shortly after the Museum's piano was built; he was in business with his twin, Adam, as J. & A. Geib & Company in 1816–17 (Fig. 207); and they were joined by William as J., A. & W. Geib from 1818 to John Jr.'s death, September 10, 1821. Adam (a music teacher) and William continued together until 1828, when William moved to Philadelphia to become a medical doctor. The only extant pipe organ ascribed to Adam and William Geib, in the Museum's collection, is discussed below. Of the three brothers, John Jr. was perhaps the most serious piano maker; he earned a patent on October 3, 1817, for a new upright model. Adam's son-in-law was a founder of the New York Philharmonic Society.

Around 1825 Adam (1790–c. 1845) and William (1793–1860) produced the Museum's piano (Fig. 208), serial number 6152, inscribed on the nameboard *New Patent, A. & W. Geib. 23, Maiden Lane New-York*. The nature of the "new patent" is unknown; perhaps it refers to this piano's damper system, in which the key tails are lifted by levers clasped by "fingers" at the ends of the keys. The nameboard is decorated with gilt neoclassical anthemia and musical stencils that simulate French-style brass inlay. Latticework replaces the more ornate scrollwork of earlier nameboards. This nameboard was modern not only in its decor and its fashionable rosewood veneer, but also in the curved ends that complement the rounded corners of the case and avoid intersecting the bass strings that pass the right corner of the key well. This curvature, however, shortens the playing surface of the top and bottom few keys.

The piano is practically indistinguishable externally from English Regency instruments then being made in London. The crossbanded mahogany and rosewood case with brass striping and molding is very similar to the Museum's example of the same size made by John Green in London; that piano, though, has a six-octave FF-f^4 keyboard, while the Geib has a smaller FF-c^4 range not suitable for the most advanced music of the period. Of course not all pianists who purchased six-octave instruments at this time were adventurous in their choice of repertoire; some may have chosen the larger compass to accommodate popular duet arrangements that called for higher notes than the standard solo literature.

This Geib piano lacks its damper pedal and support as well as the horizontal latticework panels

209. *Piano by Alpheus Babcock for George D. Mackay. Boston, Mass., 1822–23. W. 66¹¹/₁₆ in. (66.82)*

210. *Detail of nameboard of piano in Fig. 209*

212. *Detail of nameboard of piano in Fig. 211*

that flanked the key well to hide the front of the soundboard and empty space to the far left. The six legs, with unusual left- or right-handed spiral reeding below foliate carving and knurled brass collars, attach to a three-drawer skirt with the center drawer made concave for the knees. Unlike those of the earlier Geib piano, the tuning pins of this one run along the back, and the hitch pins transect the soundboard. In both pianos the function of the transecting member is to brace the right side, shorten and thus stiffen the soundboard in the treble, and reduce the unstruck portion of the strings. The triangle remaining at the back right corner is filled by a cloth-backed openwork panel.

Similar in layout and appearance, piano number 125 *Made by A. Babcock, for G. D. Mackay, Boston.* around 1822–23 (Figs. 209, 210) does not have drawers beneath the round-cornered mahogany and rosewood case and stands on only four turned and heavily reeded legs; a fifth leg holds the damper pedal. Owners of Babcock's

Sheraton-style pianos, considered among Boston's most fashionable, included Lowell Mason and the family of John Quincy Adams. Their pianos, like this one, had the lesser FF-c⁴ range. The nameboard, like that of the A. & W. Geib piano, is of rosewood with brass stringing and lattice-work, but this nameboard is straight, with an engraved brass nameplate and no stencils. The dust cover is painted green with black and gilt borders. Twelve keys run under the soundboard, their hammers striking undamped treble strings through the usual gap at the back. A plugged hole through the back framing was intended for a rod to raise a harmonic swell, but the device was never installed.

Designed to allow sympathetic resonance from the normally mute string lengths behind the bridge, the harmonic swell was patented in England by Frederick Collard in 1821 and was employed in piano compositions by his collaborator, Muzio Clementi. The device is rare in American instruments, but one appears in the Museum's

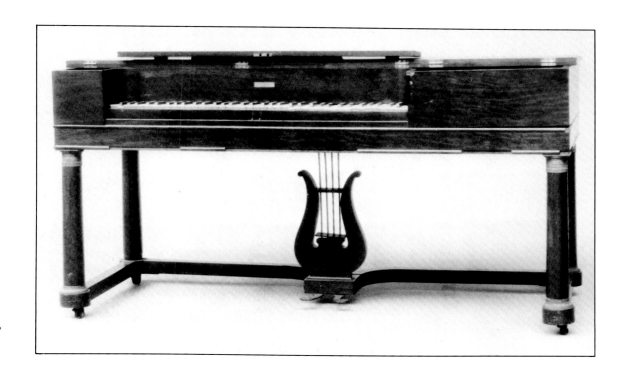

211. *Piano by Alpheus Babcock. Boston, Mass., c. 1825. W. 66¹¹/₁₆ in. (22.112)*

Babcock piano, number 376, of about 1825 (Fig. 211). This piano is of virtually the same proportions as the Babcock square previously discussed, but it has a square-cornered Restoration-style case with an inlaid brass nameplate engraved simply *A. Babcock, Boston.* (Fig. 212), indicating that it was not made to order for Mackay. The dark mahogany case's severe lines are relieved by a graceful pedal lyre centered on a brace connecting four brass-mounted columnar legs. The left pedal lifts the dampers; the right operates the harmonic swell. The FF-f⁴ keyboard has seventeen treble keys passing under the soundboard. The keys and actions are of identical workmanship in the two Babcock pianos. Even the numbering of the keys is in the same hand. Both pianos retain their original ribbon-wound bass strings, which Babcock preferred to the usual wire-wound type. The bass tuning pins are pierced to facilitate stringing, a convenience often lacking in earlier instruments. A similar piano appears in Franz Heinrich's painting of Mr. and Mrs. Ernest Fiedler and family, done in New York around 1846 (Fig. 213); that piano, still stylish even twenty years or so after its manufacture, may well have been a Babcock.

Alpheus Babcock (b. Dorchester, Mass., September 11, 1785; d. Boston, April 3, 1842), one of America's foremost piano builders, was born into a family noted on the father's side for musical ability. He and one brother, Lewis, were apprenticed to Benjamin Crehore in Milton, their boyhood home. By the age of twenty Alpheus had been taught by Peter van Hagen to tune pianos; a few years later, around 1810, the brothers were operating their own music warehouse in Boston. In 1812, while Crehore's former partner William Goodrich was on tour demonstrating Johann Nepomuk Maelzel's Panharmonicon (a mechanical instrument for which Beethoven composed a piece in 1813), the Babcocks joined Goodrich's employee Thomas Appleton to make "elegant and excellent toned" pianos, warranted for ten years. Upon his return to Boston Goodrich worked with them. After Lewis Babcock died in 1814, the others joined partnership with the merchants Charles and Elna Hayts. The new firm of Hayts, Babcock & Appleton sold lumber, umbrellas, notions, fishing poles, and small turned goods as well as instruments and music. After Alpheus opted for independent work in 1815, the firm was taken over by John and George D. Mackay, merchants who became deeply involved in piano retailing and who promoted Babcock's instruments beginning about the time he married, in 1822.

Outclassing the competition, which included William Geib and Loud & Brothers, Babcock won a silver medal for a square piano entered by his agent John G. Klemm in the second annual Franklin Society exhibition at Philadelphia in 1825. On December seventeenth of that year, Babcock patented his most important invention, a one-piece metal frame incorporating a hitch pin plate; this rigid structure strengthened and stabilized the square piano's case against the stress of the strings and climatic changes. Essential for the instrument's further development, Babcock's successful design induced progressive makers thenceforth to rely on iron castings to reinforce the cases of increasingly large square and grand pianos.

213. *Franz Heinrich.
Mr. & Mrs. Ernest
Fiedler with Their
Children at 38 Bond
Street, c. 1846. Courtesy
The Museum of the City of
New York*

Babcock moved to Philadelphia to work for Klemm around 1830 and remained there, in the employ of the dealer and exporter William Swift, between 1832 and 1837. During these productive years Babcock earned two more patents, for a new method of stringing (May 24, 1830) and for improvements in piano actions and hammers (December 31, 1833). In July and August, 1833, Babcock exchanged bitter letters in the *Daily Chronicle* with his rival Thomas Loud over the merits and originality of Babcock's controversial frame. Emilius N. Scherr entered the fray on Loud's side; neither favored metal framing at that time, but both later used iron reinforcement in their own pianos. Late in 1837 Babcock returned to Boston to work for Jonas Chickering and his backer, John Mackay (George Mackay had died in 1824). In Chickering's employ Babcock invented a quieter escapement jack (patented October 31, 1839; 1389), which Chickering used for many years; ironically, much the same type of escapement had been used by Loud nearly ten years before.

Through the excellence of his craftsmanship and the significance of his patents Babcock strongly influenced subsequent American piano manufacture, especially in Boston. He was re-

membered by a local historian, Albert Kendell Teele, as "a man of much inventive talent, constantly inventing and introducing improvements in all parts of the instrument; for many years before his death he had a private room, to which no one was admitted, where he conducted his experiments. Doubtless his patient study and mechanical ingenuity and skill did much to establish the early reputation which Chickering's pianos have so long sustained."[6]

In casting aspersions on Babcock's metal frame, Loud and Scherr were reacting against a new technology that threatened to move piano construction outside the traditional scope of the woodworker's skill. By 1850 these conservatives were losing out to the more progressive piano factories of Boston and New York. Around 1830, though, Philadelphia makers numbered about eighty, whose combined output was the highest in the nation. Of approximately twenty-five hundred pianos made in America in 1829, valued at $750,000, Philadelphia produced about nine hundred, New York about eight hundred, and Boston just over seven hundred. Pianos were a significant Philadelphia export from 1820 to 1840; in these years the eighty-eight new pianos shipped from Philadelphia in the coastwise trade numbered more than all the tables, desks, chests, bureaus, and sideboards together, while the sixty-three (plus four crates holding an unknown number) shipped in foreign trade were valued at $14,832.50, higher than any other single category of case or table furniture.

Thomas Loud and his brothers accounted for a large share of Philadelphia's pianos; the firm reportedly made some 680 in 1824 alone, an astonishing total that cannot be verified. Yet the Louds sent pianos to South America and the West Indies as early as 1821 and were certainly among Philadelphia's most prominent exporters. Their name had long been associated with piano manufacture. In 1802 a Londoner named Thomas Loud patented a portable upright piano; he may have been the same Thomas Loud from London who kept a piano shop in New York in the late 1820s and died there on January 2, 1833, at the age of seventy-one, leaving a widow, Harriet. A family of Louds, also from London, settled in Philadelphia before 1812; in that year a partnership between the piano makers Joshua Baker and Thomas Loud Evenden was dissolved. Directories of 1813 and later list Evenden variously as a piano maker and a grocer, and his son T. L. Evenden, Jr., as a piano teacher (he later earned local fame as a performer and composer). It has been supposed that Evenden Sr. was the son of the New York Loud and adopted the surname Evenden (his wife's?) to distinguish himself from his father. In any event, the Philadelphia family dropped the surname Evenden in 1817, leaving a confusion of Thomas Louds to discomfit historians.

In 1817 Thomas Loud (Evenden, Sr.?) joined his brother John in a partnership that was enlarged by two more brothers, Philologus (around 1825) and Joseph Edward (around 1828). In the next generation Thomas C., William H., and Joseph R. Loud continued to manufacture pianos, but by midcentury the whole industry in Philadelphia had begun its decline. Joseph R. was still listed as a piano maker in 1855, but as a tuner in 1860. By 1862 he was a plumber. An F. P. Loud employed by Chickering & Sons in Boston in 1865 may have been a relative.

The Philadelphia Louds were socially well connected. Thomas Sr. was active in the Musical Fund Society, which included such notables as the painter Thomas Sully and the painter and banker Francis M. Drexel. (Drexel's son Joseph

W., a trustee of the Metropolitan Museum, bequeathed to this Museum his instrument collection, which included the Albrecht piano discussed above.) Sarah Frishmuth, another prominent Philadelphian who donated instruments to the Museum's collection, still owned a Loud piano around 1900.

Loud & Brothers earned favorable comment at the Franklin Institute exhibition of 1832 for a brilliant-sounding square piano and for another more delicate one better suited to vocal accompaniment. To achieve its power the former piano was triple-strung (three strings per note, rather than the two usual in American pianos at that time). Trichord stringing later became the norm, made practical by iron framing. Thomas Loud

214. *Advertisements of Loud & Brothers and E. N. Scherr from* The National Gazette *(Philadelphia), January 2, 1830*

215. *Loud & Brothers piano salesrooms, 150 Chestnut Street, Philadelphia, Pa., c. 1825*

216. *Detail of nameboard of piano in Fig. 217*

(Sr.?) finally patented his own tubular "compensation" frame on July 7, 1835. Other Loud family patents (six between 1827 and 1865) include those of April 1, 1842 (2523) for a transposing action and of August 1, 1865 (49,127) for a swell device, both possibly anticipated in an upright piano discussed below.

The oldest extant American-made Loud piano (c. 1815; Fig. 217) is somewhat crudely built and has been altered. Its elaborate nameboard (Fig. 216) displays the makers' gilt inscription on a red-painted ground flanked by lyre-playing angels and cherubs holding music, all between large lattices. The four turned and reeded legs, with heavy brass collars and large, casterless paw feet, seem to be replacements; they do not harmonize with the plain cross- and feather-banded mahogany case, from which three drawers are suspended. The lid is hinged across the middle, with panels opening toward the front and rear. The rear panel replaces a structure that was tenoned into the sides and stood above the case, perhaps to imitate a cabinet piano's form. Extraneous slips of wood occur under the ivory key fronts; these

slips have warped, throwing off the ivories, which may in fact be a later addition. Strings of the lowest ten notes cross a separate bridge on the way to roughly forged tuning pins at the right side. Patented by Broadwood in 1788, the divided bridge allowed a piano's bass strings to be rescaled and struck closer to their center. Concern for the striking point, an important determinant of tone quality, may account for the extreme sideways displacement of this piano's hammers, which require unusually crooked key levers. The compass is a conventional FF-c^4, double-strung throughout. The damper pedal apparatus is missing.

By 1830 Loud pianos had undergone radical change. Carefully crafted by specialized workmen, they had lost any suggestion of eccentricity or sloppiness in manufacture. Loud piano number 837 (perhaps a batch number, not a serial number) carries the signature, dated 1830, of D. T. Moore, probably David Moore, a member of Philadelphia's Society of Journeymen Cabinet-Makers. The rosewood exterior of the ovolo-front case (Fig. 218) sports brass molding and gilt stripes outlining panels around tight, lightly shaded an-

217. *Piano by Thomas Loud Evenden & Son. Philadelphia, Pa., c. 1815. W. 65¾ in. The damper pedal assembly is missing* (89.4.2718)

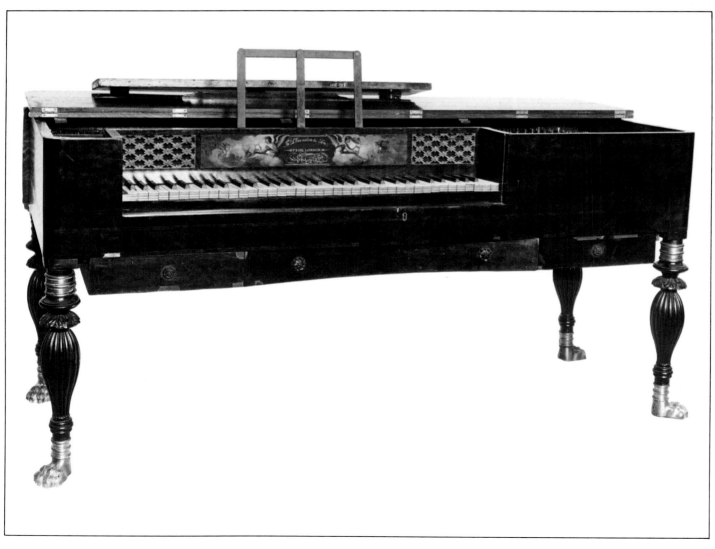

themion and vegetal stencils. Typical Philadelphia scroll-and-cornucopia brackets concealing drawers beneath the case echo the stencil motifs. Deeply reeded and carved legs with embossed collars contribute to the opulent effect; a fifth leg with the damper pedal is missing. The FF-f⁴ keyboard is stamped *D. Boggs,* doubtless David Boggs, whom directories list as a cabinetmaker in 1820 and as a piano maker from 1829 to 1840. The keyboard is flanked by flat blocks that keep the gently curved ends of the nameboard from encroaching on the playing surfaces of the extreme keys and allow clearance for removing the double action.

Even more imposing as furniture, a Loud & Brothers upright piano (Figs. 219, 220) in the form of a secretary desk has a similarly stenciled rosewood case with carved and gilt bracket legs. A fabric panel concealing the action and flanked by pivoting candleholders is surmounted by a hinged cornice. The keyboard's cylinder fall holds a folding music rack, below which is the makers' inscription (Fig. 221), exquisitely lettered with a stylus that cut through gold leaf to expose the rosewood beneath; the same sure hand inscribed the previously discussed piano. Ten horizontal swell shutters operated by the left pedal enclose the back of this unusual upright. The middle pedal shifts the FF-f⁴ action slightly sideways for an *una corda* (single string) effect; the right pedal lifts the dampers. The tuning pins are located high under the cornice, above hammers set in motion by long sticks that rise above the key tails. These "stickers" are inexplicably out of alignment with the keys, so that the f⁴ hammer is inoperative and the FF key propels the FF-sharp hammer. Perhaps a transposing action was intended but not completed.

This piano is numbered 477, but the keyboard, again made by Boggs, is stamped 986. On the back of the soundboard is the signature (dated 1831) of William Moore, another member of the Society of Journeymen Cabinet-Makers listed in directories of 1828–36. Still another woodworker made the tripod stool that accompanies the piano. The society to which both Moores belonged had begun as a benevolent club in 1806 and had grown into a labor union by 1829. Undercut by numer-

218. *Piano by Loud & Brothers. Philadelphia, Pa., 1830. W. 68⁵⁄₁₆ in. (89.4.2812)*

ous low-paid apprentices, the journeymen banded together in 1834 to open their own cooperative store. As a result they were fired by the factory owners. Labor unrest coupled with depression in 1837 spelled trouble for all manufacturers in Philadelphia and also in New York, where journeyman piano makers walked out in defiance of an influx of German newcomers who threatened their jobs.

A New York upright piano (Colorplate 11) of about 1835 resembles in classical dignity the furniture of Joseph Meeks & Sons. As in contemporary pier tables, square tapered legs with fluted corners and Ionic capitals support the key bed in front of pilasters of the same architectural order. The FF-f⁴ keyboard is enclosed by a cylinder fall bearing a recessed paper label that reads *Firth, Hall & Pond Franklin 1 Square New-York*. The label (Fig. 223) was engraved by the same W. F. Harrison who between 1831 and 1840 executed banknotes and probably also some labels for the guitar maker C. F. Martin. Like the Loud & Brothers upright, this piano employs a tall sticker action concealed behind a cloth panel, here radiating from a mercury-gilded, rose-encircled sunburst surrounding a head of Apollo. This mount and those on columns flanking the fabric probably came from France. A cornice with egg-and-dart molding surmounts the case. Similar molding surrounds the panels above and below the keyboard. The lowest thirteen notes have two strings each, the rest have three, the first instance of triple stringing encountered among the Museum's pianos discussed so far. Pedals control the dampers and *una corda* shift.

John Firth (b. Yorkshire, England, October 1, 1789; d. Newtown, Long Island, N.Y., September 10, 1864) came to the United States in 1810. He fought in the War of 1812 and afterward established himself as an instrument maker. His partner, William Hall (b. Sparta, N.Y., 1796; d. New York City? 1874), also served in that war, and both men married daughters of the prominent New York woodwind maker, music publisher, and merchant Edward Riley (d. 1831). The piano builder Sylvanus Pond, a former associate of the Meachams in Albany, joined Firth & Hall around 1833. The firm of Firth, Hall & Pond (Fig. 222) was a major musical merchandiser, publisher, and manufacturer, though who actually built the pianos sold under their name remains a mystery. The Museum's upright is numbered 337. Scratched on the lock is *Bought by Anson Baker from Firth, Hall & Pond 1835*. The lock itself is stamped *Patent T. Cadwallader*.

Altogether different in style, a late Empire square piano (Fig. 224) made in New York around 1835 by John Tallman (active c. 1825–39), then at 15 Barclay Street, shows an abundance of shaded stenciling like that associated with the Connecticut chair maker Lambert Hitchcock. Opulent vegetal stencils on the front and sides,

219. *Piano by Loud & Brothers. Philadelphia, Pa., 1831. H. 76⅛ in. (1976.317.1)*

220. *Stencil decoration on piano in Fig. 219*

221. *Detail of nameboard of piano in Fig. 219*

222. *Detail of lithographed advertisement for Firth, Hall & Pond Pianoforte and Music Warehouse, Franklin Square, New York, showing an upright piano similar to that in Colorplate 11. The same image was used by other manufacturers, who substituted their names for Firth, Hall & Pond's. Courtesy The New-York Historical Society, New York, N.Y.*

223. *Detail of nameboard of piano in Colorplate 11. The engraver's name, W. F. Harrison, appears at lower right of the central rectangle; the oval background of the number 1 resembles Harrison's designs for banknotes*

224. *Piano by John Tallman. New York, N. Y., 1835–38. W. 68⅜ in. (89.4.1198)*

225. *Work table by an unknown New York maker, c. 1835. Stylistically it has much in common with the Tallman piano, Fig. 224 (65.156)*

224

225

226. *Preface from the* Book of Prices *of the New-York Society of Journeymen Piano-forte Makers, 1835*

227. *Pages from the* Book of Prices *describing operations in the construction of typical piano cases and giving the price of each operation (51.579.1)*

228. *Piano by Jonas Chickering. Boston, Mass., 1829. W. 69⅞ in. (1983.75).* Inset: *Engraved plaque from nameboard of piano*

emblems of prosperity, are complemented by a sumptuous double-pedestal base with carved acanthus leaves and big paw feet. Similar bases support contemporary New York pianos by such makers as Thomas Gibson and Pond of Albany. All of these bases are original, though the cases look as though they could just as well have stood on six straight legs. A New York work table in the Museum's collection (Fig. 225) is closely related in style.

Tallman's piano is far advanced structurally beyond those of the mid-1820s. The soundboard extends the full width of the case, concealing and muffling the noisy double escapement action. Much of the soundboard has little acoustic function, since its front edge (behind the removable nameboard) is not rigid. The hitch pins stand above the soundboard close behind the bridge, embedded in a marbled iron plate pierced by four ovals. The range is FF-f⁴. There are five single bass strings. Each of the remaining bichords (double strings) consists of a single wire that bends around one hitch pin, with both ends wound on tuning pins arranged along the back. This economical stringing method, which depends on fairly high tension to keep the wire from slipping around the hitch pin as the strings are tuned, was patented in England by James Stewart (see below) on March 22, 1827, and adopted by Babcock in slightly more complicated form in his 1830 stringing patent. Tallman economized further by employing an interchangeable plate that held five extra hitch pins at the bass; thus, this plate could also have been used in a piano with single-strung notes down to CC.

By midcentury some manufacturers offered seven-octave pianos for concert use, but six-octave squares remained common in homes. Jonas Chickering, America's most celebrated native piano maker, sold an FF-f⁴ square now in the Museum's collection (serial number 11327) for $240 and shipped it to Detroit on April 12, 1851. In that year a similar Chickering piano won a prize at London's Crystal Palace; another of this model was supplied to the White House. Chickering's remarkable instruments caused Europeans to take American piano technology seriously at a time when the level of musical culture in the States was considered inferior.

One of seven children whose father was a blacksmith and farmer, Jonas Chickering (b. Mason, near New Ipswich, N. H., April 5, 1798; d. Boston, Mass., December 8, 1853) was apprenticed to a local cabinetmaker, John Gould, at the age of seventeen. At twenty he went to Boston to serve a further apprenticeship under Benjamin Crehore's protégé John Osborn. By 1822 he was listed independently as a piano maker, and on April 15, 1823, he entered partnership with Osborn's former associate, the Scottish immigrant James Stewart; they sold their

PREFACE.

THE social principle of man, reasonably exercised for any laudable object, must be for his individual and social advantage, whether on a large or small scale.— This principle is generally acknowledged; and in these United States it is claimed as the birthright of every individual, to associate for all honourable and lawful purposes. The Journeymen Piano-forte Makers, of the City of New-York, believed it necessary and expedient to form themselves into a Society, for the better regulating and equalizing their prices. The Society have, after much labour and expense, completed their Book of Prices, which will, they trust, be found as correct as the nature of the work would admit of, it being the first publication of the kind ever printed in the United States. The Society, therefore, now present to the Trade in general, the following Book of Prices, hoping that, (however imperfect it may be found,) it will operate to the mutual advantage of both the Employer and the Employed—an object to which the attention of the Society has been most scrupulously directed.

26

Ditto, when over ten tops at a time, each - $0 54
Hinging a top to the case, with two back hinges - 0 18
Fitting and hinging a short lock-board with three hinges - - - - - - 0 28
Ditto, ditto, a long lock-board with three hinges - 0 31
For castors on legs, &c. or extra hinges, see table, No. 1.
Making a stay, or prop stick, to support a top, tapered, the end rounded, and a hole in ditto, when six at a time or less, each - - - 0 4
Ditto, ditto, when over six at a time, each - . 0 3
Fixing a stay, or prop stick, to support a top - 0 2
For mouldings, or other extras, see tables, &c.
Fixing a pair of trusses (or consoles) between key, bottom and plinth - - - - - 0 40
Fitting and fixing a brass stay to support a lock-board, with a plate at each end, and ditto, let in flush, and making spiral spring - - - 0 12

OF OTHER WORK RECEIVED BY THE CASE-MAKER, TO BE DEDUCTED.

When the stuff for the back, the rim, lock-board, the top and all the blocking is cut out to near the size, and jacked or roughed over, also the blockings and linings, with the long bridge glued up, and the long block veneered, the veneers for the rim &c. cut out, for each case deduct - - 1 25
When only the stuff for the back, the rim, lock-board, and all the blocking is cut out to near the size, and jacked or roughed over, for each case deduct 0 50
When more or less than any of the above, see as follows.
Cutting out a top to near its size, and roughing off ditto - - - - - - 0 12
Ditto, ditto, a long bridge, and jacking off ditto, - 0 3
Ditto, the pine linings in the case - - . 0 3
Ditto, the cross-block - - - - 0 2
Ditto, all the veneers for the rim, &c. - - 0 11

27

For glueing up blocks, or veneering ditto, see tables.
For other deductions, see the prices of bottoms, blocks, &c.

A PLAIN SQUARE CABINET PIANO-FORTE CASE OF MAHOGANY, ALL SOLID.

Three feet six inches long, and five feet six inches high; the ends nine inches deep; the cheeks square, one foot three inches long, seven inches wide, tenoned into the ends of case. A straight name-board three inches wide; the inside of cheeks, and name-board, veneered with shaded mahogany. A flat fall and lock-board, with square edge to ditto, and to project over the cheeks. A fast key bottom of pine, two inches thick, or under, framed and panelled; the front edge of ditto slipped with mahogany. The cheeks square-grooved for key-bottom; rest-pin block nine inches wide, three and a half inches thick, of pine, faced with hard wood long way, one veneer on ditto cross way, the block let into the ends square, the lower end of ditto rabbeted for sounding-board, and linings on the inside of ends for ditto board. A straight angle hitchpin-block, five inches wide, three and a half inches thick, or under, of pine, faced with hard wood long way, ditto rabbeted for sounding-board. A bass hitch-pin-block, two inches thick, one foot nine inches long or under, the edge rabbeted; six braces of pine, two inches thick or under, the blocks notched a quarter of an inch thick in the edge of ditto. A half-inch pine, or white wood back, nailed or glued on, two hand-holes in ditto. The stiles and rails of the front frames, two and a half inches wide or under. The top frame to finish with a plain square rabbet on inner edge, ditto steadied with three pins. The bottom frame with one panel ploughed in, ditto steadied with two pins. A pine top and bottom to the case, slipped on the edge. A solid top fall square edge to ditto, half inch thick, forming a fillet on top of case - 22 50

CHICKERING & SONS'

PIANO FORTE MANUFACTORY,
TREMONT STREET. BOSTON.

MR. CHICKERING'S PRIVATE ROOM.

229. *Chickering & Sons' Pianoforte Manufactory, Tremont Street, Boston. The machinery was powered by a 120-horsepower steam engine, six hundred gas burners provided nighttime illumination, and six hundred buckets were kept filled with water for fire protection. From* Ballou's Pictorial Drawing-Room Companion, *May 1859*

230. *Mr. Chickering's private room at the Tremont Street factory. This engraving appears to show one of his sons marking out a new design. From* Ballou's Pictorial Drawing-Room Companion, *May 1859*

first piano for $275 on June 23 of that year. Stewart returned to Britain in 1826. On his own, Chickering secured the backing of Captain John Mackay in 1829, and the same year he built the simple mahogany and rosewood square (serial number 621) of FF-c⁴ compass, now in the Museum's collection (Fig. 228). Mackay, who had earlier backed Alpheus Babcock, exported Chickering's pianos to South America and returned with cargoes of wood for the factory. When Mackay perished at sea in 1841, Chickering came into full control of the business, in which Babcock had been employed since 1837.

As an outgrowth of Babcock's experiments Chickering introduced improved cast iron frames for square and grand pianos (patented 1840 and 1843 respectively), allowing higher string tension that greatly increased his instruments' power. At the time of his death, and by some accounts as early as 1845, Chickering was devising his version of another basic development called overstringing (more accurately known as cross-stringing), wherein the bass strings cross diagonally over the others to a separate bridge nearer the center of the soundboard. This positioning and the bass strings' consequently increased length enriched the tone; the principle was taken by the firm of Steinway in 1855 and later.

In recognition of his accomplishments, and out of respect for what Robert C. Winthrop called his "grand, upright, and square" character, Jonas Chickering was elected president of Boston's Handel and Haydn Society and of the Massachusetts Charitable Mechanic Association. On December 1, 1852, his factory burned, at a loss of $250,000. Chickering did not live to see completion of a new plant on Tremont Street (Figs. 229, 230), reputedly the largest structure in the United States at that time except for the national capitol, which the last of his three sons, George H., continued to operate until his death in 1896.

Typical of the meticulously assembled instruments produced in large numbers during Chickering's maturity, the Museum's 1851 square (Figs. 231–33) bears an inspection sticker (number 818) signed by S. Payson, an employee then of eleven years' service. The plain, round-cornered rosewood case stands on four tapered polygonal legs with circular bases enclosing recessed casters. Despite the casters, the iron plate and thick wooden members make this piano too heavy to be moved casually. Unlike earlier, lighter pianos, this one was meant to stay put as furniture, not to be carried wherever needed, like an appliance. The gold-painted plate (Fig. 232), which embraces both tuning and hitch pins and is held rigid by two integral transverse struts, incorporates foliate designs and a twelve-point star over the soundboard's right rear corner. As in the Tallman piano the soundboard extends the full width of the instrument, but the front edge is secured to an immobile beam above the nameboard, to assure stability and resonance. A removable music rack sits over this beam.

This piano is not cross-strung; its strings fan out from a single bridge. The bass hammers, curved far toward the front, have much shorter key levers than do the treble hammers near the back. The consequent difference in touch from bass to treble is compensated for, to some extent, by weighted key levers and a curved pivot line. The neatly finished keys, the naturals plain-fronted, are not only significantly wider than keys of earlier pianos, but also a bit harder to depress. Since the forceful thrust of the action

231

231. *Piano by Jonas Chickering. Boston, Mass., 1851. W. 70⅛ in. (1975.309)*

232. *Interior view of piano in Fig. 231, showing cast-iron plate and tuning pins at rear behind curved damper rail. The music rack has been folded down*

233. *Maker's decal on nameboard of piano in Fig. 231*

would quickly wear out parchment hinges, the hammer shanks are pivoted on machine-made, individually adjustable flanges. Rebounding, the leather-covered hammers are caught by back checks to improve note repetition, a feature not found in the older square pianos discussed here.

In a free-standing lyre the right pedal raises the dampers and the left interposes a row of muting tabs between the hammers and strings. The *una corda* shift used for tonal contrast in grand pianos was not feasible in squares, where the hammer shanks do not parallel the strings. Indeed, the complex geometry of square pianos (the keys, for example, being of varying length) made them more expensive to manufacture than the uprights that replaced them.

So long as cost and space posed no limits, Victorian opulence encouraged the square piano's growth. Awesome for its tremendous bulk and carving, a piano (Colorplate 12) made in New York by Nunns & Clark in 1853 is built on the scale of a billiard table. The epitome of Renaissance Revival eclecticism, this stupendous piano could have provoked the comment of dismayed judges at New York's 1853 Crystal Palace exhibition. They deplored the "vulgar, tawdry decorations of American pianos, which show a great deal of taste, and that very bad. Not only do we find the very heroics of gingerbread radiating in hideous splendors, fit for the drawing-room of a fashionable hotel, adorned with spit-boxes among other savageries; but even the plain artistic black-and-white, of the keys—that classic simplicity and harmonious distinction—is superseded for pearl and tortoise-shell and eye-grating vermilion abominations."[7] Two years earlier a Nunns & Clark piano equally deserving of this reproach had stunned visitors to London's Crystal Palace (Fig. 234).

Very likely the Museum's piano was commissioned by a rich New England whaling captain or ship owner for his wife; a circular medallion (Fig. 236) inside the removable front flap displays carved profiles of a man and woman with two dolphins (whales?) and a trident (harpoon?). The carving that embellishes the entire case is a housekeeper's nightmare to dust and polish. On the sides framed oval cartouches rest within deep moldings; elephantine legs surmounted by baroque volutes support lush bouquets carved in full relief over urns between short pilasters; vagrant finials roost on the pedal support. Scrollwork panels screen the interior on either side of an adjustable music rack vigorously modeled after Elizabethan strapwork. The natural keys are covered with mother-of-pearl, the accidentals with tortoiseshell and abalone inlay. Within, the iron plate and its separate tube and strut braces are lacquered black and embellished with painted and gilt flowers, leaves, insects, birds, and geometric designs.

Though its chaste, engraved silver nameplate

(Fig. 235) identifies only the firm's proprietors, this piano, serial number 8054, was the product of many craftsmen. The signature *Joseph Gassin Augt 20 1853* appears under the soundboard, the case is signed *Thompson*, and the top key is stamped *D. Perrin*. Of the three, only Gassin is known; he was active in New York from 1833 into the 1870s. Robert Nunns himself came from London around 1821. His brother William arrived on November twenty-first of that year, and both worked for Kearsing & Son before going into business for themselves in 1823. The Englishman John Clark joined their firm in 1833, and William withdrew in 1839. Nunns & Clark was not a progressive establishment in terms of tonal design, but the plant's employees (eighty men and three boys in 1855, when three hundred pianos worth $150,000 were produced) were provided with modern labor-saving equipment, such as a felt-hammer-covering device patented by Rudolph Kreter (June 4, 1853; 9526); the rights to this machine were purchased by the firm.

As well as having up-to-date, dense multilayered felt hammers, the Museum's piano incorporates a distinctive single action, originally of French design, in which a coil-sprung escapement jack is mounted on an adjustable "rocker" screwed to the key; this arrangement allows fine regulation of the touch. The keyboard spans seven octaves, AAA-a^4. Cross-strung bass strings reach a separate bridge set into an opening in the iron plate, in an arrangement probably derived from an 1851 patent by the New York builder Frederick Mathushek. The right pedal lifts the dampers and the left interposes muting tabs between hammers and strings.

During the decades between about 1790, when Dodds & Claus flourished and the time of Nunns & Clark, American pianos and those of New York in particular underwent revolutionary changes made possible by the nation's material wealth and the technology developed to exploit it. It remained for Heinrich Engelhard Steinweg (later Henry Steinway) and his descendants to exalt the American piano through further structural innovation and aggressive salesmanship. Steinway (b. Wolfshagen, Germany, February 15, 1797; d. New York, N.Y., February 7, 1871) arrived with most of his family in New York on June 29, 1850, a year behind his son Carl. Following a period in which father and sons gained experience in other builders' establishments (including Nunns'), the Steinways were able to open their own shop on March 5, 1853. Steinway & Sons have placed on loan to the Museum the firm's earliest extant New York square (serial number 483, 1854) and an upright from about 1863 (serial number 7765), as well as a square and a grand made by the company's founder in Seesen, Germany, around 1836–40.

In turn, the Museum has loaned to Gracie Mansion, the official residence of the Mayor of

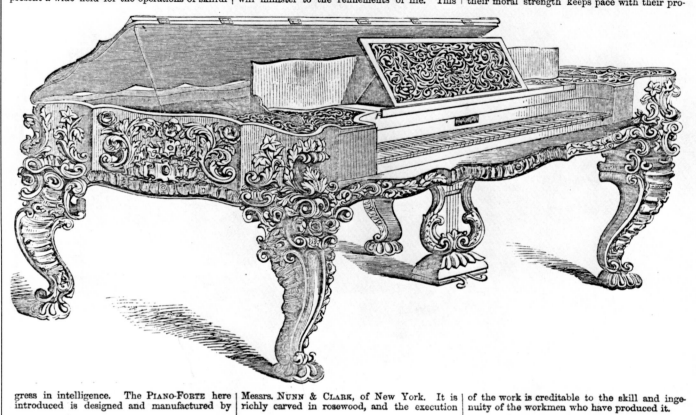

America, among her consignments of manufactured objects, contributes several worthy of being introduced into our pages. The United States present a wide field for the operations of skilful artisans in ornamental articles; as their wealth increases, so do also their taste for the elegant and the beautiful, and their desire to possess what will minister to the refinements of life. This is ever the case with nations, as they advance in intellectual power, and in the just appreciation of what confers real dignity on a people; and their moral strength keeps pace with their progress in intelligence. The PIANO-FORTE here introduced is designed and manufactured by Messrs. NUNN & CLARK, of New York. It is richly carved in rosewood, and the execution of the work is creditable to the skill and ingenuity of the workmen who have produced it.

234. *Illustration of an elaborate square piano by Nunns & Clark, New York, N. Y., exhibited at London's Crystal Palace in 1851. The picture is utterly unrealistic but indicates the taste of the times for "richly carved" casework, for which Nunns & Clark were well known. From* The Art-Journal Illustrated Catalogue, The Industry of All Nations *(Crystal Palace exhibition), London, 1851*

235. *Engraved plaque from nameboard of piano in Colorplate 12*

236. *Detail of front panel of piano in Colorplate 12, presumably showing the piano's owners and emblems of whaling*

New York, a Steinway rosewood parlor grand made in 1872 (serial number 26789, although the legs bear serial number 19904, corresponding to the year 1869). This piano, which was restored and refinished before being given to the Museum, incorporates several important Steinway patents. The cross-strung, cast-iron plate has patent marks of November 29 and December 20, 1859, and June 5, 1866; its construction features precise definition of string length behind the bridge, allowing normally muted segments to resonate in sympathy with overtones of the struck strings. A tubular metal frame (patented 1869) stabilizes the AAA-a^4 rocker action, and a patented screw device applies pressure to the soundboard to maintain its curvature or "crown." Except for the absence of a *sostenuto* pedal, introduced in 1874,

First Modern Kroeger Upright; Made in 1856

237

237. *Illustration of harp-piano by Henry Kroeger, New York, N. Y., 1856, from an advertising brochure of about 1900*

238. *Stamp of Charles Eckert on top key of Kroeger harp-piano (89.4.1187)*

239. *Advertisement of Kuhn & Ridgaway, Baltimore, Md., c. 1860, showing their "grand patent" harp-piano*

this piano is in most respects modern and represents the advanced state of America's piano craft at the time of its manufacture (Colorplate 13).

Steinway's factory made its last square piano in 1888. By that time such instruments had reached the pinnacle of their development in the hands of Frederick Mathushek, whose squares rivaled large grands in tone and power. But lack of space in middle-class apartments, rising freight rates, and mass production methods doomed the handsome, sturdy squares. To clear the market for more economical uprights, in 1903 the National Piano Manufacturers' Association (founded in 1897) staged a widely publicized bonfire in Atlantic City, New Jersey, and contemptuously burned a huge heap of square pianos to ashes.

No such drastic action was needed to condemn the so-called harp-piano, briefly fashionable in America around 1860. It was solely a parlor instrument of no musical distinction, though its imaginative shape perfectly expressed the Victorian era's romanticism. The Museum's unsigned, poorly preserved harp-piano is now attributed to Henry Kroeger of New York (Fig. 237). In the Museum's 1902 catalogue it was identified as "European, ca. 1800," an error attesting to the instrument's swift obsolescence.

Ample curves dominate this piano from its harp-inspired neck, braced by iron struts and a fluted gilt column at the bass end, to its serpentine front and rounded natural key fronts. The CC-c⁵ keyboard controls a conventional upright action with adjustable flanges and bridle straps that pull the hammers back to rest. The stringing, predominantly bichord, is novel in that the lowest seven single strings have two layers of overwinding, the inner closely spun around the core and the outer coiled openly except at the striking point, where the winding becomes close. These two layers make the strings exceptionally thick. The hammers, arranged in a horizontal line, hit the treble strings below their bridge and the bass strings above theirs; the treble strings visible above the case vibrate only sympathetically. The soundboard, behind the base, is quite small. When the piano was playable, its tone must have been thick and dull. Its overall design recalls another short-lived version of the upright piano, the English Euphonicon patented by John Steward in 1841.

Henry Kroeger (b. Germany, c. 1827) established himself in New York in 1851 or 1852. He was said to have been a Steinway superintendent for twenty years, but today that company has no record of him. Eventually Kroeger founded an independent factory; its case department moved to Stamford, Connecticut, in 1902, and the firm operated there at least until 1923. Kroeger's harp-piano closely resembles those advertised by Anthony Kuhn and Samuel Ridgaway in Baltimore (Fig. 239). A similar instrument in The Chicago

Historical Society is credited to one John Kuhn of New York under a patent of the mid-1860s. This attribution is unconfirmed; maybe he was confused with Anthony Kuhn, who disappeared from Baltimore directories after 1857 and may have moved to New York to associate with Kroeger. Supporting a New York provenance, the Museum's piano is stamped *Eckert* on the top key (Fig. 238). This was doubtless Charles Eckert, a key maker active in New York City from the mid-1850s until 1865.

Grand pianos, rare in the United States before the middle of the nineteenth century, began to be manufactured in this country in greater numbers after the Civil War. The Museum's Chickering & Sons grand, (serial number 33280, Fig. 240), was manufactured in 1868, the year after Jonas Chickering's son Charles Francis ("Frank") received on behalf of the firm a gold medal at the

Paris Exposition and the Imperial Cross of the Legion of Honor from Napoleon III. Unlike avant-garde cross-strung instruments, this one is straight-strung, having all strings on the same plane. But the AAA-c^5 range encompasses today's standard eighty-eight notes, and the repetition action, developed from an 1843 patent by Edwin Brown, has a modern "feel." Shorter than a full-length concert grand, this rosewood piano on deeply carved scroll legs is of parlor size, 7½ feet long. The keyboard lies at an obtuse angle to the spine, and carved ornaments flank the keyboard on the outsides.

The pedal lyre, stamped *G & T Alling Piano Leg Manufr's New Haven, Conn. 5252,* was obviously made outside Chickering's factory, as probably were the legs. Within the case are names of two workmen, J. Schwietzer (elsewhere spelled Schwitzer) and T. Scott, who in 1868 had been

240. *Parlor grand piano by Chickering & Sons. Boston, Mass., 1868. L. 90 in. (26.195)*

with Chickering for five and fourteen years respectively. Interestingly, lists of Chickering employees reveal that Scandinavian craftsmen began to replace British-surnamed ones in the later nineteenth century. But the 1867 list shows two Yankee names that raise historical questions: a J. Crehore of twenty years' service (possibly a descendant of John Crehore) and a G. L. Danacot, employed for twenty-five years (conceivably the misprinted name of a relative of the piano action maker George L. Darracott, discussed earlier).

Widely popular from the mid-nineteenth century until well into the twentieth, the keyless cylinder piano is often confused with the street organ. Hauled about by an itinerant busker accompanied by a begging monkey or ragamuffin, the instrument was operated by a hand crank that rotates a horizontal wooden cylinder studded with brass pins, which engage a simple upright piano action. The strings stretch vertically over the soundboard, in front of which, on more expensive models, small articulated figures move in time to the music. English makers, notably the Hicks family from Bristol, provided many such instruments for export, their cylinders programmed with tunes popular at their destination.

The Museum's typical example (Fig. 241 and Colorplate 14) dates from about 1860. Encased in stained pine and mahogany, it is stenciled *G. Hicks maker of cylinder pianos & barrel organs 101 Jay Street Brooklyn N-Y*. George Hicks (b. 1818; d. New York, N. Y., February 21, 1863) may have immigrated from Bristol. He worked in

241

Brooklyn after 1849 and maintained an office or salesroom in Manhattan from 1856 to 1858. Following his death from apoplexy, he was buried in Greenwood cemetery, leaving his widow, Harriet, and three children. Little more is known of his career. He may merely have assembled instruments from imported components; it is unlikely that he manufactured all the parts, including the pinned cylinders and crank hardware.

This piano, serial number 604, has a diatonic range f^1-e^3, plus f sharps and an isolated c^1. Ten papier-mâché figures stand on its mirrored "stage" (Fig. 242). By moving the cylinder sideways the operator selected one of eight tunes—German, Italian, Irish, Polish, the perennial "Yankee Doodle" (familiar since at least 1767) and so on—according to the ethnic character of the neighborhood. Tempo varies with the speed of the cranking. Two brass bells punctuate the rhythm as the costumed puppets bob and turn. A uniformed courtier, controlled by a knob, raises a tray to solicit coins, which he deposits in a trough.

Since the street piano impeded traffic, New York aldermen prohibited its use in 1885. This drew forth protests, including a poem beginning

I'm fond of classic music, e'en of the Vogner
    school
And dearly love to hear it sung by signor Mike
    O'Tool
But the music that I love the best, is that I
    hear each day
Played by a wandering refugee on a sweet
    street pianny.

241. *Cylinder piano by George Hicks. Brooklyn, N. Y., c. 1860. H. 36½ in. A panel enclosing the strings has been removed. (89.4.2048). See also Colorplate 14*

242. *Detail of articulated figures on "stage" of cylinder piano in Fig. 241. The woman at center plays a keyboard instrument; the man at far right collects coins on his tray and drops them into the trough below*

The instrument was usually hired by the operator and returned every six or eight weeks for a freshly pinned cylinder. Because of hard outdoor use these instruments had a limited lifetime. They needed frequent tuning, and their cylinders required careful handling. No copyright applied to the tunes, and music publishers may have appreciated the free publicity for their songs. The cylinder piano and barrel organ put popular music within earshot of poor tenement dwellers and provided a welcome diversion for people on the street:

> And yet they talk of passing laws to break up
>   strolling bands
> The organ grinder with his monk who on the
>   corner stands
> The girl with tambourine and bell! the harp
>   and fiddle too,
> If they succeed, oh dear, what will we music
>   lovers do?[8]

After a century's obsolescence the harpsichord and its relatives underwent a remarkable revival in Boston at the hands of Arnold Dolmetsch (b. Le Mans, France, February 24, 1858; d. Haslemere, England, February 28, 1940). Dolmetsch, whose father was an organ builder and piano tuner, became enchanted by antique instruments while a music student in Brussels. Pursuing this interest in London, he was influenced by William Morris's Arts and Crafts movement, a powerful force in reviving hand craftsmanship and "gothic" designs. Having gained some reputation as an advocate of historically authentic performance on old instruments, Dolmetsch came to perform in the United States late in 1904 and the next year was invited to direct a new department of Chickering & Sons' piano factory in Boston. There he supervised production of harpsichords, virginals, spinets, clavichords, and other instruments of impressive quality, many of them still in use. Aficionados of these quaint instruments included the Longfellows and also Theodore Roosevelt, for whom Dolmetsch played the clavichord at the White House on December 17, 1908. Dolmetsch also taught the harpsichord to the composer-pianist Ferruccio Busoni. Chickering & Sons was absorbed by the American Piano Company in 1908, and the recession of 1910 ended the firm's commitment to this fruitful enterprise. Dolmetsch left to work in Paris but finally settled in Surrey, where his family workshop nurtured the next generation of harpsichord builders, including several prominent Americans.

Though Dolmetsch's stay in Boston was brief, many of his finest instruments were designed and made there. A rectangular virginal (Figs. 243, 244, and Colorplate 15) with one set of strings and C-f³ keyboard is among his loveliest and most unusual works. Its deep green interior and sound hole decoration were inspired by Art Nouveau. Built in 1906 (serial number 14), it was shipped to Maine in 1913 but was returned in 1914 and subsequently sold to John S. Newberry of Cleveland.

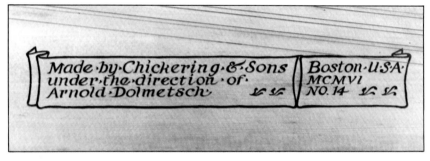

One of the inspirations for this instrument was a famous "mother and child" virginal made by Lodewijck Grauwels in 1600 and exhibited at London's South Kensington Museum in 1872. Sometime before 1902, when this Museum acquired the Grauwels virginal, Dolmetsch had built its small, removable "child" to replace the lost original. In 1907 Chickering workmen under Dolmetsch's direction restored another small virginal now in the collection, and in the same year the company produced a related octavina (serial number 48) of c-c⁴ range, shipped in 1909 to Mrs. John F. Perry of Fenway, Boston. This plain but carefully made little instrument also found its way to the Museum (Fig. 246).

Far larger than its kin, a magnificent two-manual harpsichord of 1909 (serial number 59) was also constructed under Dolmetsch's supervision (Fig. 245). This harpsichord was the first ever played by Ralph Kirkpatrick, later to become the dean of American harpsichordists. Decorated in imitation of continental instruments, it bears two mottoes in gold within the vermilion lid. The first, *SCIENTIA NON HABET INIMICVM NISI IGNORANTEM* (Knowledge has no enemy except an ignorant man), is also inscribed on the Grauwels virginal, with the medieval spelling *Sciencia*, and the second, *ACTA VIRUM PROBANT* (Deeds

243. *Virginal by Chickering & Sons under the direction of Arnold Dolmetsch. Boston, Mass., 1906. W. 68 in. (60.51). See also Colorplate 15*

244. *Maker's inscription on soundboard of virginal in Fig. 243*

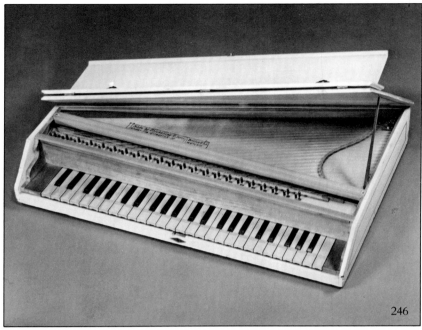

245

246

245. *Harpsichord by Chickering & Sons under the direction of Arnold Dolmetsch. Boston, Mass., 1909. L. 94⁹/₁₆ in. (1981.374)*

246. *Octavina (octave spinet) by Chickering & Sons under the direction of Arnold Dolmetsch. Boston, Mass., 1907. W. 30¾ in. (67.36)*

247. *The Reverend Charles Henry Wells playing a Daniel B. Bartlett lap organ. Wells was pastor of St. Andrew's Episcopal Church, Newark, N. J., c. 1925. Courtesy The Newark Museum, Newark, N. J.*

prove the man), appears on many seventeenth-century Flemish harpsichords. One wonders whether the choice of these mottoes reflects Dolmetsch's feelings about the termination of his project. With three sets of strings, coupler, and mute operated by six pedals fronting the turned baluster and trestle stand (another seventeenth-century derivation), and a double-curved side like those on some German baroque harpsichords, this eclectic instrument and its companion, number 60, made for Busoni, were not surpassed in distinction for some fifty years, when Boston had again become the center for harpsichord making in America.

Like square pianos, American reed organs achieved a complexity unknown abroad. The method of producing sound from wind-activated metal tongues, each fixed at one end over a close-fitting opening through which the free end vibrates, originated in East Asia, where chordal, hand-held mouth organs are still played. In the United States, hand-held types such as the mouth harmonica and accordion have mostly been imported from Germany and Italy. American manufacturers concentrated on developing larger free-reed instruments during the nineteenth century.

Several northern European makers had produced free-reed organs before the first known American-made one appeared in 1809. In that year the Boston organ builder Ebenezer Goodrich (1782–1841; brother of Benjamin Crehore's co-worker William Goodrich) presented a small organ entirely furnished with free-reed stops to the well-known organist and portraitist Gilbert Stuart. The further development of American reed organs owes much to the Huguenot refugee James A. Bazin, who immigrated from the island of Jersey and settled in Canton, Massachusetts.

248

Presumably basing his design on French accordions, Bazin built a horizontal, button-keyed model (one is preserved in the Canton Historical Society) that became known as the elbow or rocking melodeon, also called "lap organ" since it was commonly played resting across the knees of a seated player (Fig. 247). Known after about 1825, early forms of this instrument were considered "unsightly, tardy in sounding, and of harsh tone" but were useful in domestic situations where other instruments were not available.

Abraham Prescott, mentioned above in connection with Yankee bass viols, evidently purchased one of Bazin's instruments in Boston. Having moved his factory from Deerfield to Concord, New Hampshire, in 1833, to take advantage of better facilities and a more direct water shipping route to Boston, Prescott started producing his own lap organs along Bazin's lines. Prescott's sons made larger reed organs until 1891; thereafter they concentrated on pianos. Following several changes of name, the firm expired in 1917. Abra-

ham Prescott himself, a deacon of the Baptist Church, retired in 1850 covered with honors, including a silver medal from the 1837 New Hampshire State Fair.

The Museum's Prescott lap organ (Fig. 248), marked *VI* and stamped with a worker's name *L.* [or *I.*] *E. Morse* within (Fig. 249), dates from about 1837. Its ivory buttons, larger than those of a concertina, are staggered in two rows encompassing F-a^2; the accidentals have a black circle inlaid on each button. Short rods attached to the bottoms of the buttons depress leather-hinged pallets under the divided reed board, itself placed atop a wedge-shaped reservoir and pressure (feeder) bellows. As both hands finger the buttons, the player's left forearm pushes down the top, squeezing the bellows with a rocking motion. These bellows are expanded by internal springs and refill through holes in the bottom. Blocks are provided at the edges to elevate the intake holes when the instrument is played on a table. Sliding shutters operated by a horn knob in the nameplate

248. *Lap organ (rocking melodeon) by Abraham Prescott. Concord, N. H., c. 1837. W. 18^{15}/$_{16}$ in. (89.4.1194)*

249. *Stamp of L. (or I.) E. Morse on end of button board of lap organ in Fig. 248*

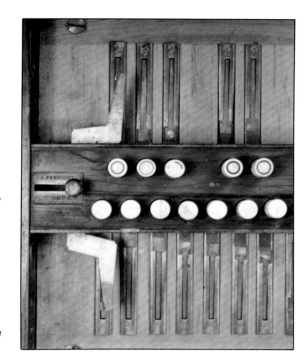

250. *Maker's mark stamped on plate for shutter knob, and view of bass reeds of lap organ in Fig. 248. The top panels and shutters have been removed*

251. *Maker's mark stamped on plate for shutter knob (shutters removed from brackets), and view of button board and bass reeds of lap organ in Fig. 252*

(Fig. 250) open and close holes above the reeds to modify the tone and loudness. Each brass reed is soldered onto a brass channel stamped with a pitch letter and fitting in an oblong vent over its pallet. At rest, the reeds bend into the channel slots; wind flowing past the open pallets blows the reeds up and out of the slots.

The encasement around the organ's upper edge, veneered with rosewood, has a cyma profile typical of French accordions. The reservoir and feeder are made of cardboard with leather corners, covered by embossed fabric. These features are characteristic of the genre. The nameplate at the left of the buttons is stamped *A. Prescott Concord N.H.* A wooden bracket at the upper left side and a wire staple below it may have held a strap that would compress the bellows when attached to a pedal on the floor.

Long before Prescott's son Joseph W. patented his version of the lap organ (April 17, 1849; 6356), the basic design had been taken up by such men as Daniel B. Bartlett, who had worked for Prescott before setting up independently in Concord, and by lesser-known makers around lower New England. The Museum's Bartlett instrument (Figs. 251, 252) looks very much like Prescott's, though it differs in having pitch letters on a raised gilt strip between the rows of buttons, and its wider reeds are riveted rather than soldered to the channels. This lap organ, number 194, dated 1847, retains its protective case, which holds in the lid Bartlett's advertising broadside printed by Morrill, Silsby & Co. This sheet (Fig. 253) shows the articles Bartlett (successor to Dearborn & Bartlett) sold: sheet music, woodwinds and brasses, plucked and bowed strings, pianos and lap organs, and the traditional umbrellas, parasols, and canes.

It is not known who first replaced buttons with piano-type keys, found on a lap organ (Figs. 254, 255) labeled *Caleb H. Packard Seraphine & Melodeon Manufacturer Bridgewater, Mass.* and lined with newspaper dated 1843. Packard (b. 1818?), of whom little is known, was descended from Samuel Packard, who came from Windham, England, to Hingham, Massachusetts, in 1638. His instrument has a smaller range (G-g²) than the previous two, even though, because of its keys, it is wider, with reeds arranged in a single row. The reeds, thinner and shorter than Prescott's, are pinned and soldered to channels that are held in place upside down by latches, so that the reeds, which are flat, are blown into their slots rather than out. Shape, twist and curvature (if any), and direction of the reeds help determine the tonal quality and were subject to much variation. This instrument is equipped with a loud-soft shutter operated by a lever in front of the keys. The feeder bellows fills through holes in the sides of the bottom rather than under it. The natural keys are covered with peculiarly flecked ivory.

A larger, anonymous instrument (Fig. 256), almost too wide to fit comfortably on a lap, has

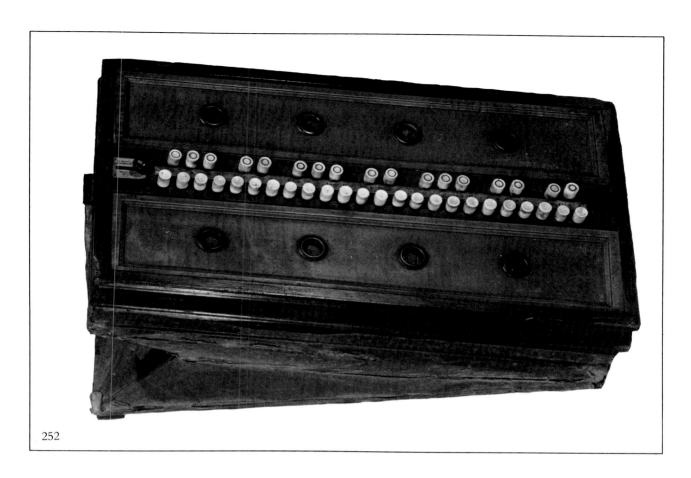

252

a C-c³ compass with keys substantially wider than Packard's. Range, octave span, and pitch were never quite standardized in these provincial instruments; this one is tuned sharper than today's standard pitch. The bellows' internal springs are made of old saw blades, and the pallets are leathered brass tongues that require no springs for closure. The name *Nellie* is written on the front. Perhaps this is a homemade composite organ, not a commercial model, yet it perfectly fulfills its function. Lap organs mainly accompanied hymns, played slowly in two parts, tune and bass. Playing too many notes at once depletes the wind supply immediately, and the reeds do not respond quickly enough for fast tempos.

The word *seraphine* (from *seraph*, a fiery guardian angel) is generally associated with John Green's Royal Seraphine, a reed organ in the shape of a small table, which came out in London in 1833. But it had been applied earlier in New York by Lewis Zwahlen, a maker of surgical pumps and reed organs, to his "harmonicon organ," patented May 5, 1832. The name *seraphine* soon identified various floor-standing reed organs somewhat larger than lap organs. These two forms overlapped chronologically.

The Museum's anonymous seraphine (Fig. 257), marked *II* in several places, has features that give it greater musical flexibility than lap organs have. Most important is the elevation of the case on legs, with swell and bellows pedals

252. *Lap organ by Daniel B. Bartlett. Concord, N.H., 1847. W. 19 in. (1976.8.36)*

253. *Maker's advertisement inside lid of case for lap organ in Fig. 252*

254. *Lap organ by Caleb Packard. Bridgewater, Mass.,
c. 1843. W. 20¹¹/₁₆ in. (89.4.1522)*

255. *Maker's label on lap organ in Fig. 254*

256. *Lap organ. New England, 1840–50. W. 28⁹/₁₆ in.
(89.4.1195)*

beneath. This frees the player's left arm and hand from pumping and operating the loud-soft shutter, and so allows a more agile technique and broader repertoire. The keys are no wider than those of the previously described lap organs but are longer and more like piano keys. The keyboard has migrated to the front of the case, where it is enclosed by a flap attached to a hinged lid. The space behind the keyboard is occupied by a rectangular reservoir with a safety valve on top to prevent overexpansion. A much larger diagonal feeder lies beneath the case; its capacity permits less frequent pumping. Higher wind pressure speeds the reeds' response.

This organ's natural keys are covered with the same flecked ivory used in Packard's; even the width and thickness of the covering are identical. This ivory must have come from a common New England source. The reeds, here pinned to right-side-up channels like those of Bartlett's organ, are shorter in the bass, longer in the treble, and slightly wider than those of the preceding lap organ. The C-c³ range is typical. The relatively wide, deep, plain rosewood case no longer has a cyma profile but takes the reed organ a step further along the road to becoming cabinet furniture. The pedal support is removable, and the square, tapered legs fold in for portability.

Of thirty-nine reed organ patents recorded between 1840 and 1856, fifteen date from 1855 and 1856. An increasing number of patents per year reflects the growing commercial importance of these instruments. Jeremiah Carhart and Emmons Hamlin, two major builders, testified during a patent investigation that Americans made fewer than three hundred reed organs altogether in the years of Prescott's ascendancy before 1846. In 1866 twenty-five manufacturers produced about fifteen thousand instruments valued at $1.6 million. In the late 1890s Sears alone was selling perhaps fifteen thousand annually, while Lyon & Healy's total output by 1890 numbered around one hundred thousand. New Hampshire inventors dominated patent statistics in the 1840s because of the role of Prescott and his disciples, but after 1850 the preponderance shifted to New York, Massachusetts, and Connecticut.

Of great significance tonally was the switch in midcentury from force or pressure bellows to suction or exhaust bellows, an innovation claimed by Jeremiah Carhart of Buffalo in his controversial patent (4912) of December 28, 1846. An earlier patent (November 11, 1818) to Aaron Merrill Peaseley of Boston had mentioned the suction principle, but that patent was lost in the Patent Office fire of 1836. When a copy was eventually found, Carhart's claim was successfully challenged by Charles Austin, whom Carhart had sued for patent infringement. Carhart's case was appealed to the Supreme Court and, after his death, by his widow, Lydia, to Congress in 1870—a measure of the claim's commercial import.

One effect of suction on free reeds is to inhibit the propagation of overtones by drawing wind pulses into the suction chamber rather than propelling them outward toward the listener. The heavier Victorian cases of suction organs, in which the reeds were buried, also muffled the sound. European makers preferred the pressure system; their reed organs had a brighter tone and crisper attack than American melodeons (the names *melodeon*, *harmonium*, and so on were used inconsistently in the nineteenth century).

Before Carhart's patent was voided, he had sold the rights to several builders, including his employer, George A. Prince & Co. At the Prince factory in Buffalo the superintendent of tuning, Emmons Hamlin, developed in 1848–49 a voicing technique that involved twisting the reeds; this refined the tone markedly. Lowell Mason, the influential advocate of American music reforms, recognized the potential of Hamlin's discovery. With backing from the Boston music publisher Oliver Ditson, Mason established his son Henry

257. Seraphine. New England, c. 1840. W. 31³⁄₈ in. (89.4.1779)

258. *Advertisement of Carhart, Needham & Co. New York, N. Y., c. 1855*

259. *Engraved nameplate on melodeon in Fig. 260*

260. *Melodeon by Carhart, Needham & Co. New York, N. Y., c. 1855. W. 46 in. (1979.288)*

260

in partnership with Hamlin on April 16, 1854. The firm of Mason & Hamlin, which donated to this Museum a model demonstrating the operation of free reeds, was destined to become a leading manufacturer of cabinet reed organs and of pianos.

Just about the time of Hamlin's innovation Carhart left Prince & Co. to start a business in New York with Elias Parkman Needham. The company, sometimes advertised by a rebus (car, heart + need, ham), was known as Carhart & Needham between 1849 and 1854 and as Carhart, Needham & Co. (Fig. 258) from 1855 to 1868, when Carhart probably died. The later name on an engraved plate approximately dates the Museum's melodeon (Figs. 259, 260), built in a late Empire rosewood case on octagonal legs, with an unusual iron support for swell and bellows pedals. This sturdy construction, needed to withstand sway, emulates the styling of square pianos. The melodeon trades easy portability for a five-octave FF-f^3 compass, still an octave or more short of a contemporary piano's. The single set of reeds shows the twist characteristic of Hamlin's method of voicing. The reeds are riveted to flat brass plates that fit into padded grooves over pallet holes beneath the key tails. Above each reed is a wind duct of graduated size. On June 10, 1856, Carhart patented (15,061) a machine for making reed boards, aimed at increasing the firm's already large output; in 1855 their steam-powered plant, which employed eighty workmen at an average monthly salary of fifty dollars, produced some fifteen hundred reed organs and five thousand reeds (which they supplied to the trade) worth $190,000. (Compared with the 1855 census figures supplied by the piano firm of Nunns & Clark, Carhart & Needham's statistics show their firm to have been vastly more productive and lucrative; at the time this was generally true for large reed organ manufacturers as compared to piano makers, whose operations were more painstaking and complex.)

The Museum's melodeon uses the suction system Carhart championed. In an arrangement that is the opposite of the seraphine's, a rectangular exhaust bellows behind the keyboard draws air from the larger suction reservoir below the case; wind is pulled down through the reeds into this reservoir.

In every respect but appearance a melodeon by Taylor & Farley (Figs. 261–63) follows Carhart & Needham's model faithfully. Simeon Taylor and John A. Farley became partners in 1855 or 1856. A year or so earlier Taylor (b. October 18, 1817) had moved to Worcester, Massachusetts, from Boston, where he had been employed since his early twenties at the piano factory of Deacon Timothy Gilbert. There Taylor had been responsible for installing free-reed "Aeolian" attachments on Gilbert's pianos. Taylor had spent his youth learning mechanical skills in his father's carriage factory in Bridgewater. While in Boston he contracted chronic bronchitis, which limited his physical activity and led to his removal to Worcester. His engineering aptitude yielded half a dozen organ-related patents between 1866 and 1870. The 1870 patent locates Taylor in Brighton, but he remained involved with the Worcester firm until shortly before his death in Haverhill on September 12, 1875.

John A. Farley (b. c. 1820; d. Worcester, Mass., November 21, 1879) was perhaps the same Farley who worked for Prescott and made bass viols. He is known to have been a reed maker in Concord, where he lived until the age of twenty-seven. Farley moved to Worcester some time before Taylor, and there in 1847 he joined the woodworker John G. Pierson (elsewhere spelled Pearson) and tuner Milton M. Morse, former Prescott employees, to found Farley, Pierson & Co., melodeon manufacturers. Morse soon went off on his own—he shared a building with the brass-instrument maker Isaac Fiske around 1851—and Pierson and a co-worker named Loring (maybe the W. Loring who went on to work for Chickering in 1867) took over the business in 1852. Farley then sought a new partner, and Taylor filled the bill. Their partnership flourished, and in 1868, the year Carhart & Needham folded, Taylor & Farley organized a stock company that provided capital for a larger factory. Five years before he died, Farley succeeded Taylor as president of the firm. Both men, active members of the Main Street Baptist Church, earned high respect in their community.

Moral integrity and visible profession of faith were vital commercial attributes for manufacturers whose products graced churches, schools, and respectable parlors. Since the better organs were fairly uniform in quality by this time, the proprietors' personal reputations mattered as much in selling locally as did any distinctive characteristics of their instruments. Unlike some unscrupulous manufacturers and dealers, Taylor & Farley avoided shameless self-aggrandizement in their advertisements; they disclaimed superiority for their instruments over those of other makers, but let their products speak for themselves. Like most makers, however, the firm relied heavily on independent specialty houses for parts. The Museum's Taylor & Farley organ incorporates reeds (Fig. 263) produced by the neighboring manufacturer Gustavus W. Ingalls; each reed plate is stamped with his patent date, October 23, 1866 (59,027). Ingalls was yet another former Prescott employee, who had made seraphines in Bristol, New Hampshire, before going on to supply reeds to the trade.

This melodeon, which bears several serial or batch numbers, is also signed *Made Oct 26 1867 A. M. Knight*, while the keyboard, like the Carhart & Needham melodeon's, has an illegible stamp of another craftsman. The Rococo Revival case, with rounded front corners and cabriole legs with

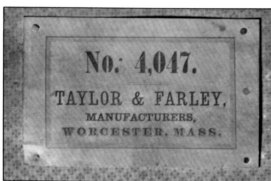

261. *Melodeon by Taylor & Farley. Worcester, Mass., 1867. W. 49⁷⁄₁₆ in. (45.54)*

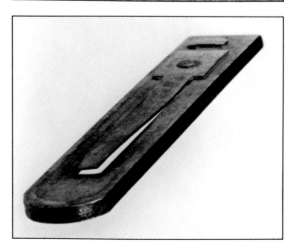

262. *Printed label inside melodeon in Fig. 261; elsewhere the case is stamped 1624, probably the serial number*

263. *Brass plate and riveted reed from melodeon in Fig. 261, showing twist in reed for the purpose of voicing*

264. *Reed organ and piano. Probably Baltimore, Md., after 1860? H. 44³/₁₆ in. (89.4.2776)*

scroll feet on oval pads, may have been made locally by Partridge & Taber, known suppliers to Taylor & Farley. The wide skirt's scalloped lower edge, curvaceous pedal lyre, and scrollwork music rack contribute to a feeling of opulence. This voluptuous style is borrowed from the Victorian square piano; the case itself is nearly identical to one in which Ezra Durand of Norwich, Connecticut, installed a hammer dulcimer from around 1868, now in the Smithsonian Institution's collection.

Between about 1840 and 1870 the reed organ developed rapidly, but it reached a technological plateau in the last quarter of the nineteenth century. Thereafter innovation occurred chiefly in regard to appearance and size. False organ pipes embellished the most pretentious models. One reed organ built by Lyon & Healy in 1892 had thirty-six stops and 1,948 reeds controlled by three manuals and a pedal board. Since the player could no longer directly control the wind pressure in such a mammoth instrument, the expressive nuances possible on smaller reed organs were lost to it.

Unlike the piano, the reed organ seldom needed maintenance or tuning and was virtually indestructible in normal use. It was also relatively simple to manufacture and therefore inexpensive compared to the average piano. By 1900, when piano makers were embarking on a well-organized campaign to expand their sales by aggressively marketing upright pianos to replace old squares, reed organs were declining in popularity because of dreary associations with cold churches, funeral parlors, and charity bands. Few serious composers were attracted by their saccharine, tubby sound, beloved of Victorian hymn writers. With a sluggish response and a limited compass, the typical reed organ lacked the grandeur of the pipe organ and the brilliance and range of the piano. Inevitably it came to be perceived as a stale compromise. As though ashamed of their identity, cheap melodeons made around 1900 were often disguised as fashionable upright pianos.

During the reed organ's heyday builders on the fringe of the market were apt to tinker with unusual hybrid designs. One such instrument in the Museum's collection combines a simple one-rank reed organ with a short upright piano (Fig. 264). Both sections have crudely crafted mechanisms. The limited range c-e³ suggests a function as a rehearsal instrument used to give pitches or to accompany a choir. It is lined in places with mid–nineteenth-century Baltimore newspaper. The atypical style of its construction and case further indicates an origin outside the Northeast. There are no makers' marks or part numbers.

A far more imposing piano and reed organ combination (Fig. 265) may also have come from the mid-Atlantic states. The upright case's Greek Revival design, disturbed by the loss of some components, may be dated to about 1835. Neither the piano nor the organ part resembles the work of any known maker, yet the craftsmanship is fully professional. The neatly finished keyboard has a peculiar range EE-c⁴, symmetrically displaying the extreme accidentals in groups of three. The action is of the English sticker type. In addition to a bellows pedal, there are five pedals that control the dampers, as well as a bassoon stop, a mute, and a drum effect (by striking all the strings at once), and that disengage the piano action. A knob brings on the reed organ. Most unusually, the top thirteen notes are quadruple-strung; the remainder are trichords. A dark oval on the nameboard, in which a maker's name should appear, is cryptically blank. The instrument seems to be unique.

For people who could not afford or were unable to play a conventional instrument, musical automata such as cylinder pianos, barrel organs, and music boxes offered a practical, satisfying alternative. Among the cheapest, simplest, and most widespread music machines were those invented by Henry Bishop Horton (b. Winchester, Conn., September 1, 1819; d. before 1887?). Horton's compact free-reed instruments, extensively furnished with current tunes in the form of punched paper strips or pinned wooden cylinders, were nearly foolproof, did not need tuning, and could be easily mailed; thus they appealed greatly to rural families. Until rendered obsolete by radios and phonographs, that however had the disadvantage of requiring electricity, Horton's manually operated automata and others like them disseminated popular music throughout the land, helping to homogenize American taste.

For three years, starting at the age of nineteen, Horton worked for the cabinetmaker George Whiton in Ithaca, New York. Thereafter Horton built organs for several years. In 1845 he moved to Akron, Ohio, where with B. T. Blodgett he developed a free-reed Aeolian (patented June 19, 1849; 6531) and a "music registering machine" (patented December 18, 1855; 13,946). After fifteen years Horton returned to Ithaca and started a clock factory. He invented a calendar clock and a machine for imprinting pencils, as well as various other devices. Two important patents (October 30, 1877; 196,529, and December 3, 1878; 210,424) relate to his Autophone, the first of a family of organettes (small free-reed automata) that the firm he founded, The Autophone Company (Fig. 266), produced until the 1920s.

Before this company was incorporated in 1879, the Autophone was manufactured in a corner of Horton's clock factory. Perhaps the idea for its sprocket drive came from clockwork. The Museum's example (Fig. 269) has twenty-two reeds mounted in a vertical wooden frame flanked by a wedge-shaped bellows and matching reservoir. The reeds sound when a perforated strip uncovers their apertures in sequence as it advances by means of a sprocket linked to the hand-squeezed

265. *Piano and reed organ. Possibly Philadelphia, Pa., or New York, N. Y., c. 1835. H. 83½ in. Front panel over strings and panel over organ mechanism removed (89.4.2098)*

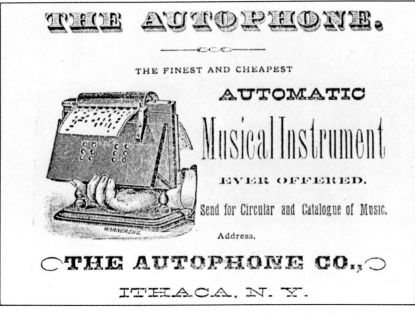

266. *Advertisement of The Autophone Co. Ithaca, N. Y., c. 1880*

267. *Article describing the Autophone, from* Popular Science Recreations, *London, c. 1885*

Perhaps the present opportunity will be the most convenient to speak of the AUTOPHONE, although it is more a musical than an acoustic instrument. Until lately Barbary organs and piano organs have been the only means by which poor people have been able to hear any music, and that not of a very elevated class. Besides, there is a good deal of expense connected with the possession of an organ. But the Americans, with a view to popularize music, have invented the AUTOPHONE, which is simply a mechanical accordeon, manufactured by the Autophone Company, of Ithaca, New York.

The principle of the instrument is represented in fig. 186, and is extremely simple. An upright frame carries within it on one side a bellows, and on the other a flexible air chamber, which serves as a reservoir.

The upper portion contains a set of stops like an accordeon, but the escape of the air through the small vibrating plates can only take place by the upper surface of the frame work, upon which slides a thin plate of Bristol board pierced with holes at convenient distances, and set in motion by the mechanism shown in the annexed diagram (fig. 187).

The figure represents an axle furnished with a series of "washers," which, acting upon the plate, cause it to move round. It is the bellows

Fig. 186.—The Autophone.

movement that turns the axle by the aid of two "catches," B and C, which work upon a toothed wheel fixed upon it.

The "catch" B moves the paper on which the tune is "perforated," when the bellows is empty, the other catch when it is distended; but a counter catch, D, represented by the dotted lines in the illustration, is so arranged that the paper cannot pass on except the tooth of the catch D is opposite a hole pierced upon the plate above. In the contrary case there is no movement of the paper during the dilatation of the bellows. The effect of this very ingenious arrangement is to give to the "musical" band of "board" an irregular movement, but it economises it in the case of sustained notes. The whole action of the instrument depends upon the correct working of the bellows.

The effect, from an artistic point of view, certainly leaves something to be desired, but the instrument is cheap, and not cumbersome, and the

Fig. 187.—Detail of the Autophone.

slips of paper upon which the music is "cut out" can be made by machinery, and consequently are not dear. So far, the Autophone is fitted for popular favour and use, and may supersede the barrel organ.

bellows. The operation was illustrated and explained in *Popular Science Recreations*, an English journal, around 1885 (Fig. 267).

Around the time Horton's name disappears from published records, one Henry B. Morris took out several music-related patents that he assigned to The Autophone Company (Morris also invented looms and a wire netting machine). From Morris's patents came the roller organ. Produced in models called Concert and Gem, these organettes had crank-operated bellows and rotating pinned cylinders known as corncobs. Each "cob" played one tune, and hundreds of them were available, offering sacred music, popular songs and dances, and patriotic airs of various nationalities. The cobs, patented on July 14, 1885 (322,390), had one advantage over larger cylinders: Only one size of pin was used, which could easily be inserted by machinery. Long notes were produced by clusters of pins, rather than by staples of varying length. The roller mechanism received its patent on May 31, 1887 (363,841), with credit shared among Morris, S. R. Tisdel, and F. Labar. In 1902 Sears claimed to have contracted for the entire output of the manufacturer, perhaps fifteen thousand organettes and two hundred fifty thousand cobs annually. Sears sold the twelve-pound Gem together with three cobs for $3.25. Additional cobs cost $2.16 per dozen, a price competitive with sheet music.

The Museum's Concert roller organ (Figs. 268, 270), larger than the Gem, has a twenty-note range, with brass reeds mounted in two rows on a wooden block within the wind-chest. The block is stamped with the manufacturing date *July 2, 1891*. The reeds sound when pins engage pivoted tabs that seal the reed ducts; springs return the tabs when the pins disengage, stopping the notes. A hinged glass panel gives access to the cob and tabs, while the rear part of the top, opening toward the back, can be raised to increase loudness. A crank protruding from the front rotates the cob and pumps a small bellows in the bottom of the case. Operating instructions are glued under the lid. The instrument is stamped under the wind-chest cover *Luigi Lombardi Accordatore e Restauratore di Piano-Forti ed altri Strumenti Armonici Livorno* (Luigi Lombardi, tuner and restorer of pianos and other musical instruments, Livorno) and was acquired abroad. Its cob plays a piece called "Boccaccio Racket." Roller organs were enormously popular abroad; even Princess Beatrice of England had one.

In size and operation the roller organ resembles a small type of French barrel organ known as the *serinette*, which produces sound from pipes rather than reeds; serinettes were sometimes used to teach tunes to singing birds. Larger barrel organs were popular in Britain, where they served much the same function as cylinder pianos on the street, and also were used in churches. Large and small barrel organs were imported to America, and

268. *Concert Roller Organ by The Autophone Co. Ithaca, N. Y., after 1887. W. 18¹/₁₆ in. (89.4.2813)*

some were made locally.

An attractive, unsigned example encased in cherry and satinwood veneer has a classical portico and shaded paterae inlaid on the front (Fig. 271, and Colorplate 16). The portico recalls the shape of some tall Federal clocks. A colored paper lining the case interior is typical of Federal wallpapers (Fig. 273). The big barrel shifts laterally in sixteen increments, each corresponding to a tune or pair of tunes named on a sliding indicator panel. The tunes represent an interesting assortment of Anglo-American dances, hymns, and airs popular in the northeastern United States around 1800 (Fig. 272). Four knobs extending through the front panel control three ranks of wooden pipes (the lowest ones mitered to reduce their length) and six special-effect pipes set horizontally on a separate wind-chest and operated manually by buttons inside the case. Two of these special pipes have cane reeds like a clarinet's. The range of the complete ranks is two diatonic octaves starting on a D, plus the upper C-sharp.

The donor related that this organ came from a man named Beach, whose great-great-grandfather and his brother made it in East Hamilton, New York. The brothers played it at fairs and on Erie Canal and Mississippi River boats, including the *Robert E. Lee.* Stranded in New Orleans, the brothers played on the streets to earn their fare back home. This account presupposes extraordinary skill in an out-of-the-way village; pinning

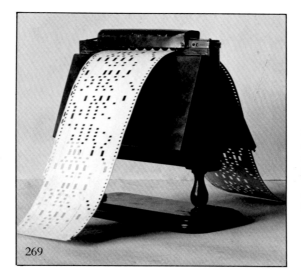

269

270

271

269. *Autophone by The Autophone Co., Ithaca, N. Y., c. 1880, with punched strip encoding "The Star-Spangled Banner." H. 10¼ in. (07.195)*

270. *Interior of roller organ, Fig. 268, showing the "cob" and flaps over the reeds operated by means of pins on the cob*

271. *Barrel organ by brothers named Beach. East Hamilton, N. Y., c. 1800. W. 34⁵/₁₆ in. (1972.166). See also Colorplate 16*

The handwritten list (Fig. 272):

- Major Andres Farewell
- 16 McDonalds reel
- 15 Montgomery
- Henry 4th
- 14 Hail Columbia
- 13 Soldiers Joy
- 12 Durangs Hornpipe
- 11 Sherburne
- Maggie Lawder
- 10 St. Michael
- 9 St. Helens
- 8 For the 4th July
- 7 Fulton
- Yankee doodle
- 6 Masons Childs
- 5 Bridgewater
- 4 Handels Clarionet
- Masonic Ode
- 3 Newburgh
- 2 Flowers of Edinburgh
- Ocean Science
- 1 The New Years Festival's

the barrel and machining the hardware were highly specialized operations. Perhaps the organ was assembled from parts purchased elsewhere. In any event, no record of the builders has been found, and there is no reason to suppose they were related to the organ builder Giles Beach (1829–1906) of Gloversville, New York.

Barrel organs were not only used for entertainment but found their way into public worship. In a sermon preached on May 7, 1807, celebrating a new barrel organ for the Society of Goshen in Lebanon, Connecticut, Rev. William Lyman addressed the question of the instrument's propriety:

> But it will be said, perhaps, the expense is too great, and societies in general cannot easily defray it. I know not the proportion of expense between such an instrument as is now before us, and the frequent expense of time and money, in hiring and attending upon a teacher of musick. But, I believe, in the compass of a few years, the balance would be in favour of the instrument; and many societies, by adopting this mode, would find themselves gainers on the score of interest. Besides, it would be a constant and unvarying aid in this part of service: nor would it, like the vocal singers, desert the seat assigned, through disgust, or from indifference. On the construction which distinguishes the present noble machine, the expense is greatly reduced, and society is freed from the burthen of an organist.[9]

272. *List of tunes from barrel organ in Fig. 271*

273. *Interior of barrel organ in Fig. 271*

274. *Chamber organ by Adam and William Geib. New York, N. Y., 1822–27. H. 69 in. An electric switch and bellows pedal formerly fit in holes in the case (1983.440)*

Keyed pipe organs, though not indispensable in worship and indeed eschewed by some Protestant denominations, were nevertheless prized by churches able to afford an instrument and player. Although Catholic Mexico's organ-building tradition dates back at least to 1527, and organs were installed in New Mexico's Spanish missions in the seventeenth century, the earliest recorded use of an organ in a northern settlement was in 1703 by German pietists at Philadelphia's Gloria Dei Church. Before 1775 German immigrants in Pennsylvania included several skilled organ builders besides Johan Clemm, active especially in German communities, but in New York and New England competent local makers were few. The first known native-born organ builder, Edward Broomfield, Jr., of Boston (1723–46), died before completing "for exercise and recreation, with his own hands" a two-manual organ "exceeding anything of the kind that ever came here from England." It is said that by 1815 only four organs were to be found among Boston's major churches.

During the Revolution, and for a long time thereafter, American organ builders suffered from a shortage of lead and tin, pipe alloy ingredients kept in short supply by British trade restrictions imposed on behalf of the Worshipful Company of Pewterers. Since pewter was in great demand for essential housewares, American organs relied heavily on wood for pipes. In Pennsylvania, "beautiful and excellent cedar trees are the greatest ornament of the forests. . . . Their wood has a strong smell, is light as foam, and is especially valuable for the construction of organ pipes. For organ pipes made of cedar wood have a far finer and purer tone than those made of tin."[10]

The use of wooden pipes put the building of organs within the ability of any painstaking joiner or intelligent mechanic. For professional builders who bought large amounts of lumber, the introduction of the circular saw around 1814 and of the steam-driven band saw in the 1820s meant lower costs and consequently a growing market. Before 1850 native builders in the Northeast were regularly supplying modest one-manual organs with predominantly wooden pipes for use in homes and small churches.

The New York City builders Adam and William Geib, discussed above in connection with square pianos, dealt also in pipe organs, though whether they manufactured organs or only sold other people's under the Geib name is uncertain. Only one organ with the firm's label is known to survive (Fig. 274); it dates from the mid-1820s. The mahogany case, cross-banded with rosewood and surmounted by a simple cornice, displays on either side of the fabric front panel a group of three ornamental pipes, shaded and gilded but merely two-dimensional. The real pipes within are not entirely original; of the two ranks (labeled on the stop knobs, Fig. 275, *Open Diapason Treble*, *Stop Diapason Treble*, and *Stop Diapason Bass*, the latter two a single divided rank) the metal open diapason is a replacement, suggesting that, as often happened, the original pipes were at some time melted down, perhaps for bullets. The stopped diapason pipes are of wood and have survived in good order. To save space, the wooden bass pipes are mounted horizontally at the back of the case, one resting atop another. The keyboard spans five octaves, C-c⁴. Unfortunately, the organ, which was discovered in Ulster, Pennsylvania, has lost its foot-pumped bellows; an electric blower was substituted, and a square hole was cut into the front of the case to accommodate the switch. Though not in keeping with the builder's intent, the replacement pipes and blower at least show that this organ has had a useful life of about a century and a half. Few American organs of the same age have fared so well.

William Crowell (dates unknown) was one of half a dozen cooperating builders active in Mont [*sic*] Vernon, New Hampshire, between about 1830 and 1850. Most of the parlor organs made by this group are of closely related design, exemplified by the Museum's Crowell instrument, which is dated November 28, 1852, on the windchest. The village of Mont Vernon (next to Milford, less than thirty miles from Concord) at midcentury supported a lumber mill, a tannery, and two box factories as well as the organ works. Six-horse wagons passing through on the pike from Boston to Vermont carried merchandise to market and delivered raw materials until railroads, bypassing the town, caused the decline of its manufactures. The local pipe organ industry was hard hit by mass production of reed organs nearby and failed shortly after the Museum's organ was built.

275. *Engraved stop knobs of organ in Fig. 274*

276. *Detail of nameboard of Crowell organ in Colorplate 17*

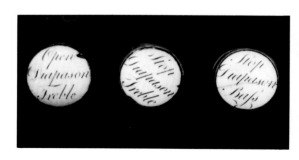

Crowell's instrument (Colorplate 17) is a fine example of provincial cabinetry combining Empire and Rococo Revival styles. Of special interest are the descending bellflowers applied to engaged pilasters, an attractive scrollwork grille backed by cloth in front of the pipes, ornamental rosettes, and an applied rinceau on the cornice. The variety of materials is impressive: the cabinet is of Honduras mahogany with American walnut side panels, the stop knobs and nameboard veneer are of Brazilian rosewood (Fig. 276), the pipes are pine with cedar caps, the keyboard is covered with ebony and ivory, and so on. Leathers for the bellows and mechanism may have come from the local tannery, the native woods from the town mill.

The organ's six stops allow considerable tonal flexibility. The eight-foot diapason and four-foot principal ranks divide into bass and treble stops; the eight-foot dulciana and two-foot fifteenth operate only above middle C. Crowell's tonal ideal may have been influenced by melodeon sound, sweet and subdued. His method of voicing by cutting windways into the pipe caps is typically

277. Chamber organ by George Clisbee. Marlboro, Mass., 1845–60. H. 72½ in. (49.90)

278. *Back of organ in Fig. 277 showing arrangement of pipes and wind supply*

English, but the pipe work is unusual in other respects: The scaling of open pipes in all ranks is nearly identical and very narrow, and the mouths are very low. The gentle voicing is further softened by swell shutters located behind the cloth-backed grille. The left pedal opens these shutters, while the right inflates the bellows. The keyboard encompasses fifty-eight notes, C-a³. Intricate channeling conveys wind to the pipes, which directly adjoin and support one another and thus inhibit sound transmission even more.

A later chamber organ (Fig. 277) attributed to George Clisbee (b. Marlborough, Mass., March 30, 1828; d. Marlborough, 1885) is said to be only the second he made. Its construction is clever though unorthodox. The range is short, only fifty-three notes, F-a³. A bellows suspended under the wind-chest and pumped by a swinging pedal feeds a reservoir above the case. The three ranks are of wood: eight-foot stopped flute, eight-foot open flute (sharing a common stopped bass), four-foot principal. Two stops control the open flute and principal; the third rank always sounds. The pallet valves are located atypically, at the back of the wind-chest instead of the front (Fig. 278). The darkly varnished mahogany case has gilt dummy pipes on the facade. The ungainly, curved front legs are decorated with machine-carved leaf designs. Horizontal scallops ornament the ends of the keyboard.

Clisbee's father, John (b. 1791), whose ancestors came to Marlborough from Lynn around 1788, probably started out as a house carpenter, but later he owned the small pipe organ factory cited in Marlborough's industrial index of 1855 as having an annual output valued at two thousand dollars. The firm was listed in 1861 as John Clisbee & Son. Tax records locate their factory and house across the street from the Second Parish Unitarian Church, where John installed an organ in September, 1824. (In 1865 the firm supplied another organ to a Unitarian church in neighboring Hudson; no other organs of theirs are known to survive.) The 1824 organ was begun by Aaron Howe, who reportedly went insane "from excessive study upon it." George himself, who may, like his father, have first been a carpenter, was considered "a genius whose talents were undeveloped from lack of appreciation from those who could not understand him." He "sacrificed his life in devotion to his mother who died only nine days after his own death."[11]

Little evidence survives as to how domestic chamber organs in this country were tuned, at times and places where professional maintenance was not available. A hitherto unpublished letter in The Chicago Historical Society, acquired with a Joseph Foster chamber organ made around 1837 in Winchester, New Hampshire, sheds light on the procedure followed by owners of such instruments. The instructions for setting the basic temperament are imprecise but would yield a tolerable result. Of special interest is the implication that equal temperament, standard today, was not the only system used for organs at that time; the implication is borne out by evidence from the instruments themselves.

INSTRUCTIONS FOR TUNING THE ORGAN

Commence tuning by striking C between the treble and bass staff. If the equal temperament be the one chosen, tune next after C, G above, a perfect fifth; next G, the octave below a perfect octave. Proceed in this way, until you arrive at B [sic]. After this tune your fifths a little flat, and you will probably come out right. This you can tell by trying your last letter tuned, (F) with C the first one tuned. If they are in tune, a fifth, your tuning is good. If not, which will be most probable, the better way will be to make F perfect with C. Then smooth up your tuning by going back, tuning up by octaves and down by fifths, not exceeding the compass of about an octave and a half. In the equal temperament the thirds of every key will be a little sharp, and the fifths a little flat i.e., not strictly perfect.

A majestic pipe organ (Colorplate 18) by the Boston builder Thomas Appleton (b. Boston,

Mass., December 26, 1785; d. Reading, Mass., July 11, 1872) crowns the collection. It is one of the most imposing objects of American craft in any museum, and perhaps the most important organ of its kind located in a secular building in this country.

Appleton, the son of a house carpenter, was apprenticed to the cabinetmaker Elisha Larned before going to work for William Goodrich, from whom he learned the basic skills of organ construction during the years 1807–11. In 1812 Appleton married Goodrich's sister. After several years' collaboration with the Haytses and the Babcocks, and later with the Mackays (discussed above), Appleton was on his own for the first time in 1821. At first he hired the more experienced Ebenezer Goodrich to finish the organs he was building. Later (1824–28), assisted by Henry Corrie, an expert English builder, Appleton became adept at all aspects of his craft. His reputation grew rapidly as he completed about forty organs by 1833. In 1839 he received a gold medal from the Massachusetts Charitable Mechanic Association, in which he had been active alongside Jonas Chickering.

Appleton's best work was accomplished by 1850, when he moved to Reading, to a new factory built for him by his son. By the time he retired, in 1869, his many fine organs were being played in churches as distant as California. According to a Reading historian, Lilley Eaton, "His organs, like himself, were honest clear through. He never counted the cost, but made every instrument as thoroughly as possible. He said he should be

279. *Inscription* Maid 1830 *inside case of organ in Colorplate 18. Photograph by William T. Van Pelt*

280. *Engraved nameplate of Appleton organ. See Colorplate 18. Photograph by William T. Van Pelt*

ashamed to pass a church that had in it an organ of his that was imperfectly built. He designed his work to last one hundred and fifty years as the best monument he could leave to perpetuate his memory."[12]

The Museum's organ, now Appleton's oldest and best preserved, was built in 1830 (Figs. 279–81) for South Church in Hartford, Connecticut, whence it was removed in 1854 by William Johnson in trade for a new instrument. Its whereabouts for the next twenty-nine years are unknown, but in 1883 it was installed by Johnson's former employee Emmons Howard in Sacred Heart Church, Plains, Pennsylvania. The organ was discovered there in 1980, unused and neglected but virtually unaltered except for Howard's addition of a pedal register. Now restored, it reveals Appleton as a masterful but conservative builder, strongly oriented toward the late eighteenth-century English style of construction. Appleton's carving and joinery are of superior quality. The sixteen-foot-tall Greek Revival case of Honduras mahogany with gold-leafed facade pipes testifies to his aesthetic sense. No less elegant is the aural impression afforded by the 836 meticulously voiced pipes, their tone enhanced by the resonant acoustics of the Museum's Equestrian Court, which the organ overlooks from a high balcony (Fig. 281).

Two manuals (GG-f³, omitting GG-sharp) and pedal board (CCC-D, added by Emmons Howard) control sixteen ranks of pipes for which wind is provided by hand-pumped bellows. The disposition of the stops is as follows:

GREAT (lower manual)		SWELL (upper manual)	
Open diapason	8′	Open diapason	8′
Stopt diapason	8′	Stopt diapason	8′
Stopt diapason bass	8′	Stopt diapason bass	8′
Dulciana	8′	(unenclosed)	
Principal	4′	Principal	4′
Flute	4′	Hautboy	8′
Twelfth	2⅔′		
Fifteenth	2′	COUPLERS	
Sesquialtera	III		
Trumpet treble	8′	Swell to Great	
Trumpet bass	8′	Swell to Pedal	
		Great to Pedal	

PEDAL	
Subbass	16′

The organ is tuned in unequal temperament at a pitch slightly lower than today's norm. Wind pressure of 2¼ inches is maintained by marble slabs that weight the air reservoir. The intricate mechanism, comprising hundreds of moving parts, is accurately fashioned and literally good as new. The case incorporates bronzed ornaments, Ionic capitals, carved pipe shades, and cornices that provide an effect that is architectural rather than decorative, but the elements are all in keeping with Boston furniture of the period.

Perhaps better than any other contemporary American instrument, this organ demonstrates the large-scale integration of functional and ornamental elements that combine with mechanical sophistication and tonal integrity to characterize a musical masterpiece. With instruments such as this the United States has built a musical heritage of enduring excellence.

281. *Appleton organ installed overlooking the Equestrian Court, The Metropolitan Museum of Art*

Notes

(The titles referred to are fully cited in the Bibliography.)

1. Frances Densmore, *Handbook of the Collection of Musical Instruments in the United States National Museum*, pp. 15–16.
2. Olive Logan, "The Ancestry of Brudder Bones," p. 689.
3. A. Hyatt King, "The Musical Glasses and Glass Harmonica," p. 103.
4. William Billings, *Continental Harmony*, p. 26.
5. Gottlieb Mittelberger, *Journey to Pennsylvania*, pp. 42–43.
6. Albert Kendall Teele, *A History of Milton, Mass.: 1640 to 1887*, pp. 379–80.
7. *Dwight's Journal of Music IV* (1853–54), p. 133, quoted in Edwin M. Good, *Giraffes, Black Dragons, and Other Pianos* (Stanford, Cal.: Stanford University Press, 1982), p. 170.
8. Quoted in Henry Collins Brown, ed., *Valentine's Manual of Old New York: 1927*, pp. 119–20.
9. William Lyman, *The Design and Benefits of Instrumental Musick*, p. 10.
10. Gottlieb Mittelberger, *Journey to Pennsylvania*, pp. 42–43.
11. Ella A. Bigelow, *Historical Reminiscences of the Early Times*, pp. 246, 248.
12. Lilley Eaton, *Genealogical History of the Town of Reading* (1874), quoted in Barbara Owen, *The Organ in New England . . .* , p. 91.

Selected Bibliography

Aaron, Amy. "William Tuckey, A Choirmaster in Colonial New York." *Musical Quarterly* 64/1 (January, 1978): 79–97.

Albrecht, Otto E. "Opera in Philadelphia, 1800–1830." *Journal of the American Musicological Society* 32/3 (Fall, 1979): 499–515.

American Cyclopaedia. New York: D. Appleton & Co., 1889.

The American Magazine of Useful and Entertaining Knowledge. Vol. 1. Boston, 1835.

American Musical Directory. New York: Thomas Hutchinson, 1861.

Armstrong, William H. *Organs for America: The Life and Work of David Tannenberg.* Philadelphia: University of Pennsylvania Press, 1967.

Ayars, Christine M. *Contributions to the Art of Music in America by the Music Industries of Boston, 1640–1936.* New York: H. W. Wilson Co., 1937.

Badger, Alfred G. *An Illustrated History of the Flute & Sketch of the Successive Improvements Made in the Flute. . . .* New York: Firth, Pond & Co., 1853.

Bailey, Jay. "Historical Origin and Stylistic Development of the Five-String Banjo." *Journal of American Folklore* 85 (1972): 58–65.

Bigelow, Ella A. *Historical Reminiscences of the Early Times.* Marlborough, Mass.: Times Publishing Co., 1910.

Bill, Edward Lyman, ed. *General History of the Music Trades of America.* New York: Bill & Bill, 1891.

Billings, William. *Continental Harmony.* Boston: Isaiah Thomas and Ebenezer T. Andrews, 1794.

Bjerkoe, Ethel Hall. *The Cabinet Makers of America.* Garden City, N.Y.: Doubleday & Co., 1957.

Blades, James. *Percussion Instruments and Their History.* London: Faber & Faber, 1970.

Boalch, Donald H. *Makers of the Harpsichord and Clavichord 1440–1840.* Oxford: Clarendon Press, 1974.

Boston, Canon Noel, and Langwill, Lyndesay G. *Church and Chamber Barrel-Organs.* Edinburgh: Lyndesay G. Langwill, 1967.

Bowers, Q. David. *Encyclopedia of Automatic Musical Instruments.* Vestal, N.Y.: Vestal Press, 1972.

Boyd, Julian, et al. *The Papers of Thomas Jefferson.* Princeton, N.J.: Princeton University Press, 1950–.

Brown, Henry Collins, ed. *Valentine's Manual of Old New York: 1927.* New York: Valentine's Manual Inc., 1926.

Caba, G. Craig. *United States Military Drums 1845–1865: A Pictorial Survey.* Harrisburg, Penn.: Civil War Antiquities Ltd., 1977.

Campbell, Margaret. *Dolmetsch: The Man and His Work.* Seattle: University of Washington Press, 1975.

Catalano, Kathleen M. "Cabinetmaking in Philadelphia 1820–1840: Transition from Craft to Industry." In *American Furniture and Its Makers* (Winterthur Portfolio 13). Ed. by Ian M. G. Quimby. Chicago: University of Chicago Press for the Henry Francis du Pont Winterthur Museum, 1979.

Chase, Gilbert. *America's Music.* New York: McGraw-Hill, 1955.

Crehore, Charles L. *The Benjamin Crehore Piano: An Account in the Form of Notes.* Boston: For the author, 1926.

Cripe, Helen. *Thomas Jefferson and Music.* Charlottesville: University Press of Virginia, 1974.

Densmore, Frances. *Handbook of the Collection of Musical Instruments in the United States National Museum*. Bulletin 136. Washington, D.C.: United States Government Printing Office, 1927.

Dolge, Alfred. *Pianos and Their Makers*. Covina, Cal.: Covina Publishing Co., 1911.

Eliason, Robert E. *Early American Brass Makers*. Brass Research Series, no. 10. Nashville: The Brass Press, 1979.

———. *Graves & Company Musical Instrument Makers*. Detroit: The Edison Institute, 1975.

———. *Keyed Bugles in the United States*. Washington, D.C.: Smithsonian Institution Press, 1972.

———. "Recently Discovered Information About Graves & Company, Musical Instrument Makers." *The Herald* 5 (April, 1976): 58–63.

Epstein, Dena J. "African Music in British and French America." *Musical Quarterly* 59/1 (January, 1973): 61–91.

———. "The Folk Banjo: A Documentary History." *Ethnomusicology* 19 (September, 1975): 347–71.

Ervine, Beverly Ann. "Francis Hopkinson Smith and His Grand Harmonicon." M.A. thesis, Ohio State University, 1975.

Falcon, Amy H. B. Crehore. *Crehore and Kin 1620–1961*. Evanston, Ill.: A Crehore Format, 1962.

Falconer, Joan O. "The Second Berlin Song School in America." *Musical Quarterly* 49/3 (July, 1973): 411–40.

Frankenstein, Alfred V. *William Sidney Mount*. New York: Harry N. Abrams, 1975.

Franklin, Benjamin. *The Papers of Benjamin Franklin*. Vol. 10. New Haven: Yale University Press, 1974.

Freedley, Edwin T. *Philadelphia and Its Manufacturers: a Handbook.* . . . Philadelphia: Edward Young & Co., 1867.

Gardiner, William. *The Music of Nature.* . . . Boston: Wilkins, Rice & Kendall, 1852.

Gellerman, Robert F. *The American Reed Organ: Its History, How It Works, How to Rebuild It*. Vestal, N.Y.: Vestal Press, 1976.

Gemunder, George. *George Gemunder's Progress in Violin Making.* . . . Astoria, N.Y.: By the author, 1881.

Gerson, Robert A. *Music in Philadelphia*. Westport, Conn.: Greenwood Press, 1970.

Gildersleeve, Alger C. *John Geib and His Seven Children*. New York: By the author, 1945.

Glassie, Henry. *Pattern in the Material Folk Culture of the Eastern United States*. Philadelphia: University of Pennsylvania Press, 1969.

Gottesman, Rita Susswein. *The Arts and Crafts in New York, 1726–1804*. New York: New-York Historical Society, 1938–65.

Grafing, Keith G. "Alpheus Babcock: American Pianoforte Maker (1785–1842); His Life, Instruments, and Patents." D.M.A. dissertation, University of Missouri at Kansas City, 1972.

Groce, Nancy Jane. "The Hammered Dulcimer in America." In *Festival of American Folklife* (1977 program book). Washington, D.C.: Smithsonian Institution, 1977.

———. "Musical Instrument Making in New York City During the Eighteenth and Nineteenth Centuries." Ph.D. dissertation, University of Michigan, 1982.

Hart, G. "H. C. Eisenbrandt in Baltimore." *Das Musikinstrument* 13 (February, 1974): 276.

Heintze, James R. "Music of the Washington Family: A Little-Known Collection." *Musical Quarterly* 56/2 (April, 1970): 288–93.

Henley, William. *Universal Dictionary of Violin and Bow Makers*. 5 vols. Brighton: Amati, 1959–60.

Hindle, Brooke, ed. *America's Wooden Age: Aspects of Its Early Technology*. Tarrytown, N.Y.: Sleepy Hollow Restorations, 1975.

Hoover, Cynthia A. *Music Machines—American Style*. Washington, D.C.: Smithsonian Institution Press, 1971.

———. "The Steinways and Their Pianos in the Nineteenth Century." *Journal of the American Musical Instrument Society* 7 (1981): 47–89.

Horton, Charles A. "Serious Art and Concert Music for the Piano in America in the One Hundred

Years from Alexander Reinagle to Edward MacDowell." Ph.D. dissertation, University of North Carolina, 1965.

Hurd, D. Hamilton. *History of Hillsborough County, New Hampshire.* Philadelphia: J. W. Lewis & Co., 1885.

Jackson, Joseph. *Encyclopedia of Philadelphia.* Harrisburg, Penn.: National Historical Association, 1932.

Johnson, H. Earle. "The John Rowe Parker Letters." *Musical Quarterly* 62/1 (January, 1976): 72–86.

————. *Musical Interludes in Boston, 1795–1830.* New York: Columbia University Press, 1943.

Journeymen Piano-forte Makers' Society. *The New York Book of Prices for the Manufacturing of Piano-Fortes.* New York: For the Society, 1835.

Karnath, Timothy A. "The History of Musical Glasses in America, 1760–1830." M.A. thesis, Kent State University, 1979.

Kaufman, Charles H. "Musical-Instrument Makers in New Jersey 1796–1860." *Journal of the American Musical Instrument Society* 2 (1976): 5–33.

Kettlewell, David. "The Dulcimer." Ph.D. dissertation, Loughborough University of Technology, 1976.

King, A. Hyatt. "The Musical Glasses and Glass Harmonica." *Proceedings of the Royal Musical Association*, session LXXII (April, 1946): 97–120.

Krivin, Martin. "A Century of Wind Instrument Manufacturing in the United States: 1860–1960." Ph.D. dissertation, State University of Iowa, 1961.

Lindsley, Charles Edward. "Scoring and Placement of the 'Air' in Early American Tunebooks." *Musical Quarterly* 58/3 (July, 1972): 365–82.

Logan, Olive. "The Ancestry of Brudder Bones." *Harper's New Monthly Magazine* 58 (December, 1878–May, 1879): 687–98.

Longworth, Mike. *Martin Guitars: A History.* Cedar Knolls, N.J.: Colonial Press, 1975.

Lyman, William. *The Design and Benefits of Instrumental Musick.* New London, Conn.: Ebenezer P. Cady, 1807.

McClinton, Katharine. *Antiques of American Childhood.* New York: Clarkson N. Potter, 1970.

McKay, David. "William Selby, Musical Emigré in Colonial Boston." *Musical Quarterly* 57/4 (October, 1971): 609–27.

Malone, Bill C. *Southern Music/American Music.* Lexington: The University Press of Kentucky, 1979.

Mann, Walter Edward. "Piano Making in Philadelphia Before 1825." Ph.D. dissertation, University of Iowa, 1977.

The Manufactories and Manufacturers of Pennsylvania of the Nineteenth Century. Philadelphia: Galaxy Publishing Co., 1875.

Massachusetts Charitable Mechanic Association. *Exhibition & Fair.* Boston: Dutton & Wentworth, 1837–50.

Mercer, Henry C. "The Zithers of the Pennsylvania Germans." *A Collection of Papers Read Before the Bucks County Historical Society* 5 (1926): 482–97.

Messiter, A. H. *A History of the Choir and Music of Trinity Church, New York.* New York: Edwin S. Gorham, 1906.

Metropolitan Museum of Art. *Catalogue of the Crosby Brown Collection of Musical Instruments of All Nations.* Vol. 1, *Europe.* New York: The Metropolitan Museum of Art, 1902, 1904.

————. *Catalogue of the Crosby Brown Collection of Musical Instruments of All Nations.* Vol. 2, *Oceania and America.* New York: The Metropolitan Museum of Art, 1914.

————. *The Crosby Brown Collection of Musical Instruments of All Nations: Catalogue of Keyboard Instruments.* New York: The Metropolitan Museum of Art, 1903.

Miles, Clarence Francis. *The History and Romance of "Rattling" Musical Jaw Bones.* [Pamphlet.] Worcester, Mass.: Privately printed, 1936.

Mittelberger, Gottlieb. *Journey to Pennsylvania.* 1756. Ed. and trans. by Oscar Handlin and John Clive. Cambridge, Mass.: Harvard University Press, 1960.

Montgomery, Charles F. *American Furniture: The Federal Period, 1788–1825.* New York: The Viking Press, 1966.

Nolan, Carolyn. "Thomas Jefferson: Gentleman Musician." Master's thesis, University of Virginia, 1967.

Ochse, Orpha. *The History of the Organ in the United States*. Bloomington, Ind.: Indiana University Press, 1975.

Official Catalogue of the New-York Exhibition of the Industry of All Nations. New York: George P. Putnam & Co., 1853.

Ogasapian, John. *Organ Building in New York City: 1700–1900*. Braintree, Mass.: The Organ Literature Foundation, 1977.

Oja, Carol J. "The Still-Life Paintings of William Michael Harnett: Their Reflections upon Nineteenth-Century American Musical Culture." *Musical Quarterly* 63/4 (October, 1977): 505–23.

Owen, Barbara. *The Organ in New England*. . . . Raleigh, N.C.: Sunbury Press, 1979.

Parker, Richard C. *A Tribute to the Life and Character of Jonas Chickering*. Boston: Wm. P. Tewksbury, 1854.

Payton, Rodney J. "The Music of Futurism: Concerts and Polemics." *Musical Quarterly* 62–1 (January, 1976): 25–45.

Pennsylvania Chapter of the Society of the Colonial Dames of America. *Church Music and Musical Life in Pennsylvania in the Eighteenth Century*. Lancaster, Penn.: Wickersham Printing Co., 1926–47.

Pilling, Julian. "Fiddles with Horns." *Galpin Society Journal* 28 (April, 1975): 86–92.

Prescott, William. *The Prescott Memorial or a Genealogical Memoir of the Prescott Families in America*. Boston: Henry W. Dutton & Son, 1870.

Price, Carl F. *Yankee Township*. East Hampton, Conn.: Citizen's Welfare Club, 1941.

Redway, Virginia L. *Music Directories of Early New York City*. . . . New York: New York Public Library, 1941.

Ritter, Frederick Louis. *Music in America*. New York: C. Scribner's Sons, 1890.

Romaine, Lawrence B. *A Guide to American Trade Catalogs 1744–1900*. New York: R. R. Bowker Co., 1960.

Schulz, Russell Eugene. "The Reed Organ in Nineteenth-Century America." Ph.D. dissertation, University of Texas at Austin, 1974.

Seeger, Charles. "The Appalachian Dulcimer." *Journal of American Folklore* 71/279 (January–March, 1958): 40–51.

Selch, Frederick R. "Early American Violins and Their Makers." *Journal of the Violin Society of America* 6/1 (Spring/Summer, 1980): 33–42.

Silverman, Kenneth. *A Cultural History of the American Revolution*. New York: Thomas Y. Crowell Co., 1976.

Simpson, Mary Jane. "Alfred G. Badger (1815–1892), Nineteenth-Century Flutemaker. . . ." D.M.A. dissertation, University of Maryland at College Park, 1982.

Smith, Charles J. *History of the Town of Mont Vernon, New Hampshire*. Boston: Blanchard Printing Co., 1907.

Smith, Francis H. *Preceptor for the Grand Harmonicon, or Musical Glasses*. Baltimore: John D. Toy, 1831.

Smith, Helen Burr. "Nicholas Roosevelt—Goldsmith." *The New-York Historical Society Quarterly* 4 (October, 1950): 301–14.

Smith, L. Allen. *A Catalogue of Pre-Revival Appalachian Dulcimers*. Columbia and London: University of Missouri Press, 1983.

Sonneck, Oscar. *Early Concert-Life in America (1731–1800)*. Reprint. New York: Musurgia, 1949.

———. *Francis Hopkinson . . . and James Lyon*. . . . Washington, D.C.: For the author by H. L. McQueen, 1905.

Southern, Eileen J. "Musical Practices in Black Churches of Philadelphia and New York, ca. 1800–1844." *Journal of the American Musicological Society* 30/2 (Summer, 1977): 296–312.

Spillane, Daniel. *History of the American Pianoforte: Its Technical Development, and the Trade*. New York: D. Spillane, 1890.

Steinberg, Judith T. "Old Folks Concerts and the Revival of New England Psalmody." *Musical Quarterly* 59/4 (October, 1973): 602–19.

Taricani, Jo Ann. "Music in Colonial Philadelphia: Some New Documents." *Musical Quarterly* 65/2 (April, 1979): 185–99.

Tawa, Nicholas E. "Secular Music in the Late-Eighteenth-Century American Home." *Musical Quarterly* 61/4 (October, 1975): 511–27.

Taylor, Vincent [interviewed]. "On the Street." *The New Yorker* 49/50 (February 4, 1974): 27–28.

Teele, Albert Kendall. *A History of Milton, Mass.: 1640 to 1887*. Boston: Rockwell & Churchill, 1887.

Toll, Robert C. *Blacking Up: The Minstrel Show in Nineteenth Century America*. New York: Oxford University Press, 1974.

Tunis, Edwin. *Colonial Craftsmen and the Beginnings of American Industry*. New York: World Publishing Co., 1965.

United States Department of Commerce, Bureau of the Census. *Statistical Abstract of the United States: 1981*. Washington, D.C.: United States Government Printing Office, 1981.

Wagner, John W. "James Hewitt, 1770–1827." *Musical Quarterly* 58/2 (April, 1972): 259–76.

Waring, Janet. *Early American Stencils on Walls and Furniture*. New York: William R. Scott, n.d.

Washburn, Charles G. *Manufacturing and Mechanical Industries of Worcester*. Philadelphia: J. W. Lewis & Co., 1889.

Wolf, Edward C. "Music in Old Zion, Philadelphia, 1750–1850." *Musical Quarterly* 53/4 (October, 1972): 622–52.

Young, Phillip T. "Asa Hopkins of Fluteville." Master's thesis, Yale University, 1962.

Index of Works by Accession Number

*All objects with the accession number prefix 89.4 are part of The Crosby Brown Collection of Musical Instruments.

Coe Moore, 1959

63.85   William Harnett. Wolfe Fund, Catharine Lorillard Wolfe Collection, 1963

63.205   Piano. Gift of John W. Castles and Dorothea J. Castles, 1963

64.114.2   William Johnston. Anonymous gift, 1964

65.156   Work table. Rogers Fund, 1965

65.235   Mather Brown. Gift of Caroline Newhouse, 1965

66.82   Piano. Gift of Mrs. Kenneth H. Volk and Mrs. Roy A. Duffus, Jr., 1966

67.36   Octavina. Gift of Elizabeth M. Riley, 1967

69.259   Piano. Gift of Eric M. Wunsch, 1969

1971.152.2   Harp. Gift of Mrs. Edward V. Jones, in memory of Nella Vason Jones, 1971

1972.111.1   Mandolin. Gift of the family of Angelo Mannello, 1972

1972.111.2   Mandolin. Gift of the family of Angelo Mannello, 1972

1972.166   Barrel organ. Gift of Eric M. Wunsch, 1972

1974.114   Piano pans and beaters. Gift of Vincent Taylor, 1974

1974.193   Chamber organ. Rogers Fund, 1974

Inst. 1975.22   Five snares. Gift of the Roslyn Landmark Society, Inc., 1975

1975.122   Appalachian dulcimer. Rogers Fund, 1975

1975.309   Piano. Rogers Fund, 1975

1975.357.1   Lyre-mandolin. Rogers Fund, 1975

1975.357.3   Plectrum banjo. Rogers Fund, 1975

1975.364   Flute. Gift of Philip L. Worcester, 1975

1976.7.10   Oboe. Funds from various donors, 1976

1976.8.36   Lap organ. The Crosby Brown Collection of Musical Instruments, by exchange, 1976

1976.229   Bentside spinet. Purchase, Anonymous Gift, Friends of the American Wing Fund, Sansbury-Mills, Dodge and Pfeiffer Funds, and Funds from various donors, 1976

1976.317.1   Piano. Purchase, Rogers Fund, Funds from various donors, Alice M. Hufstader Gift, Richard B. Kellam Gift, and The Crosby Brown Collection of Musical Instruments, by exchange, 1976

1976.644.1-2   Certificates. Gift of Maris Mannello, 1976

1977.246.1   Cornet. Purchase, Anonymous gift, 1977

1977.246.2   Calliope. Purchase, Anonymous gift, 1977

1977.266.1   Toy piano. Gift of Beatrice Paynter, 1977

1977.266.2   Stool. Gift of Beatrice Paynter, 1977

1978.136.4   Flute. Rogers Fund, 1978

1978.217   Violin. Gift of Mrs. John H. Lufbery and Shirley Sammis Foulds, 1978

1978.265.2   Flute. Gift of Firm of Wurlitzer-Bruck, 1978

1978.274   Bandonian. Gift of Mr. and Mrs. Harry C. Wolfson, 1978

1978.369   Hammer dulcimer. Purchase, Rogers Fund, Bequest of Dorothy E. Swenson and The Crosby Brown Collection of Musical Instruments, by exchange, and George D. Skinner Gift, 1978

1978.379   Piano. Purchase, The Crosby Brown Collection of Musical Instruments, by exchange, 1978

1978.552.1   Flute. Gift of J. George Adashko, 1978

1979.21   Folk fiddle. Funds from various donors, 1979

1979.204   Yankee bass viol. Gift of Margaret Hodges Warren, 1979

1979.288   Melodeon

1979.380   Guitar. Rogers Fund, 1979

1979.443   Clarinet. Rogers Fund, 1979

1979.444   Mandolin. Rogers Fund, 1979

1979.552.2   Hammer dulcimer. Gift of The Chicago Historical Society, 1979

1979.522.3   Hammer dulcimer. Gift of The Chicago Historical Society, 1979

1980.215.1   Pitch pipe. Rogers Fund, and Funds from various donors, 1980

1980.215.2   Fiddle case. Rogers Fund, and Funds from various donors, 1980

1980.301   Flute. Rogers Fund, 1980

1980.332   Cornet mouthpiece. Rogers Fund, 1980

1980.492   Double bass. Rogers Fund, 1980

1980.504   Grand Harmonicon. Gift of Richard T. Button, 1980

1980.544   Electric guitar. Gift of Arthur N. Becvar, 1980

1981.137   Ocarina. Gift of the artist, 1981

1981.217.1-3   Group of ocarinas. Gift of the artist, 1981

1981.221   Free-reed pitch pipe. Purchase, Mark R. Murray Gift, and Funds from various donors, 1981

1981.374   Harpsichord. Gift of Mr. and Mrs. Richard H. Dana, 1981

1981.479   Snare drum. Gift of D. Judith Ledwon, in loving memory of Mildred H. Ledwon-Lawless, 1981

1982.18   Clarinet. Rogers Fund, 1982

1982.42   Clarinet. Purchase, The Crosby Brown Collection of Musical Instruments, by exchange, Rogers Fund, and Funds from various donors, 1982

1982.59   Church organ. Purchase, Margaret M. Hess Gift, in memory of her father, John B. McCarty, 1982

1982.101   Yankee bass viol. Gift of Genevieve Vaughn and Laurence Libin, in memory of Mary Ruth McClane, 1982

1982.240   Appalachian dulcimer. Gift of the artist, 1982

1983.58   Clarinet. Funds from various donors, 1983

1983.75   Piano. Gift of Newcomb Debevoise Cole, 1983

1983.118   Bass bow. Funds from various donors, 1983

1983.119   Cornet. Funds from various donors, 1983

1983.129   Bass bow. Funds from various donors, 1983

1983.267   Boehm-style piccolo. Purchase, Gifts of Samuel and Eva Eisenstein and Helen C. Lanier, by exchange, 1983

1983.346   Harp. Bequest of Mildred Dilling Parker, 1982

1983.348   Guitar. Gift of Louise Ransom, 1983

1983.425   Alto violin. Gift of Walter and Harriet Michel, 1983

1983.440   Chamber organ. Purchase, Gift of Mr. and Mrs. Gregory W. Mandeville, by exchange, 1983

1984.130   Guitar. Gift of Mr. and Mrs. George P. Hergen, 1984

N.A. 11.1983   Parlor grand piano. Gift of Mr. and Mrs. Robert P. Freedman, 1983

Index

Page numbers in *italics* refer to illustrations.